PERSPECTIVES ON POSITIVE POLITICAL ECONOMY

POLITICAL ECONOMY OF INSTITUTIONS AND DECISIONS

Editors

Professor James E. Alt, Harvard University
Professor Douglass C. North, Washington University
in St. Louis

Other books in series

Gary W. Cox, *The efficient secret: the Cabinet and the
development of political parties in Victorian England*

Mathew D. McCubbins and Terry Sullivan, eds., *Congress:
structure and policy*

Leif Lewin, *Ideology and strategy: a century of
Swedish politics*

Robert H. Bates, *Beyond the miracle of the market: the
political economy of agrarian development in Kenya*

Charles H. Stewart III, *Budget reform politics: the
design of the appropriations process in the
House of Representatives, 1865–1921*

Yoram Barzel, *Economic analysis of property rights*

Gary D. Libecap, *Contracting for property rights*

Douglass C. North, *Institutions, institutional change
and economic performance*

Elinor Ostrom, *Governing the commons: the evolution of
institutions for collective action*

PERSPECTIVES ON POSITIVE POLITICAL ECONOMY

Edited by
JAMES E. ALT
KENNETH A. SHEPSLE
Harvard University

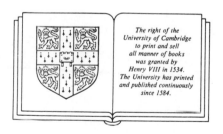

The right of the
University of Cambridge
to print and sell
all manner of books
was granted by
Henry VIII in 1534.
The University has printed
and published continuously
since 1584.

CAMBRIDGE UNIVERSITY PRESS

Cambridge
New York   Port Chester   Melbourne   Sydney

Published by the Press Syndicate of the University of Cambridge
The Pitt Building, Trumpington Street, Cambridge CB2 1RP
40 West 20th Street, New York, NY 10011, USA
10 Stamford Road, Oakleigh, Melbourne 3166, Australia

First published 1990

Printed in the United States of America

Library of Congress Cataloging-in-Publication Data

Perspectives on positive political economy / [edited by] James E. Alt
and Kenneth A. Shepsle.

p. cm. – (Political economy of institutions and decisions)

"A number of commissioned pieces for a series of seminars on
political economy held in Cambridge, Massachusetts, at Harvard University
in the fall of 1987." – P.

Includes bibliographical references.

ISBN 0–521–39221–7. – ISBN 0–521–39851–7 (pbk.)

1. Institutional economics – Congresses.   2. Social choice –
Congresses.   3. Decision-making – Congresses.   I. Alt, James E.
II. Shepsle, Kenneth A.   III. Series.
HB99.5.P47   1990
338.9 – dc20   90–1567
                                                        CIP

British Library Cataloguing in Publication Data
Alt, James E.
Perspectives on positive political economy. – (Political
economy of institutions and decisions).
1. Economic policies
I. Title   II. Shepsle, Kenneth A.   III. Series
330.9

ISBN 0–521–39221–7 hardback
ISBN 0–521–39851–7 paperback

Contents

Contents

PART III
REFLECTIONS ON THEORETICAL FOUNDATIONS

Contributors

Robert H. Bates
Department of Political Science
Duke University
Durham, NC 27706

Harold Demsetz
Department of Economics
University of California
Los Angeles, CA 90024

David M. Kreps
Graduate School of Business
Stanford University
Stanford, CA 94305

Paul Milgrom
Department of Economics
Stanford University
Stanford, CA 94305

Douglass C. North
Department of Economics
Washington University
St. Louis, MO 63130

Mancur Olson
Department of Economics
University of Maryland
College Park, MD 20742

Peter C. Ordeshook
Division of Humanities and Social
  Sciences
California Institute of Technology
Pasadena, CA 91125

William H. Riker
Department of Political Science
University of Rochester
Rochester, NY 14627

John Roberts
Graduate School of Business
Stanford University
Stanford, CA 94305

Gordon Tullock
Department of Economics
University of Arizona
Tucson, AZ 85721

Series editors' preface

The Cambridge series on the Political Economy of Institutions and Decisions is built around attempts to answer two central questions: How do institutions evolve in response to individual incentives, strategies, and choices, and how do institutions affect the performance of political and economic systems? The scope of the series is comparative and historical rather than international or specifically American, and the focus is positive rather than normative.

The simultaneous treatment of these two central questions is at the heart of the field of positive political economy. On the whole, the chapters collected in this volume avoid normative judgments and steer a course midway between broad historical generalization and detailed microtheoretical reasoning. Within these limits, they contain a broad set of views of the theoretical structure of the field. Chapters survey both microroots and macrophenomena in the evolution of First World and Third World political economies. Much of the volume is addressed to organizational development, discussed from diverse perspectives that stress the roles of reputation and unforeseen contingencies, of factional competition for amenity potential, and of the cost of attempting to influence collective actions. In later chapters, several contending approaches are represented in discussions of varied units of analysis that have founded research programs: individual decisions, exchange transactions, rent seeking, and indivisibilities.

Nevertheless, while displaying much diversity of approach and content, the chapters of this volume share an underlying unity of purpose: to demonstrate how economic and political outcomes reflect choices constrained by institutions while also explaining why and how, in view of the outcomes, such institutions should have developed.

Acknowledgments

The present volume consists of a number of commissioned pieces for a series of seminars on political economy held in Cambridge, Massachusetts, at Harvard University in the fall of 1987. Financial support in the form of a grant to Harvard from the Andrew W. Mellon Foundation is gratefully acknowledged. This grant supported lectures by Robert H. Bates, Harold Demsetz, Douglass C. North, Mancur Olson, William H. Riker, John Roberts, and Gordon Tullock. Revised versions of these lectures are contained in the following pages. They are joined by two previously unpublished (in English) essays by David M. Kreps and Peter C. Ordeshook.

The editors also thank James Hamilton, an economics graduate student at Harvard, for his substantive and editorial advice, and Tonya Koenker for compiling a unified bibliography and for other manuscript-preparation tasks.

James E. Alt
Kenneth A. Shepsle

Cambridge, Massachusetts

Editors' introduction

JAMES E. ALT AND KENNETH A. SHEPSLE

POSITIVE POLITICAL ECONOMY

Recent advances in interdisciplinary research in economics and politics have created the field of positive political economy. This new research tradition is distinct from both normative and historical approaches to political economy. The former emphasizes value judgments about the distribution of wealth and power and derives optimal outcomes or arrangements according to postulated standards of evaluation. The latter focuses atheoretically on thick historical description. In contrast, positive political economy, on the one hand, seeks out principles and propositions against which actual experience can be compared in order to understand and explain, not judge, that experience. On the other hand, although ultimately interested in real phenomena, positive political economy is explicitly theoretical. Its focus is on microfoundations, and it is grounded in the rational-actor methodology of microeconomics. Thus, its most distinguishing characteristics are its coherent and unified theoretical view of politics and economics, its strongly interdisciplinary nature, and its concern with explaining empirical regularities.

Moreover, in contrast to either of the separate fields of economics and political science, positive political economy emphasizes both economic behavior in political processes and political behavior in the marketplace. In emphasizing the former it uses an economic approach – constrained maximizing and strategic behavior by self-interested agents – to explain the origins and maintenance of political institutions and the formulation and implementation of public policies. In emphasizing the latter it stresses the political context in which market phenomena take place. By focusing on how political and economic institutions constrain, direct, and reflect individual behavior, positive political economy attempts to explain in a unified fashion social outcomes such as production, resource allocation, and public policy.

1

James E. Alt and Kenneth A. Shepsle

In short, positive political economy is *the study of rational decisions in a context of political and economic institutions*. It deals with two characteristic questions: How do observed differences among institutions affect political and economic outcomes in various social, economic, and political systems, and how are institutions themselves affected by individual and collective beliefs, preferences, and strategies? In effect, these are questions about equilibrium in institutions and about institutions as equilibria. In providing answers to these questions, positive political economy seeks both to furnish an understanding of optimal choices in various institutional settings and to endogenize those institutional settings.

Superficially, there is nothing new and distinctive in these two questions. However, the distinguishing characteristic of positive political economy is that it always considers these two questions to be related. Take the first question, with its emphasis on performance. Political scientists studying legislatures might investigate the policy consequences of changes in procedural rules or in the powers of committees. Historically oriented students of international political economy, to take another example, might investigate the effects of creating and maintaining an international regime or of the breakup of an existing international agreement. What seems to us to distinguish the political-economic approach from the approaches of other disciplines is the recognition that those responsible for changing an institution can anticipate any effect of an institutional change; the effect may thus have been a source of that institutional evolution. But then in addressing the first question, on institutional effects, we are answering the second question (on institutional change) as well. The reverse also holds. One would naturally expect that those seeking to change an institution have some result in mind when they try to do so and that that result (among others) would show up among the consequences of institutional change. In principle, any consequence can be anticipated, at least to some extent. Thus, it is inappropriate to explain institutional change without invoking anticipated effects. Positive political economy, recognizing this, is distinctive because it insists on treating its two central questions simultaneously.

DIRECTIONS OF DEVELOPMENT

Much of the impetus for the study of positive political economy stems from an appreciation of both the power and limits of neoclassical economic models. Generally, the results of these models derive from market equilibria. These equilibria are the outcomes of voluntary exchanges among individuals in a decentralized context, free of transac-

2

tion costs and involving no market power or externalities. Neoclassical models typically do not refer to institutions, or at most treat them as some sort of exogenous constraint on or parameter of self-interested maximizing behavior. (Even this more generous interpretation of the neoclassical approach exaggerates, for rarely are comparative statics conducted on institutional features.) By contrast, positive political economy tries to relax or even to do away with one or another of the central neoclassical assumptions in order to take account of the origins and workings of institutions.

Research in positive political economy has developed in several directions, which are by no means mutually exclusive. One main theme centers on work replacing the assumption of purely decentralized exchange among individuals with models involving collective action, collective decisions, and, thus, collective choice processes, rules, and procedures. Peter Ordeshook's chapter in this volume reviews many of the main contributions in this area. He starts with the logic of collective action, the spatial model of elections and legislatures, and committee decision making and leads us through an array of recent research that has attempted to integrate these concepts into coherent, rational-choice-based models of the sorts of political processes that are frequently found in industrialized, democratic societies.

An alternative line of development explores situations involving market power or other sorts of competitive market failure. Reviewing the political and economic development literature, Robert Bates takes the view that models of neoclassical economic growth fail to recognize the actual organization of markets and of other exchange arenas as foci of political competition in the Third World. Thus, neoclassical models are unable to explain patterns of import substitution, labor subsidy, and protection for inefficient industries, which typically occur as governments attempt to control economic outcomes in order to create or maintain political support.

A third major line of development in positive political economy, transaction-cost analysis, replaces the neoclassical assumption of frictionless exchange with the possibility that at least some positive costs are attributable to discovering and exploiting transaction opportunities. This analysis recognizes that complete contracting – the ability to specify and enforce contracts covering all aspects of an economic transaction – is impossible in a world in which enforcement and measurement are costly, human cognitive abilities are limited, and opportunistic behavior (self-seeking, with guile) is risky. Some transactions that might be made in a frictionless world, this approach presumes, will not actually occur. The approach, then, describes the search for institutions that allow maximum exchange net of the costs

of transacting to take place. The first part of the chapter by Milgrom
and Roberts surveys the approach and its links to agency problems,
to the organization of firms, and to the possibilities for opportunistic
rent extraction.

SUBSTANTIVE CONTRIBUTIONS

Part I of this volume sets the stage by surveying the evolution of positive political economy. Peter Ordeshook provides a *tour d'horizon* of
the intellectual history of positive political economy, rejecting along the
way the proposition that it constitutes economic imperialism. Whereas
Ordeshook emphasizes microroots, Robert Bates completes the intellectual tour with his emphasis on macrophenomena. He especially focuses
on how the rational choice paradigm and positive political economy
have transformed the studies of political and economic development,
principally in the Third World. He also suggests that the time is now
ripe for political economy to reconcile the rational choice paradigm
with cultural and sociological insights, which theoretical political scientists and economists have heretofore ignored.

Part II elaborates some of the findings from game theory and from
the general liberation of political economy from its earlier neoclassical
moorings. Paul Milgrom and John Roberts examine the proposition
that the choice to do things collectively in organizations, instead of
individually in markets, hinges not only on the costs of transacting but
also on the (wasted) resources devoted to trying to influence decisions
in collective institutions. David Kreps's chapter, written some years ago
and appearing in English for the first time, surveys the intuitions derived from modern, extensive-form game theory about formal organizations. Although written explicitly about firms, his insights are
general and should be understood as broad propositions about the effects of reputation and unforeseen contingencies on organizations.
Harold Demsetz's chapter, which compares firms and political parties
as institutional arenas for self-interested behavior, offers an original
and controversial perspective – namely, that these organizations should
not be distinguished merely by their agency costs. Rather, he suggests,
organizations often differ in terms of the contending factions they consist of and in terms of the degree to which those factions compete to
capture the organization's amenity potential.

Each of these chapters represents a sort of middle ground between
the broadbrush historical generalization that is typical of scholarship in
historical political economy and the detailed theoretical reasoning that
is typical of the micro- and macromodels reviewed by Ordeshook and
Bates and of the game-theory principles discussed in passing by Mil-

4

grom and Roberts and Kreps. In each case a microstructural feature, or "vignette," figures prominently in the analysis: bargaining and influence costs (Milgrom and Roberts), reputation and unforeseen contingencies (Kreps), and amenity potential (Demsetz). These features may serve as building blocks for understanding more general phenomena like institutional form, institutional culture, coordination and leadership, commitment, and delegation and specialization.

Part III of this volume provides a forum for several well-known authors who have made seminal scholarly contributions in the field. Each focuses on a unit of analysis that has served as the foundation for a research program. William Riker emphasizes individual decisions; Douglass North, exchange transactions; Gordon Tullock, the extraction of surplus (or rent seeking); and Mancur Olson, indivisibilities. Each reflects on the important questions and promising lines of development in positive political economy that follow from his choice of unit.

While this wide variety of theoretical perspectives might appear to separate scholars in positive political economy, we believe the field has an underlying unity of purpose and content. The contributions collected in this volume provide information on broad trends in the field, yet give an overview of its structure and contending approaches.

PART I

The new political economy

1

The emerging discipline of political economy

PETER C. ORDESHOOK

That political and economic processes cannot be separated seems self-evident. Markets are regulated by the coercive institutions of the state, and the state dictates the supply of that most efficient accounting of exchange – money. Simultaneously, regardless of a state's form, as long as two people perceive mutual advantages from exchange, markets, however primitive, will persist. Thus, the hard-learned lesson of political conservatives is that the state establishes the context in which markets operate and stands ready at any time to upset any particular market outcome. People are not merely consumers and producers, they are also citizens in a variety of polities that can not only regulate markets but can also expropriate directly the resources markets allocate. Correspondingly, it is impossible to predict market outcomes without also predicting the political responses that alternative outcomes engender. On the other hand, the hard-learned lesson of the left, and of cruder forms of Marxism in particular, is that whatever institutional structure the state takes, the laws governing market forces cannot be abrogated – the forces of supply and demand operate regardless of culture, ethnic identity, socialization pattern, ideology, and political system.

From this view, it is surprising to find economics and politics divided into distinct disciplines, with their joint study impeded by bureaucratic divisions at universities, by the specialization of scholarly journals, and by the prevalent use of modes of inquiry in political science that are seemingly at odds with those used in economics. Indeed, we cannot even say that the two disciplines provide the primary external stimulation to each other; political science in particular has been the beneficiary as well as the victim of many intellectual currents from other disciplines, especially sociology and psychology. Nevertheless, an emerging intellectual synergism promises to blur boundaries altogether.

9

Some scholars view this synergism as a manifestation of the "imperialism of economic theory." We argue here, however, that it is little more than the natural evolution of a paradigm that had previously integrated both disciplines but that economists refined in the first part of this century after shedding many of the encumbrances reality places on theorizing. And although the rational choice paradigm may not yet be the dominant paradigm of political science, it is the most prominent. It serves today as the successor to the behavioralist revolution of the 1950s and 1960s, and so it seems only reasonable to anticipate that the study of politics and economics can once again become wholly integrated. This is not to say, of course, that we can anticipate the imminent demise of disciplinary boundaries at universities. Bureaucratic inertia is a heavy burden, and political scientists and economists do not always share substantive concerns. Nevertheless, the time has long since passed when practitioners of one discipline can ignore the theoretical advances and problems of the other.

In its simplest form, the reemergence of political economy as a discernible field, with a significant, integrated, and mathematically rigorous literature, represents the reintegration into a refined paradigm of those features of reality that economists discarded in order to facilitate theorizing. The particular feature of reality that economists shed, of course, was politics. Although we might bemoan this distortion of reality, it permitted economics to proceed unencumbered. Left to study decentralized markets and the allocation of money, economists uncovered the requisite details of a paradigm. They developed axioms of choice and preference, along with formal representations of preference and alternative choice contexts. Aided in no small way by noneconomists such as Savage and von Neumann, they extended the paradigm to reveal the underlying structures of preference, subjective probability, and interdependent choice. The separation of the disciplines of politics and economics resulted in the formulation of an abstraction that might not otherwise have been delineated, and it permitted the development of that most powerful of social theories, classical microeconomics.

Because the rational choice paradigm's mathematical structure first appeared in the domain of microeconomic theory, the adoption of this formalism by political scientists seems to support the case for economic imperialism rather than the more benign notions of synergism and cross-fertilization. That is, a discipline of political economy appears to emerge because economists extended their paradigm beyond its initial boundaries. Even if we object to this supposition because we can discern this paradigm in the writings of political scientists such as Arthur Bentley, David Truman, Robert Dahl, Hans Morgenthau, Charles

Lindblom, and V. O. Key, the case for imperialism is bolstered by observing that these scholars did not incorporate the deductive rigor of economics and that the interdisciplinary research most apparent today began in the period bracketed by Arrow's *Social Choice and Individual Values* (1951) and Mancur Olson's *The Logic of Collective Action* (1965). This period encompasses four seminal volumes: Duncan Black's *The Theory of Committees and Elections* (1958), Anthony Downs's *An Economic Theory of Democracy* (1957), William H. Riker's *The Theory of Political Coalitions* (1962), and James Buchanan and Gordon Tullock's *The Calculus of Consent* (1962). Today, research stimulated by these volumes is published across the full gamut of journals representing the mainstreams of both disciplines, and few people can keep abreast of it and the attendant flow of articles, books, and working papers. In this flow the rational choice paradigm's impact on political science is now fully apparent. By any accounting, an increasing percentage of essays in political science journals either are designed to extend the paradigm explicitly or are set in the paradigm's context. Further, the labels "formal political theorist" and "positive political theorist" are not applied to political scientists who merely use mathematics in their arguments – they are reserved for those who specifically work within the paradigm. However, only one person in this list of seminal contributors – William Riker – can be identified as a card-carrying political scientist, and therein lies the argument that economics is imperial and is supplanting political science at its own trade.

With this argument as background, this chapter has three themes. First, if economics is imperial, then that imperialism is merely of a sort in which the eighteenth- and nineteenth-century rationalist paradigm of social theorists is once again serving its integrative function. Only at a rudimentary level does this presumed imperialism transport economic models and laws into political science. More generally, it results in political scientists once again explicitly using a theoretical view that previously unified politics and economics and that economists have refined for the past seventy-five years. Second, a theoretical structure is now emerging that does not merely promise a comprehensive basis for modeling political processes but that also integrates the studies of politics and economics. Finally, however, this theoretical apparatus suffers from fundamental inadequacies, many of which are especially evident in the study of politics. The inadequacies of special concern involve the treatment of strategic and cooperative action. Game theory, which is the part of the paradigm pertaining to such actions, is only now being developed in a theoretically satisfactory way, after languishing as a theoretical backwater of economics. Later we show how political science, because of the special problems common to nearly all political processes, contributes to game theory's development.

EARLY RESISTANCE TO INTELLECTUAL INVASION

Although its details are constantly questioned, criticized, defended, and reformulated, the rational choice paradigm – founded on methodological individualism and the assumption that individuals are motivated by self-interest – forms the thread uniting politics and economics. Despite the fact that the paradigm's adaptation to the study of political processes is commonly cited as evidence of imperialism in political science of economic theory, it is tempting to assert that this imperialism is illusory. After all, even though their writings lacked an economist's mathematical rigor, we can discern the paradigm in the research of political scientists such as Bentley, Dahl, Key, Morgenthau, and Truman. Hence, we might believe that economists have merely contributed a mathematical formalization. Nevertheless, we cannot fail to notice the facts that political scientists did not universally embrace the efforts of Black, Downs, Riker, Buchanan, and Tullock and that they largely ignored the impact of Arrow's Impossibility Theorem for decades. Scholars who followed the behavioralist tradition and who gained their theoretical sustenance from psychology and sociology were at best skeptical about the paradigm's relevance, believing that its definition of rationality was too restrictive, that its concept of self-interest precluded motivations such as altruism, and that the hypothesis of methodological individualism made the study and accommodation of "group-oriented" ideas such as socialization, norms, and culture impossible. Moreover, students of public policy and foreign affairs saw the paradigm's formalism and the assumptions required to render a mathematical argument tractable as lethal impediments to an adequate understanding of their subjects. Hence, the paradigm's explicit use in political science was often limited to isolated instances at professional meetings with panels devoted to formal political theory, mathematical models, or public choice. Only infrequently in the 1960s or the early 1970s did the paradigm's proponents participate on panels dealing with traditional topics such as legislative processes, elections, the presidency, international affairs, the courts, or public policy formation.

How do we reconcile the fact, then, that although central practitioners of the trade of political science implicitly used the paradigm, they strongly resisted its explicit adaptation to the discipline? The answer to this question has two parts. First, those who followed in the intellectual footsteps of Downs, Riker, and others emphasized deductive rigor at the apparent expense of substantive content; their work, therefore, was viewed as mere mathematical manipulations. As terms like fixed-point theorem, Euclidean space, multidimensional median, and subgame-perfect equilibrium replaced more familiar jargon, many political scientists questioned whether the substantive concerns of their field were being sacrificed for mathematical rigor and tractability. However, the use of mathematics alone cannot account for the political scientist's skepticism. Statistical methodologies gained broad acceptance and often legitimated learning mathematics, despite the fact that heroic assumptions about the nature and quality of data were required in order to proceed with even the simplest application of statistical methods. Instead, the second part of our answer concerns the political scientist's lack of understanding about the role of mathematics in scientific explanation and about the nature of general theory. Our answer also concerns the natural and healthy reluctance to abandon one approach in favor of another until the usurper's relative value is evident.

Political science's explicit adaptation of the paradigm's formalism was not preceded by any readily apparent insight that lit the way for all to see. No understanding of a specific empirical phenomenon compelled others to follow. No startling discovery or critical experiment preceded theoretical developments. Rather, the paradigm's entry was marked by the formalization of ideas that seemed merely reasonable – that unless candidates are constrained by special interests and the threat of abstention, they are drawn to advocate the median voter's preference on an election's salient issue; that candidates should not build coalitions that are too large or they will have no losers to expropriate from; that committees might agree to some middle position when debating a single issue; and that political institutions are the products of the self-interest of those who establish them. Although the authors of these ideas began a revolution within a discipline, the ideas themselves hardly grab the intellectual imagination. Indeed, in a discipline possessing a surfeit of ideas but not of theory, they are easily lost in the noise; or, as is almost always the case with general theoretical ideas, their intellectual antecedents can be found in a great many places.

Economics did not bring a particular substantive insight to political science; rather, it brought a method of conducting research tied to a general and malleable theoretical structure. Because this method was distinct from many of the established research methodologies in political science, Arrow, Olson, Downs, Riker, Buchanan, and Tullock were not viewed as the intellectual kin of Bentley, Truman, Morgenthau, Dahl, and Key. Understanding gained of experience and time-consuming empirical study, and explanation based on wisdom and ad hoc speculation cannot suffice with this paradigm. Hypotheses must

13

be shown to follow logically from explicit assumptions before they qualify for a test of empirical validity. Hence, the initial rejection of this method as mere mathematical manipulation failed to appreciate the fact that the mathematics of the method represented the desire to understand phenomena generally, logically, and scientifically.

We might assert that the innovations introduced in the 1960s went largely unrecognized and were even boldly resisted because political scientists were not sufficiently scientific to appreciate their promise. Too often, authors of essays were confronted with referees who offered the criticism that "by rendering their assumptions explicit, the limitations of their analysis are apparent." However, accusing it of being unscientific neglects the fact that political science is a discipline that has had its share of innovative thinkers. We can sympathize with those who viewed the erection of mathematical edifices as more often than not an exercise in logic with little substantive significance. More fundamentally, however, the early skepticism seems warranted and in the spirit of any scientific enterprise. If a general theoretical perspective is the new idea – a more efficient route to explanation and understanding – then no single research effort proves the case. Instead, unswerving cynics as well as potential converts can rightly demand an extensive theoretical development before acquiescing. Data and ideas must be demonstrably organizable in some more useful form, and new unanticipated insights must follow before paradigms change or before one becomes dominant.

THE AGENDA ESTABLISHED BY PUBLIC CHOICE

Even though Arrow's monograph preceded the publication of *The Calculus of Consent* by eleven years and Downs's seminal contribution preceded it by five years, Buchanan and Tullock's volume is an important milestone, because its premise sets the stage for the influence of earlier and subsequent research. That premise today seems self-evident: The institutions and procedures that affect the allocation of scarce resources are human creations. As such, their development, form, and operation can be understood only by understanding the purposes they serve, the individual objectives they satisfy, and the consequences to individual decision makers of alternative institutions. Understanding why groups adopt even so simple a procedure as majority rule rather than other voting methods necessitates understanding, from each participant's perspective, the potential costs and benefits of one rule as against another, as well as the opportunities and costs of changing rules and procedures.

Buchanan and Tullock's premise, however, extends to more than the choice of voting rules: It includes the choice to make social decisions by decentralized market institutions, by the centralized mechanisms of the state, or by hybrid institutions that await invention. This premise, then, demands the integration of economics and political science, because to abide by it, the operations of all rules and institutions must be understandable in the same terms – in terms of the same paradigm. To understand why governments regulate markets, why and how legislators redistribute income, and how market forces influence political outcomes, we must understand the subject matter of political science and economics not merely rigorously but from the same theoretical perspective.

The consequences of these ideas have been profound not just for economists but for political scientists as well. We can trace to them the establishment of the interdisciplinary Public Choice Society and its journal *Public Choice*, the publication of Mancur Olson's *The Logic of Collective Action*, William Niskanen's *Bureaucracy and Representative Government*, and even perhaps the development of models of principal-agent relationships. Since the appearance of *The Calculus of Consent*, political scientists have felt compelled to become more familiar with indifference curves, supply and demand curves, and the concepts of elasticity, market equilibrium, efficiency, public and private goods, and consumer surplus, as well as the content of essays appearing in journals such as the *Journal of Political Economy, Public Finance, The National Tax Journal,* and *The Journal of the Public Economics.*

It follows from these developments that if there is a case for arguing that economics is imperial, that case is strongest in the broadly defined field of public choice. An example of this imperialism – of the transformation of ideas that extends beyond the mere adaptation of the paradigm – is Olson's influential *The Logic of Collective Action.* From the view of economic theory, little in this monograph cannot be attributed to economists such as Samuelson, Pigou, or Pareto (for example, the distinction between private and public goods and the conclusion that decentralized mechanisms typically yield a less than optimal supply of or demand for public goods). Hence, we can regard the development of its thesis as the direct transfer of economic laws to politics. Indeed, its contribution is the political interpretation given to the concepts of public goods and externalities and to the sources of market failure. Olson revises our thinking about interest-group politics, neo-Marxist theories, and the nature of revolution. New ideas enter the political scientist's dialogue, ideas such as political entrepreneurship and the possibility that the causes of government failure may be as general and as theoretically identifiable as the causes of market failures.

What cleared the path for this incursion of economic theory is that political scientists somehow forgot their roots even as they studied them – roots derived from the writings of Rousseau, Locke, Hume, and Hobbes. In fact, even a cursory acquaintance with the writings of these early political thinkers should lead to the question of why political scientists failed to develop the ideas of private versus public goods in conjunction with a formalization of ideas such as the prisoners' dilemma implicit in classical writings. Why did political science not assume the imperialistic mantle attributed to economics? It is beyond the scope of this essay to seek satisfactory answers to these questions but this much is evident: Twentieth-century economics precisely defines and formally refines ideas such as Pareto optimality, externalities, and jointly supplied goods and exactly formulates the relationships of these ideas for decentralized social processes. "Refines" is the proper word, because many of those same ideas were perceived by social theorists at least 200 years earlier. The ideas remained central to political thinking in this century, but with no explicit paradigm to hold them in place, we were not assured that all thinking remained consistent with them. Economics appears imperialistic, then, because adherence to the formalism of a paradigm cements these concepts into an integrated theoretical structure, thereby allowing us to see their generality and connection to other aspects of economic theory.

Despite the case for economic imperialism that exists in this context, a hint of the political scientist's special contribution can be found in the attempts of public choice theorists to understand governmental growth. A principal empirical regularity in social processes today is the increasing size and domain of the public sector in nearly all democratic societies. This growth is especially perplexing if we also accept the proposition that much of what governments do is economically inefficient – that a variety of decentralized mechanisms can achieve equivalent ends at considerably reduced social cost. The question then becomes, what accounts for this seemingly pervasive and increasingly prevalent form of social irrationality? Economists have sought answers to this question using tools such as the concepts of fiscal illusion and the relative costs of labor- versus capital-intensive activity. None of these explanations is adequate, however, and instead research has focused on more game-theoretic ideas, such as the inefficiencies associated with prisoners' dilemmas and the split representative institutions cause between the incentives of legislators and those of voters. Out of this research comes the idea that if markets fail whenever costs are private and certain goods are public, then the public sector can fail as well because, even in regulating the supply of public goods, it must confer private benefits (e.g., benefits to interests groups) at public cost. Thus, the public sector mirrors the private sector, and the inefficiencies possible in markets find their counterparts in governmental activity. To proceed further, however, these ideas must be augmented with a serious effort at modeling political institutions: the simple translation of economic concepts into politics no longer suffices. Mathematical relationships among marginal utilities that show the inefficiency of the private sector with respect to public goods are not enough to show how such inefficiencies arise and are maintained in the public sector. The processes of representative governments must be modeled, the imperatives of elections and voting uncovered, and the qualities common to diverse democratic institutions understood. Thus, although economics provides the initial insight in the form of a precise representation of key concepts (externalities and public goods), theorizing must proceed anew.

Today, then, the ideas of Rousseau, Hobbes, Hume, Riker, Dahl, Key, Buchanan, Tullock, or Olson can be compared, and their logical connections can be assessed. What emerges from volumes such as *The Calculus of Consent* and *The Logic of Collective Action* is an economic imperialism that takes the form of a heightened sensitivity to the advantages of the rational choice paradigm's formal structure and even of an initial adaptation of theorems about supply and demand and the sources of inefficiency in decentralized systems. What also emerges, however, is an appreciation of the paradigm's incompleteness with respect to its treatment of political institutions.

THE INTEGRATION OCCASIONED BY THE SPATIAL PREFERENCE CONCEPTUALIZATION

Buchanan and Tullock made explicit that political and economic choices cannot be sharply distinguished and that economic and political processes affect one another. The challenge for us, then, is to model the great diversity of political and economic institutions using the same theoretical tools. To do otherwise precludes learning scientifically how such institutions function. However, although economic imperialism is supported by scholars who have accepted this challenge and by the rational choice paradigm's impact in political science, examining the attendant development of a unified theoretical structure for studying elections, legislatures, and international politics reveals the unique contribution political scientists have begun to make toward the development of a general theory of political-economic processes.

This contribution takes two forms: modeling specific institutions and uncovering, in the process, deficiencies in the paradigm's structure. The primary example of the first form, unsurprisingly, concerns elections.

17

If the study of decentralized markets helps define economics, then the study of elections serves the same function for political science. Correspondingly, we can credit Downs's seminal modeling of elections and voting as the first major inroad of the paradigm and its mathematical formalism into theorizing about a particular political institution. Although an exhaustive search of the literature might reveal prior inroads, research into the spatial theory of elections (and its publication in the 1960s in traditional political science journals) marked the sustained effort at developing a complete theoretical structure for one important political institution. Nevertheless, as we penetrate this theory, the contributions of economics, other than its paradigm and its requirement that essential decision makers be seen as pursuing well-defined goals, become obscure.

It is tempting to consider as Downs's contribution the hypothesis that parties or candidates are self-interested and motivated solely by the desire to win elections. An equivalent view of political processes is found, however, in the writings of realpolitik theorists like Morgenthau, in their assumptions about the power motivations of national leaders. In fact, Downs's more profound contribution was the idea that electoral competition occurs over a Euclidean "issue space" in which each voter's preferences are characterized by the distance of an ideal policy from alternative policies or party platforms defined as points in that space. This conceptualization is especially important because it links candidates' strategies and goals and voters' motives in a simple, unified, geometrically interpretable structure – a structure that forms an important part of the connection between contemporary political and economic theory.

In microeconomics, Euclidean coordinate systems, which represent items subject to trade, and preference sets and indifference curves, which summarize preferences for these items, are powerful tools. The proposition that commodity bundles that maximize a consumer's utility are characterized by the tangency of an indifference contour and a budget constraint marks the beginning of the use of mathematics in economics. It also marks the beginning of the use of the scientific generality that mathematics affords, occasioning the application of Kuhn-Tucker maximization conditions and the formal definitions of a plethora of ideas with substantive significance, such as homogeneous goods, consumer surplus, and elastic and inelastic demand. In the same way, coordinate systems, used to represent the political issues that concern the electorate and that candidates compete over, and indifference curves with interior satiation points, used to summarize voter preferences, are equally powerful devices for those who model political processes. Instead of interpreting the decision to vote and the choice

18

of a candidate as the product of childhood socialization or partisan loyalties, those choices are explained by mathematical proximity to candidates on broadly defined issues, and victorious candidates are characterized by the positioning of median lines and the like in this issue space. This representation, then, gives rise to the application of mathematical ideas such as multidimensional medians, distributions of ideal points, and metrics for representing preferences.

Downs, of course, merely borrowed from Hotelling's spatial model. Earlier, however, Black postulated a more general idea. His notion of single-peaked utility functions on issues, which he formulated as an empirically meaningful violation of Arrow's universal admissability axiom, was used to establish that processes involving majority rule can escape the dilemma of welfare economics posed by Arrow's Impossibility Theorem. And although the concept of single-peakedness applies to situations involving a single issue, Black, in conjunction with R. A. Newing, sought to extend it to multiple dimensions. Subsequently, an economist (Plott) and a statistician collaborating with an economist (Hinich and Davis) generalized and formalized many of Black's ideas about preferences with internal satiation points.

Not fully realized at first, however, was the fact that the use of single-peaked preferences, or the more general conceptualization of convex preference sets with internal satiation points, contributes importantly to the reintegration of the fields of political science and economics. This reintegration is a consequence of the close connection between these so-called political and economic preferences. The classical microeconomic representation presumes that consumers prefer more to less. The most preferred, feasible commodity bundle – the point corresponding to the tangency of the highest indifference curve to the budget constraint – is then determined by a consumer's income and the market prices of the goods in question. This tangency marks the consumer's decision, and the market outcome is merely the sum of individual choices. However, if, as in politics, goods are publicly supplied and if a centralized mechanism such as majority rule dictates their level of supply, then we must have a complete accounting of preferences over the feasible set in order to predict outcomes. This is because no voter nor legislator determines any component of the social outcome; indeed, participants may have to compromise their ideals before a final outcome is chosen. What is interesting, though, is that if we make the same assumptions an economist does about preference and trade-offs, then preferences over the budget constraint (assuming two goods) are single-peaked – a person's ideal lies at the point of tangency, and preference decreases as we move along the constraint on either side away from this point. Thus, we see quite directly that microeconomics con-

19

cerns those decentralized mechanisms in which each person determines one component of the social outcome – his or her consumption of market goods and services; on the other hand, politics concerns the centralized choice of a particular point in the feasible space, with no person dictator necessarily over any component of the decision. The central questions of politics, then, concern how political institutions (such as elections, representative assemblies, and committees) together with the procedural details of these institutions translate preferences over this feasible set into a social decision.

With respect to the first theme of this chapter – the presumed imperialism of economics – we note that many economists regarded the notion of spatial preferences with internal satiation points as merely a peculiar special case; they thereby resisted the supposition that general theorizing could proceed with it. However, with the derivation of such preferences from neoclassical assumptions, we now see that such preferences are not merely a special case but that they follow from what distinguishes political institutions from decentralized markets. Hence, because what substantively distinguishes economics from politics is reflected in the formal representation of preferences, this distinction becomes part of the paradigm and can be manipulated and recombined by anyone operating within the paradigm.

SUBSEQUENT THEORETICAL DEVELOPMENTS

With the formal representation of election processes that the spatial model provides, political theorists maintained the analytic mode of the rational choice paradigm by hypothesizing a primary objective for key decision makers. Replacing the behavioralist model, which assumes that people's behavior merely reflects early socialization, theorists now modeled political actors as active decision makers. Candidates maximize the probability of election, and voters maximize the consumptive utility of candidates' policies. The study of electoral processes, then, devolved less on measuring and weighing the dimensions and patterns of socialization and more on generalizing the structure of models and on testing the implications of alternative hypotheses about citizens' and candidates' goals.

Despite this parallelism, initial developments gave rise to a great disappointment. Nearly all spatial election models fail to yield the simple equilibrium found in microeconomic models of perfectly competitive, decentralized markets. Unless restrictions are imposed on the number of issues before voters or on the distribution of preferences in the issue space, or unless voting is modeled as a probabilistic act, there is no equilibrium platform for candidates – every election platform can be defeated by some other election platform. Thus, we can describe no specific outcome as being directly implied by preferences and institutional arrangements. Moreover, research by political scientists revealed that matters become even more muddled if we allow for more than two candidates or parties, if we permit abstention, if we look at a campaign as a sequence of elections in which candidates must first secure their parties' nominations, if we allow candidates to make campaign promises that are uncertain prospects, or if we take account of the incomplete information about politics voters possess. Thus, although economists characterize market outcomes in terms of some simple equations relating aggregate supply and demand, political scientists found themselves unable to offer a simple characterization of the relationship between voter preferences and the policies candidates advocate or might implement if elected.

However, this initial disappointment, which itself illuminates the differences in the traditional subject matters of economics and political science, became the inspiration for new theoretical ideas. Political theorists concluded from their unsuccessful attempts at replicating the equilibrium results of microeconomic theory that research should pursue two avenues. These avenues were generally regarded by economists as refinements of their theory, not as centerpieces. One elaborated the abstract description of elections to include a more dynamic element (Kramer 1977), and the other developed more general notions of equilibrium (McKelvey and Ordeshook 1976). The result of such efforts to date is a focus on the second avenue (but not a rejection of the first), accompanied by the application of ideas drawn directly from noncooperative game theory and aided by the development of other ideas drawn from social choice theory, such as the uncovered set (Miller 1980; McKelvey 1986).

This change in research intent is important for understanding the influences of political science and economics on each other. The early applications of game theory to economics generally sought to show how old results could be reformulated and generalized with an alternative structure (for example, that the core of a market game contracts to the competitive equilibrium as the number of consumers increases). But as it became apparent that the classical equilibrium results of microeconomics could not be replicated in political models, the application and development of game theory itself became a central activity of political theorizing. Although the general idea that key actors efficiently pursue well-defined goals is common to the economist's models of markets and the political scientist's models of elections, important differences in theoretical emphasis emerged. In economics, research sought to uncover the factors that lead competitive equilibria to assume one form

21

rather than another – for example, the conditions under which outcomes are efficient or inefficient. Some of the same issues motivated models of elections; but generally research there was directed at discovering the factors that yield equilibria or, when traditional equilibria did not exist, the conditions under which outcomes were assured of belonging to sets described by newly invented concepts (the uncovered set) or to sets with minimal application in microeconomic theory (the support set of mixed strategies).

A close look at a particular model illustrates the point that, after Downs's initial idea was accepted, theorizing about elections did not parallel the imperialistic pattern of Olson's reformulation of interest-group politics. Presently, the importation of ideas from rational expectations models of markets allows us to understand better how democracies function with the incomplete information available to electorates (McKelvey and Ordeshook 1986). However, aside from the insight that cues provide information and follow a dynamic that can yield an equilibrium that would exist if everyone were perfectly informed, no specific law or theorem can be borrowed to complete the theoretical enterprise. Instead, modeling must proceed from scratch so that the rational expectations hypothesis is adapted to the specific situation under consideration. In elections, although public opinion polls and the endorsements of interest groups can offer signals similar to those provided by prices in financial markets, the ways in which these mechanisms operate are quite different, because markets and elections are organized differently. Because decision makers may have a special influence on parameters (such as candidates and interest groups), we must look at the opportunities for strategic misrepresentation of preferences; because elections are infrequent events, we must pay closer heed to the temporal dynamics governing convergence to an equilibrium.

We do not want to emphasize the details of theoretical developments. Rather we stress that with the paradigm's application to elections political scientists moved to the forefront of the effort to formulate a rigorous deductive theory and that this research did not merely apply ideas borrowed from economics. Indeed, to emphasize the contributions of political scientists, we can look at the differing responses of economists and political scientists to Downs's election theory. The simplest, least general, but most widely cited result is the Median Voter Theorem. This states that if an election between two candidates decided by majority rule concerns a single issue, if the information voters have about candidates and candidates have about voters is perfect, if all citizens vote, and if there are no constraints on candidate strategies, then both candidates should converge to the electorate's median preference. Polit-

22

ical scientists agree that such a model captures but a small part of the forces operating in even the simplest election. Thus their instinct has been to generalize the result to include multiple issues, nonvoting, incomplete information, interest-group influences, and nomination procedures. Economists, on the other hand, often take the result as an excuse to eliminate politics altogether from their analyses. With a quick reference to the result, levels of consumption of public goods and services in a consumer's utility function, as well as taxes that constrain individual budgets, are assumed to be dictated by a median preference. Thus, the economist's contribution falls short and provides but the initial structure and perspective.

THE ANALYSIS OF COMMITTEES

This story is repeated again by a review of the research into legislative and parliamentary processes inspired by Arrow and Black. Here, however, research has drawn an even more diverse collection of scholars, not only from economics and political science but from philosophy as well. To give it some coherence, this research can be divided into two categories: social choice theory and the study of committees. We can take social choice theory to mean the normative study of social welfare and its axiomatic relationship to individual preferences. Again, the mode of analysis is primarily economic, with that field's dependence on individuals as the primary units of analysis and its assumption that individuals seek to maximize utility. However, after this is said and after Arrow's seminal contribution is cited, it is difficult to assert that economics is the home base of even a majority of subsequent research.

Arrow's demonstration that most rules for aggregating individual preferences into a social preference need not yield a transitive social-preference relation resulted perhaps most importantly in Gibbard's (1971) and Satterthwaite's (1975) conclusion about the manipulability of aggregation mechanisms. Those two writers found that reasonable rules are manipulable – that for a broad class of social choice mechanisms, one or more persons in some circumstances will not find it in their interest to reveal their sincere preferences. The conclusion, of course, places strategy, and thus game theory, at the heart of the study of decision making in social processes. But Gibbard is not an economist, but a philosopher. The extension of Arrow's theorem to cyclic preferences (as against the weaker form of intransitive social orders) was accomplished by another philosopher, Thomas Schwartz, a political science teacher who published in the eclectic journal *Theory and Decision*. Economists such as Amartya Sen, Peter Fishburn and Charles Plott have made seminal contributions to social choice theory, but the publication of Arrow's volume was not followed by research demonstrating the imperialism of economic thought so much as it was by the development of a new subdiscipline with roots in a great many disciplines.

In the study of committees, Black's research is seminal and, as already noted, closely connected to Arrow's. But the differences between the research of Black and Arrow are important. Although Arrow's work profoundly influenced how some scholars approached the topic of welfare economics, Black's work has had a more profound impact on political theory. Arrow sought to delineate the general properties (if not the impossibility) of social welfare functions. Normative theory, however, can play only a small role in a discipline not yet armed with a universally accepted descriptive theory. Black's research, on the other hand, was more descriptive and can be viewed retrospectively as following traditional microeconomic theory. There, specific topological assumptions about consumer preferences yield equilibrium outcomes (and their properties) in a particular institutional arrangement – unregulated competitive markets. Black's seminal contribution, presented in *The Theory of Committees and Elections* as well as in his short monograph (written with R. A. Newing), *Committee Decisions with Complementary Valuation* (1951), was to supply a conceptualization of preferences that is especially germane to politics and that provides the basis for a genuine micropolitical theory. We do not cite Black's work as an instance of economic imperialism, and we note that Black can hardly be classified as a mainstream economist. Were it not for the interest his research generated in political science, that research almost certainly would go unappreciated. Indeed, much of the research on committees that follows Black's lead has been conducted by political scientists. Fused with the insights into the theoretical nature of voting provided by Robin Farquharson in *The Theory of Voting*, and alerted by results such as McKelvey's (1979) cycling theorem to the possibility that institutions play a profound role in setting the strategic options of decision makers, that research is the basis for what political scientists call the new institutionalism.

This new institutionalism, although motivated by theoretical results derived from the rational choice paradigm, is less an attempt at synthesizing economics and political science than it is an effort at recombining behavioralist research with more traditional concerns of political science. Traditionally, political science focused on the structure and impact of institutions – legislative structures, electoral rules, constitutional provisions, and the like – but during the behavioral revolution this emphasis was somehow lost in defining, measuring, and correlating concepts such social class, partisan identification, attitudes, childhood socialization, norms, and socioeconomic status. Contemporary research is a synthesis that builds on such research and depends on it for an understanding of preferences and perceptions. However, this synthesis examines attitudes, preferences, and perceptions in the context of constraints set by institutions. In turn, these institutions (legislative committees, regulatory agencies, budgetary procedures, agendas, voting rules) are viewed not only as important determinants of preferences over alternative actions, but also, in accordance with the premise of Buchanan and Tullock, as endogenously determined by individual preferences, tradition, and transaction costs. Thus, with everything connected to everything else, the study of institutions that emerges as the hallmark of modern political theory potentially forms the basis for a synthesis of several intellectual traditions within political science.

As in modeling elections, then, economics provides the paradigm's formal structure and perhaps even the initial insights about outcomes and the corresponding representation of preferences. But its imperialism stops short of actually taking over the discipline of political science. No theorems from economics are grafted onto theories of legislative or parliamentary processes. Rather, assumptions particular to the institutions under investigation are developed, and research proceeds using the tools and insights from game theory rather than from economic theory. This process is most evident in the study of institutions involving majority rule. We know, of course, that such institutions encompass more than the simple mechanisms Downs or Black dealt with. We also know that with multiple issues, majority rule equilibria in the form of Condorcet winners – outcomes that defeat all others in a majority vote or that cannot be defeated – are rare. However, various procedures, such as voting on issues one at a time, or agendas, such as those used in the U.S. Congress that pair alternatives in some specific order, can yield a determinate outcome. Now, however, learning the properties of such outcomes must follow the logic of Gibbard's and Satterthwaite's results about strategic manipulability – a logic that is irrelevant to microeconomic models in which the topic of interdependent choice is rendered mute by "appropriate" assumptions. Specifically, this logic must model the strategic sophistication of voters and their knowledge and beliefs about the preferences of others. What, for example, are the strategic incentives for voting on one issue rather than on another? Who chooses the order in which issues are considered? If an agenda is used to choose from some finite set of alternatives, who determines the type of agenda? What types of outcomes prevail if everyone is strategic? What happens when new alternatives are introduced to the agenda? What are the consequences of incomplete information about preferences and the revelation of preferences as an

25

agenda proceeds? In answering these questions, political science expands the paradigm's domain and adds substance to it. Our purpose here, of course, is not to survey these answers but merely to note that this research is well under way and that the task of constructing theories no longer rests with economists.

JOINT EXPLORATIONS OF THE PARADIGM'S FRONTIERS

Establishing the theoretical properties of alternative institutional arrangements is not simple, and our survey to this point does not dispute that the paradigm's spread is a one-way street of fundamental theoretical ideas, from economics to political science. However, economics itself is being changed in the process. Although political science does not have a paradigm to transmit to economics, its concern with institutions, which economists frequently trivialize, yields a special sensitivity to the paradigm's inadequacies for studying those institutions.

Perhaps no assumption contributed more to the development of microeconomic theory and to contemporary economic thought than the assumption that markets contain a sufficient number of consumers and firms so that no decision maker affects price. This assumption decouples decisions and removes from the scene a great bugaboo – interdependent decision making. With this bugaboo absent, classical decision theory is all that economists need to pursue their craft, and students can understand professional manuscripts after a single course in calculus or in real variable analysis. Indeed, although a part of the paradigm, game theory, wrestles with the issue of interdependent decision making, and despite the fact that this bugaboo cannot be removed from any other social process, all but a handful of economists (such as Shapley, Shubick, Morgenstern, Scarf, and Aumann) resisted incorporating this part of the paradigm into their models for nearly twenty years. In this resistance, we find a failure of economists to develop their paradigm fully.

This resistance has several explanations. First, game theory once again reveals the necessity for cardinal rather than ordinal conceptualizations of utility. Second, early applications of game theory to economics provided few new theoretical insights. Game theory was deemed either to be irrelevant to the central problems of duopoly and oligopoly or to provide unsatisfactory answers. However, while economists fretted over the necessity of cardinal utility and over alternative ideas for modeling interdependent choices in markets dominated by a few firms, political scientists quickly learned that game theory was the key element of their enterprise. In some instances, such as modeling two-candidate elections and committee agendas, research could proceed with the tools that noncooperative theory provided. But others, such as Riker in *The Theory of Political Coalitions*, cast a broader substantive net and sought to explore the application of the cooperative game theory that von Neumann and Morgenstern offered. This net ranged from predicting coalitions in legislatures and parliaments to understanding stability in international systems. In fact, problems that might appear susceptible to simple reinterpretation by economic laws, such as vote trading (i.e., the legislative market for votes might be like any other), were soon found to exhibit externalities (vote trading was therefore more appropriately modeled as a cooperative game). These efforts, however, revealed the far more disquieting fact that the notion of cooperation and rationality concepts like utility maximization were ill defined. If von Neumann and Morgenstern, aided by Nash's definition of noncooperative equilibria, showed that interdependent choice per se was not a bugaboo, they failed to show that the paradigm had much to say about cooperative decision making.

Ostensibly, von Neumann and Morgenstern's *The Theory of Games and Economic Behavior* makes two profound contributions. It shows us how to model and analyze two seemingly distinct situations: those in which interdependent decisions are noncooperative (participants cannot form binding contractual arrangements) and those in which decisions are cooperative (binding agreements are possible). Although their theory of noncooperative decisions, when expressed in its extensive form, could be connected to the classical form of the paradigm, no such connection was evident for their theory of cooperative decisions. Both their characteristic function representation of the value of coalitions – of alternative contractual arrangements – and the V-set solution that they proposed to treat cooperative games were ad hoc. Certainly, these two ideas could not be deduced from any general assumptions about utility maximization. Even one of the theory's founders surmised that, as formulated, it had a fundamental flaw: that if people learned the theory, they might also learn to avoid its consequences, thereby invalidating its predictions (Morgenstern and Schwodiauer 1976).

Not surprisingly, then, aside from reformulating classical microeconomic theory as a cooperative game, economists largely ignored cooperative game theory as originally formulated. Rather than grapple with developing a better theory, economists' research here – consisting of the formulation of market games, of nonatomic games, and of the development of value theory – was less fundamentally conceptual and more an exercise in pure mathematics. Instead, in the 1960s and 1970s game theorists such as John Harsanyi and a diverse set of political scientists, sociologists, and psychologists were left to develop a fuller explication of the paradigm's inadequacies and to attempt to resolve

Peter C. Ordeshook

unanswered theoretical questions. Much of this research, admittedly, was not less ad hoc than the original effort of von Neumann and Morgenstern. Certainly the notions of connected or minimal variance coalitions that some researchers hypothesized to explain and predict coalitions in parliamentary governments in a spatial context could not be deduced from rationality postulates. Riker's size principle dealt with a special case and assumed the inadequate characteristic function representation of situations. And theories about coalitions in the triad or theories applied to majority voting games were hardly general. Although the mathematical formulations of these ideas were frequently inelegant, these efforts reveal a groping with the paradigm's fundamental inadequacy not by economists but by others.

The source of much of this groping was the realization that, just as elections failed to yield equilibria of the sort that describes markets, cooperative political processes failed to yield equivalent equilibria as well. Thus, while economists could remanufacture much of the theory using the concepts of the characteristic function and the core, the cooperative equilibrium the core describes was merely a special case in most political games. In this way, then, a small subset of political scientists showed that the various solution hypotheses game theorists offered as generalizations of or alternatives to the core were inadequate.

Today economists again are interested in the problems that cooperative game theory in particular and game theory in general seek to treat. Part of this interest derives from a branch of social choice theory – implementation theory. Briefly, this theory is inspired by two concerns. The first and more traditionally economic concern focuses on the design of tax schemes guaranteed to circumvent Gibbard's and Satterthwaite's result and to elicit honest preferences about public goods. The second and more theoretically general concern evolves directly from social choice theory. In this instance, general properties of social choice functions are specified, and the theoretical question researchers seek to answer is whether in principle institutions exist that satisfy those properties. In much the same spirit as Arrow's work, then, this research consists of possibility and impossibility theorems. The special feature of implementation theory, though, is that it legitimized game theory in economics, since the usual method of economic analysis was to establish the equilibrium choices in institutions that are not necessarily decentralized.

Another source of the economist's interest in game theory is the development of new equilibrium concepts and more sophisticated methods for studying sequential and extensive form games, as well as games with incomplete information. Indeed, so pervasive is the application of

28

game-theoretic reasoning in economics today that the distinction between game theorist and economist is blurred. The result is the promise that noncooperative game theory will soon accommodate the choice situations that von Neumann and Morgenstern sought to treat with their cooperative theory. However, even if we admit that economists are on the forefront of developments in game theory, those developments are not confined to their discipline. Although most political scientists are content with consuming the game theorist's product, the problems political science brings to this research have a profound effect on theory. For example, if we approach cooperative game theory along the same avenue as the one proposed originally by von Neumann and Morgenstern (via the characteristic function representation), we learn quickly that derivative solution hypotheses such as the V-set and the various bargaining sets do not exist or that they make silly predictions when preferences are spatial. Indeed, spatial preferences provide an especially valuable function here for determining the viability of alternative solutions. With this particular topological structure for preferences, ideas that fail (i.e., are empty or yield intuitively implausible predictions) only for very special economic cases (i.e., particular games in characteristic function form with transferable utility) are now known to be inadequate for a well-defined, broad class of political games. Political science is also especially concerned with the impact of institutional structures or, in the case of international relations, with systems that either have no structure or have structures that must be treated as endogenous. This concern forces game theorists to be especially aware of aspects of the environment that constrain individual decisions and to be involved in developing a theory that includes institutional structure within the strategy set of decision makers.

The desire to model all interactive decision making using noncooperative game theory, the rekindling of interest in the economics of institutional structure, and dissatisfaction with the classical treatment of cooperative games have, nevertheless, revealed the paradigm's inadequacy in a new form. Today the literature on repeated games and games with incomplete information is characterized by an array of folk theorems; these state, in effect, that nearly any reasonable outcome can be sustained by some equilibrium of individual strategies. Thus, in nearly all complex situations, a plethora of nonequivalent, noninterchangeable equilibria exists. Unfortunately, despite the various refinements of equilibria that have been proposed, we do not yet possess the tools for identifying which equilibria are most likely to prevail or how players choose one equilibrium strategy over another. Stated differently, contemporary research shows us that the notion of rationality itself is ill defined.

29

Confronted with this dilemma, game theorists, economists, and political scientists now reach to other disciplines for ideas, such as to genetics and learning theory. Rather than review this research, we merely emphasize that it differs importantly from previous applications of the paradigm to politics. In following Downs, Black, and Arrow, political scientists accepted the paradigm and molded new theoretical results around it. Here, however, we see the joint development of a fundamental part of the paradigm itself. There can be no economic imperialism in this context simply because economists do not have a fully developed theoretical structure to transmit. The danger for political science, of course, is that, without ready solutions, a significant part of the discipline will reject the paradigm, leaving its developments to others. In this event, we can readily envision essays seventy-five years from now discussing the "new imperialism of economics" and the belated reintegration of disciplines.

2

Macropolitical economy in the field of development

ROBERT H. BATES

The study of developing societies as a distinct field of contemporary political science began in the 1950s. Cambridge, Mass., provided the birthplace for important traditions in the field, whose content was shaped by the intellectual interests of the scholars who were its parents. Early researchers focused on the modernization of traditional societies and in particular on the political significance of mass communications and of human culture.

As did so many of my generation, I made my way to Cambridge to train with the pioneers of development studies. In my early work, I essentially adopted their definition of the field. But later I changed. The seeds of doubt had been planted early on, and they propelled me toward a perspective based on political economy.

INTERESTS AND OPTIMIZING BEHAVIOR

My dissertation focused on the roles of the Mineworkers' Union and of the United National Independence Party in implementing the government's labor policy in postindependence Zambia. Adopting the social-psychological approach that had dominated my graduate training, I attempted to explain that policy's failure in terms of the inability of the union and the governing party to communicate the foundations for the government's labor policy effectively. That policy consisted of a wide national perspective, specific development objectives, and the appropriation of an investable surplus from the mining industry. The fact that the union and political party provided poor communication be-

John Aldrich, William Bianco, James Alt, Kenneth Shepsle, Peter Evans, John Waterbury, James White, and participants at seminars at Harvard University, Princeton University, and the University of North Carolina have commented on this paper. I wish to thank them for their criticisms and to acknowledge the support of the National Science Foundation under grant SES = 8821151.

31

tween the government and the labor force, I argued, helped to explain the continued militancy of the laborers.

I still recall one of my professors, Myron Weiner, peering at me while clutching a marked-up copy of my thesis and saying, "Bob, I think you are wrong. I bet the workers know the government's position. I bet they understand the government's policies. They simply disagree." He was right, of course.

Upon reflection, it became apparent that the broader problem was that the study of communications and persuasion simply failed to deal adequately with the role of interests. Contemporary research into framing and judgments has begun to span the divide between social-psychological theories and theories of optimizing behavior (Hogarth and Reder 1986). But while I was a graduate student in the mid-1960s, the gap remained too wide to be easily transcended.

As I became more deeply involved in the study of Africa, I encountered data that weakened my commitment to a second mainstay of the development field: the notion of culture. Largely through the work of Melville Herskovitz, Africa had provided a key illustration of the power of culture – the so-called cattle complex (Herskovitz 1926). Students of African culture noted the myriad ways in which people used cattle – not only, or even principally, for sustenance, but also for social and religious purposes. They stressed the noneconomic role of cattle, arguing that the value placed on them exceeded any possible value warranted by the market. In support of this argument, they cited studies documenting the unwillingness of pastoralists to reduce herd sizes by selling their cattle to meat packers, even when faced with high costs for herding and low-quality grazing land. Pastoralists caught up in the cattle complex, students argued, proved uniquely resistant to change. They did not, for example, send their children to school, they did not become literate, and they did not pursue modern occupations. Students concluded, therefore, that their attachment to their cattle demonstrated the power of culture and by implication also demonstrated the limited value of economic reasoning when applied to developing areas.

As I immersed myself in African data, I found persuasive reasons to doubt the accuracy of this hypothesis – and the intellectual position it supported. I learned, for example, that much of the data on pastoralists' sale of cattle had been gathered from official government sources; the principal source for the government's data was a meat packing firm that the colonial government had licensed to function as a monopsony when purchasing cattle and as a monopoly when selling meat. Government regulations were imperfectly enforced. It was therefore not surprising that the official data, which the licensed buyer of cattle collected, showed a low rate of cattle sales and that informal accounts, which took note of the unlicensed market where prices were competitive, suggested a much greater willingness by pastoralists to market their cattle (Munro 1975; Tignor 1976; Jacobs 1980).

Further reading disclosed other weaknesses in the notion of the cattle complex. In accordance with comparative advantage, Africans practice pastoralism in semiarid zones and run their herds on lands where private rights are sometimes poorly defined. For both reasons, they tend to keep larger herds than Western observers would consider optimal. But the outsider would not appreciate the level of risk pastoralists face in their semiarid environment. The outsider might also not initially appreciate how property rights weaken incentives to restrict herd size so as to safeguard grazing lands. Rather than representing the tendency to keep large herds, an attachment to cattle, therefore, could represent a rational response to economic incentives – incentives created by an environment of risk and of imperfectly defined property rights (Fiedler 1972).

What, then, of the pastoralists' resistance to change? Why their apparent reluctance to invest in literacy, modern skills, or new occupations? One possibility, of course, was that cultural theorists had again got their facts wrong. But a careful appraisal of the data on cattle keeping, literacy, and urban migration suggested that theorists were right – that pastoralists were less likely to educate their children, send them to the cities, and place them in modern occupations (Bates 1976). Fieldwork revealed, however, that pastoralists' behavior did not reflect unique cultural values but rather unique opportunities.

I drew this inference on the basis of intensive fieldwork that I carried out in rural Zambia in the early 1970s. In the villages I studied, parents invested in their children. They did so by paying for their education and by giving them the skills needed to acquire high-paying jobs, which, given patterns of development in Africa, meant jobs in the urban sector, particularly in public administration. Expenditures on schooling and educating children yielded, by my calculations, roughly a 9 percent rate of return in terms of financial support received by parents in their old age (Bates 1976).

This reasoning suggests an explanation for the failure of pastoralists to adopt a modern life-style. For if literacy, education, and urban migration represent forms of investment, then the extent of a group's devotion to them should vary with the magnitude of the costs of devoting resources to them. These costs are determined by the return the resources could earn in other activities. In rural Africa, raising and breeding cattle represents the major alternative investment. Investment in cattle yields a rate of return equivalent to the biological rate of increase in the herd, appropriately discounted for risks. Given the growth

33

of per capita income in Africa and the wealth-driven preference people generally have for meat, the economic rate of return is even higher than the physical rate of increase.

The implication is clear: Behavior that has been interpreted to be the result of tradition, passed on by socialization and learning, can instead be interpreted to be the result of choice, albeit choice made under constraints. Pastoralists do not resist modernization because their culture imposes constraints on them, they resist modernization because they choose to do so. An explanation based on choice theory proves more powerful, for it explains as well the behavior of those who do in fact choose to modernize.

In the broader field of development studies, the cattle complex stood as a distinctive phenomenon – almost a curiosity – trotted out, as it were, to demonstrate the power of culture. Although the development of alternative explanations for pastoralists' behavior should have proved unsettling to development theorists, because of the marginality of the phenomenon, it did not. Far more powerful and persuasive, rather, was the growth of rural rebellions.

Modernization theory classified rural, agrarian societies as "traditional" and urban, industrial societies as "modern." As members of traditional societies, rural dwellers were held to be poorly informed, conservative, and politically passive; under the impact of education, the mass media, and urbanization, they became well-informed, innovative, and politically aggressive. According to Daniel Lerner's parable of the grocer and the chief, the modernization of traditional societies required the psychic transformation of those living in rural areas (Deutsch 1953; Lerner 1958; see also Rogers 1962).

In conducting fieldwork in rural Africa, I rapidly discovered how misleading this framework could be. The rural dwellers I and others encountered were not poorly informed. Fieldworkers found themselves repeatedly grilled by rural Africans about recent political events in the United States and queried about contemporary U.S. fads.[1] Nor did villagers appear all that conservative. In the village I studied I found repeated efforts at entrepreneurial behavior; in an adjacent field site, Thayer Scudder chronicled the introduction of at least three major economic activities – fishing, raising cattle, and cultivating cotton – in less than two decades (Scudder 1966). Nor did villagers prove to be politically inactive. The village I studied had led an insurrection that tied down the Rhodesian army for several months in the early 1960s. The accomplishments of this insurrection paled beside those of peasant revolutions that were beginning at this time in Vietnam.[2]

Thus, many of us learned that rural dwellers were not poorly informed and bound by tradition; rather, many were well-informed and capable of altering their behavior. Rural dwellers did not change because of the power of the media, of education, or of urban-industrial society. Rather, they were the initiators of change. Above all, they proved perfectly capable of initiating political action.

RADICAL POLITICAL ECONOMY

Rural rebellions in Vietnam drew attention to the writings of Che Guevara, Frantz Fanon, Mao Zedong, and others who championed the peasantry as a revolutionary class (Miller and Aya 1971). Because it had labeled peasants politically passive, the modernization school was discredited by peasants' revolutionary ardor. What rose in its place was a new form of political economy – the dependency school.

The dependency school has a fascinating intellectual parentage (see Palma 1978; de Janvry 1981). Basically, however, it is an analysis of the way imperialism transforms capitalism from an intranational into an international phenomenon. It holds that exploitation takes place not just among the classes in industrial nations but throughout the world, where industrial nations extract surplus from underdeveloped nations.

To Marxists, this analysis explains why labor movements in industrial nations resisted militant appeals and why class revolutions instead broke out in preindustrial societies. To others, it provided a framework for understanding political violence in developing nations, particularly in colonial societies. The dependency school provided a framework for understanding why the penetration of international markets and centralizing states into Third World agrarian societies resulted in political violence.

However, the dependency school itself proved unsatisfactory, in large part because it possessed many of the same limitations of its predecessor. It held that rural, agrarian societies were passive victims and that international capitalism was the active agent. More broadly, it assumed that peripheral, developing societies lacked the capacity for choice, constrained by their location in the world economy. Both assumptions proved wrong.

The dependency perspective found it anomalous that members of rural, agrarian societies could prosper as economic entrepreneurs, seeking foreign investment and utilizing it to enhance productive capacity (Hill 1960, 1963). It also found anomalous the fact that rural political leaders could act as political entrepreneurs and overwhelm the power of developed nations. Moreover, as Bill Warren and others were quick to recognize, the dependency school strikingly underestimated the capacity of Third World nations to manipulate international trade to their advantage and to transform their domestic economies (Warren 1973).

Robert H. Bates

Trimberger (1972), Alavi (1972), and others argued that Third World governments proved capable of exercising an autonomous political capacity for economic choice. In particular, they chose their positions with respect to international markets. Some, as in Africa, sought to withdraw defensively from markets; others, especially in Asia, chose to compete aggressively in them. A primary difficulty with the dependency perspective in political economy, then, was that it failed to recognize the scope for choice in the Third World and the magnitude of its significance.

The limitations of microlevel reasoning

In their search for choice theoretic foundations for the study of developing societies, many scholars turned to economic reasoning. Some turned to decision theory, others to microeconomics. But all encountered severe difficulties, the most significant of which proved to be the problem of aggregation.

Decision theory. Peasant rebellions in the underdeveloped world shifted the intellectual center of development studies from the modernization school to radical political economy. James C. Scott, in his classic *The Moral Economy of the Peasant* (1976), shifted the center of the field by approaching a radical theme from microfoundations borrowed from rational choice theory.

Peasants live on the margin of subsistence, Scott argued, and they are therefore averse to risk. Employing an elementary model of risk aversion, Scott explained the apparent preference peasants have for economic, social, and political arrangements that yield a relatively low but certain reward over those that yield a higher average reward but also are more likely to let them fall below the subsistence margin. In so doing, Scott "accounted for" many of the characteristics of agrarian societies:

In the economic realm:
  The conservative commitment to traditional crops that, while low yielding on average, yield reliably in good years and bad.
  The preference for the growing of food crops as opposed to cash crops.
  The failure to specialize in production.

In the social realm:
  The preference for incorporative institutions, such as extended kinship and common property.
  The preference for redistributive institutions.

In the political realm:
  Patron–client relations, in which low wages are exchanged for certainty of employment.
  The preference for proportional as opposed to fixed rate taxes.

(Scott 1976)

More significantly, Scott accounted for peasant revolutions. Colonial powers promoted the spread of private property and the market and thus undermined peasants' social defenses against risk. In Vietnam, at least, they also changed the tax system. The result was that under colonialism the peasantry faced a greater risk of living below a subsistence level. Colonialism therefore violated an ethical foundation of peasant society – that society be arranged so that no one should lose an entitlement to subsistence. The resultant moral outrage fueled the political insurrections that led to the overthrow of colonial governments.

Scott based his analysis on choice theory. He accounted for collective behavior by showing that it was consistent with the rational behavior of individuals, given their individual preferences. And yet, as Popkin (1979) was quick to point out, Scott's account proved profoundly deficient. Scott may well have correctly characterized peasant preferences (although Popkin expresses doubts), but, Popkin argues, he failed to account for social outcomes. Between individual preferences and social outcomes falls the problem of aggregation. As Popkin so devastatingly exposed, Scott left this problem unexplored.

For Scott, preindustrial society's practices and arrangements supplied outcomes that fully accorded with individual preferences. All risk-averse agents were assured of subsistence. Moreover, when society violated peasant values, the peasants rebelled.

The problem, of course, is that there is no reason to expect social outcomes to be systematically related to individual preferences. For a variety of powerful and fundamental reasons, rational individuals can make decisions that result in socially irrational customs (the classic analysis is Arrow 1968; see also Hardin and Barry 1982). As argued by Popkin, this problem arises with particular clarity over the provision of public goods, and it proves devastating to Scott's analysis of peasant rebellions.

A pure public good is neither exhaustible nor excludable; if one person consumes it, its value to others remains undiminished. As a consequence, rational individuals will not pay to create a public good; each person does better to wait for someone else to pay for it and then enjoy its benefits for free (Mueller 1979). Everyone might prefer that the public good exist, but no one is willing to supply it. Therefore, a

37

fundamental disjunction exists between individual values and social outcomes. Equally as important, the preferences of actors and the assumption of individual rationality fail to explain collective outcomes, for the outcome may well be unanimously nonpreferred.[3]

With respect to collective goods, it is therefore inappropriate to reason from the level of individual values to the level of collective outcomes. As Popkin and others pointed out, attention must therefore focus on the key intermediate step – the process of aggregation, whereby individual preferences gain collective expression.

Market-based reasoning. The search for choice theoretic foundations for the study of development also led to the use of market-based reasoning. This was particularly true of the work of scholars who sought to account for divergent rates of economic development among contemporary developing nations. They stressed that the open economies of newly industrialized nations did better than those that sheltered themselves from world markets. This was true historically, they argued. It was particularly true during the 1970s, when countries that altered domestic prices in response to the shift in world market prices brought on by rising oil prices recovered more quickly than did those that failed to pass on world market prices to domestic markets (Balassa 1981, 1982; World Bank 1987).

Other scholars examined historical variations in growth rates. They too explored the role of markets in leading rational decision makers to achieve the social good of rapid development. Some explained the successful rise of particular economies in terms of property rights. Given appropriate property rights, market forces would set prices that would make the private costs and benefits of economic alternatives equal to their social costs and benefits, thereby generating incentives for private decision makers to promote the efficient allocation of resources (North and Thomas 1973). Still other scholars emphasized the role of government policies. Some economies failed to grow because government policies generated deadweight losses by creating monopoly rents, by distorting prices, and by diverting resources from their most efficient uses (Little 1982; Lal 1983).

Particularly since the late 1970s, market-based reasoning has won renewed respect in the development field. Some speak of a neoclassical revival, with a stress on the capacity of markets to orchestrate socially desirable outcomes from individually optimizing choices (Little 1982). Others speak of the new development economics, with its assertion of the desirability of markets and its skeptical appraisal of the role of governments (Bates 1988). Whatever its theoretical stance or its view of governments, this thrust in the development field represents a sustained and concerted attempt to refound development studies on choice theoretic foundations. It too, however, confronts several basic problems.

In some cases, market-based theorists invoke Pareto optimality to compare allocations made by politicians with those that would be generated by the market; in this way, they gain insight into the impact of politics on the economy (Bates 1981). In other cases, they employ the Pareto criterion normatively, to assess the social costs of political decision making. In this way, they critique government actions (Little 1982; Lal 1983).

It is difficult, however, to employ Pareto optimality in either fashion. When used normatively, Pareto optimality presumes that economic efficiency provides a measure of what is socially best; but it can serve as a measure of welfare only if endowments are more justly distributed in an exchange economy. In development studies, this assumption is difficult to defend. In many of the markets of greatest significance to developing countries, prices result from bargaining between agents from developed countries, who enter the market richly endowed, and agents from developing countries, who enter it impoverished. It is therefore difficult to impute ethical qualities to efficient allocations induced by market forces or to censure on normative grounds politically induced departures from them.

In addition, the strongly normative orientation of those who employ market-based reasoning often detracts from positive analysis. According to this reasoning, political institutions making allocations that are not Pareto-efficient impose social costs. They are therefore more condemned than studied by market-oriented scholars. Decision makers who allocate resources in ways that do not conform to markets are often called irrational. By implication, their behavior is beyond the scope of systematic study. Those seeking a choice theoretic framework for studying development therefore often find the works of market-oriented theorists disappointing.

The work that has grown out of the public choice tradition is illustrative. Much of it is based on the theory of the predatory, the rent-seeking, or the revenue-maximizing state. The common theme of this tradition is that political activity imposes economic costs on society (Krueger 1974; Collander 1984; Lal 1984; Scrinivasan 1985; for a corrective, see Ames 1987 and Levi 1988). The point, while perhaps a valid one, so dominates the analysis that it obscures deeper political questions. Why would rational political elites make socially irrational (i.e., inefficient) decisions? If groups in fact impose economic costs on the rest of society while reaping economic benefits, how do they get away with it? The failure to address such questions leaves the politics of the process underanalyzed, even while highlighting the normative lessons.

Lastly, market-oriented approaches fall victim to the same problem that bedevils the attempt to ground the study of development on decision theory – the problem of aggregation. Microeconomic theory contends that markets generate prices which furnish incentives for agents to allocate their resources such that no agent will alter its behavior. At such a point, no agent can be made better off without making some other agent worse off, and no agent will willingly agree to depart from that allocation. As a method of aggregating individual preferences into collective outcomes, voluntary exchange in markets yields a predictable result: it generates an equilibrium.

Economic theory also indicates, however, that markets behave this way only under very special circumstances. Strategic behavior is common to many forms of market failure. Where one agent's conduct affects the value of the outcomes associated with other agents' choices, then other agents must choose strategically – that is, choose while taking into account other agents' behavior. In strategic environments, individuals' rational choices no longer aggregate in well-behaved ways. Equilibria may no longer exist; if they do exist, they may no longer be unique. Under such circumstances, market-based reasoning may no longer give insight into collective outcomes.

Developing economies possess all the usual sources of market failure: poorly defined property rights, production externalities, incomplete markets, and so forth.[4] Like all economies, developing economies require public goods. Law, order, justice, and security, as well as roads, health, and education, are relatively scarce, but highly desired in many developing societies. The inappropriate incentives that surround all public goods and the difficulty of organizing collective action to secure their supply keep them from being provided. In a public goods environment, private individuals' maximizing behavior simply will not yield the market equilibrium. Under such circumstances, market-based reasoning cannot explain how individually rational choices generate collective outcomes. Rather, attention must be turned to politics.

In an attempt to provide microfoundations for the study of development, then, some social scientists turned to decision theory; many others turned to microeconomics. The two approaches sought to establish choice theoretic foundations for the study of development but diverged radically in their normative position. For Scott and others, the market was unjust; it did not guarantee subsistence to poor people. For many market economists, by contrast, market allocations furnish the basic measure of public welfare. It is ironic, then, that the two approaches ultimately proved vulnerable to the same shortcoming: an inadequate theory of how individual choices will yield collective outcomes.[5]

Toward a political economy

What is needed, then, is a theory of aggregation, and the theory must stress institutions other than markets. One such theory – the theory of collective action – stresses the role of interest groups; another – democratic theory – stresses the role of parties and elections. Both contribute much to the political economy of development; both also possess severe limitations.

The theory of collective action. The theory of collective action (Olson 1965; Hardin 1982) provides a form of political economy. As most often applied, it examines the behavior of individuals in markets in which actors possess incentives to engage in strategic behavior. It is frequently used to account for political intervention in markets.

The theory begins by recognizing that market prices constitute public goods; arbitrage ensures that all agents face a single price in a market and that all agents on a single side of a market therefore stand to benefit from a favorable shift in that price. Governments possess the power to affect prices. They can regulate prices directly or, by imposing tariffs, issuing licenses, or regulating production or marketing, can help determine the prices. But lobbying to secure government intervention is costly. Efforts to secure favorable protection from government therefore run afoul of the same incentives that confound the provision of other public goods. Behaving rationally, individuals do better to let someone else bear the costs of lobbying; they then receive benefits for free. But when all agents free ride, favorable policies are not supplied, and economic interests remain unprotected.

How, then, do we explain the forms of protection that we commonly observe? For example, why in developing areas do small numbers of people, those working in large-scale urban industries, receive tariff protection while most people, who work on small farms, find their incomes undercut by cheap foreign imports? Why are markets subject to political rationing, so that they become political machines? Why are large, inefficient firms protected by governments, while the small-scale, relatively efficient informal sector is taxed? And why do fights over economic distribution become conflicts among ethnic communities?

Several factors clearly affect incentives to organize to shape government policy. They affect the incentives to free ride, and they thereby

41

help to explain why some interests prevail and others lose out in the struggle for economic advantage.

One factor is size, which means market share (Olson 1965). When, for example, a market contains only one firm, it will lobby for protection if the benefits of protection exceed the costs. It will have no incentive to free ride, because even though it pays all costs, it also captures all benefits. When a market contains only a few large actors, then single actors may act rationally by bearing the costs of supplying the collective good by lobbying for government protection; each actor may be large enough that the benefits of lobbying exceed the costs. But when a market contains many small agents – and large fixed costs of organizing – then the benefits to each from securing a higher price may not exceed the costs of lobbying. Therefore, each, behaving rationally, may seek to free ride.

Partially for these reasons, then, the few large firms may secure better deals from governments than the numerous small firms. In the developing world, the fact that the modern sector may consist of only a small number of large firms indicates that those firms lobby more actively to defend their interests than do the large number of smaller producers in the rural sector. In many poor countries, family farmers "employ" the greatest number of workers, and their output renders them the single largest economic sector. But having small businesses, peasant farmers also have little incentive to engage in collective action.[6] The size distribution of production weakens their incentive to organize to support policies that enhance their collective economic standing. Government intervention therefore rarely promotes positive pricing policies for peasant farmers; to the contrary, it often violates their interests. Rural dwellers in the developing world are often subject to low prices, and collective action helps to account for that.

The theory of collective action also helps to account for behavior that otherwise may appear anomalous or irrational. Most people in Africa, as elsewhere in the developing world, live in rural areas, and most of them are ill-favored by government policy. But rather than organize to defend their collective interests as peasant producers, they instead tend to organize to defend traditional ethnic claims. Instead of calling for the collective benefit of higher prices, these ethnic claims tend to demand political spoils – the group's fair share of roads, clinics, and other divisible benefits.

Some have labeled this behavior irrational – an example of the persistence of primordial loyalties and traditional cultural values. The theory of collective action provides an alternative interpretation. It stresses that organization is costly, if only because the incentives to free ride must be overcome. Those seeking to organize are therefore more likely to appropriate existing organizations than to form new ones. Ethnic associations already exist in rural Africa, whereas farmers' associations must be created. Moreover, given the numerous linguistic communities in Africa, politicians often find it far easier to mobilize within language groups than across them. Those trying to secure resources may therefore attempt to organize subsets of the rural community rather than farm interests as a whole. The costs of organizing therefore help to account for the relative attractiveness of narrower appeals, made on ethnic lines.

The theory of collective action also stresses selective incentives – costs or benefits that are conferred when a desired act is performed. Armed with selective incentives, political entrepreneurs can reward those who contribute to the collective good and penalize those who do not; political contributors then no longer find it in their interests to free ride. Political entrepreneurs can therefore manipulate selective benefits in efforts to build effective political organizations. It is not surprising, then, that rural political organizations demand divisible benefits such as schools, roads, and clinics rather than collective benefits such as higher prices.

Selective incentives and the costs of organizing help us to understand why rural political organizations consist of ethnic groups rather than producer associations and seek divisible improvements from governments rather than more favorable producer prices (Young 1976; Rothchild and Olorunsula 1983; Horowitz 1985). Ethnic groups do not form because producers and politicians are irrational. Rather, they form precisely because rural dwellers – and political organizers – respond rationally to incentives.

The theory of collective action thus provides insight not only into the incidence of effective political action but also into its form. The theory has significant limitations, however, and these warrant great emphasis.

As a theory of government, the theory of collective action is a type of capture theory. It provides a theory of the political action that reduces public sector interests to the subset of economic interests that are organized. But, as already suggested, politicians organize groups. The theory of collective action too often does not consider politicians and the institutional incentives that motivate them.[7] The theory may, therefore, provide an explanation of policy formation that is incomplete or wrong.

The theory of collective action explains market intervention as a response to organized interests. But many accounts of government intervention suggest a different dynamic: that organization follows rather than precedes government intervention.

Robert H. Bates

In developing areas of the world, politicians intervene in markets, often because of ideology or to try to achieve development (such as by shifting resources from agriculture to industry). Often the consequence of such intervention is the alteration of prices in some market; for illustrative purposes, we can assume that prices are lowered. This shift in prices results in a failure to achieve market equilibrium; when prices are lowered, demand exceeds supply. Governments thereby gain the opportunity to ration; they can channel benefits to those who support them, withhold benefits from those who oppose them, and thereby build a loyal constituency for themselves and the programs they control. The benefits politicians allocate are, of course, worth more to large economic interests. Those interests therefore become the most vocal clients of public programs, lobbying to maintain them and the benefits they provide.

The theory of collective action would suggest that large interests organize, support politicians who promote key programs, and thereby extract collective benefits from governments. But the causal process may actually run in the opposite direction. (An example is provided by the literature on campaign contributions by interest groups in the United States; see, for example, Jacobson 1980.) If it does, then we must look to factors that the theory of collective action ignores. We must look to the political incentives that shape politicians' economic choices; for, by this analysis, politicians are not perfect agents of economic interests but rather have distinctive political incentives of their own. We must therefore understand the nature of the political problems politicians try to solve when making economic policy. We must also look at the ideologies that motivate their interventions. If politicians do take the initiative, we must turn our attention from the economic forces that demand political intervention to the political forces that supply it.[8]

These comments underscore the significance of another factor left out of the logic of collective action: the institutional structure of politics. If economic interests can collude by free riding, then the interests with access to state power may be in a position to organize to defend their interests more effectively than those who are excluded from power. Backed by the coercive power of the state, they can sanction free riders and police and enforce agreements that restrain competition. The implication is clear: If the constitutional order facilitates access to state power, it apportions the capacity to organize. The constitutional structure thus determines which interests can shape collective outcomes by engaging in collective action. It determines which economic interests are politically effective.

44

Macropolitical economy in the field of development

In the nineteenth and early twentieth centuries, for example, industrializing states considered trade unions illegal, even while stabilizing cooperative agreements that restricted competition among firms. Later changes in the franchise that gave greater power to the working classes allowed defenders of labor's collective interests to pass new laws. Legislation allowed labor to coerce free riders, as by imposing closed shop agreements. These politically supplied innovations enhanced labor's economic power. The significance of the legal order in less developed countries is evident in the contrasting positions of agricultural interests in colonial Africa. In Ghana, farmers were excluded from the interests represented by the colonial government; in Kenya, white settlers – many of whom were farmers – dominated the colonial legislature. Farmers in Kenya could legally promote collusive behavior by their own kind, actions that in Ghana were treated as illegal restraints of trade. The result was that farmers in Kenya used their control over the state to combine, to restructure markets, and thereby to extract profits that exceeded those attainable in competitive markets. By contrast, farmers in Ghana had to compete with one another; collusion was illegal. As a result, other economic interests, in particular the large commercial trading firms that the state allowed to organize, set prices against the farmers and extracted revenues from them (Bates 1983). The constitutional order allocated the right to organize and thus determined which economic interests became organized and could effectively engage in collective action.

The theory of collective action provides a means of analyzing the incidence and form of interest aggregation. It does not take into account the impact of political forces, such as the motivations of politicians and the structure of political institutions. It thereby threatens to mis-specify the relationship between policy choice and the formation of interest groups. This and other instrumentalist theories – capture theory, the theory of rent seeking, and so forth – thus may need to be reinterpreted. The analysis should, it would appear, begin with the political.[9]

Democratic theory. Perhaps no other field in the social sciences has focused so centrally on the problem of aggregation as has democratic theory. Those studying voting and majority rule have analyzed how the preferences of rational individuals translate into collective choices. The principal lesson is that, in general, one cannot expect an equilibrium to exist; and, because any outcome can be defeated, political decisions represent arbitrary outcomes. The most general elaboration of this conclusion is contained in the famous chaos theorems, which indicate that the absence of a majority rule equilibrium implies that virtually any policy outcome is possible (see, for example, McKelvey 1976).

One implication is normative: Superior ethical properties cannot be attributed to the outcomes a majority supports. Equally as significant are the implications for positive analysis. Clearly political outcomes tend to be more stable and predictable than we would expect, given that the choices made under democratic procedures could in principle result in many possible outcomes. Research, then, must identify the additional constraints that systematically restrict and thereby account for the range of political outcomes.

Some scholars have investigated the impact of control over the agenda (Levine and Plott 1977). If any outcome can defeat any other outcome, then the order in which alternatives are considered determines which outcome survives. This insight has been exploited to examine the impact of rules and procedures on policy making; to account for the political power of parliamentary leaders (i.e., those who control the sequence and order of legislative deliberations); and to explain the power of legislative committees (Shepsle and Weingast 1987).

Scholars have also investigated the impact of institutions. Shepsle and Weingast, for example, demonstrate how the rules of the U.S. Congress make public policy stable and predictable when it might be expected to be arbitrary (Shepsle 1979; Shepsle and Weingast 1981). Subsequent researchers have investigated the roles of amendment procedures and the committee system in influencing legislative choices (McCubbins and Sullivan 1987).

The progress of this research can only frustrate development specialists. Democratic institutions are far less common in developing nations than in industrialized nations. Moreover, political institutions in the developing world tend to be more fragile: They are less constraining and more frequently changed. The analyses that have so powerfully illustrated the way institutions aggregate the preferences of individuals into collective outcomes in democratic societies therefore offer little assistance to those attempting to develop a theory of governmental behavior relevant to developing societies.

Some general lessons are apparent, of course. Faced with the lessons of chaos theorems, for example, development specialists can readily critique policy proposals that stress political participation as a way of securing optimal levels and mixes of public services. Social democrats and public choice theorists advance these policy proposals, the former believing that more participation is better than less, the latter seeking decentralized means of bidding for public goods. Black's Theorem helps shed light on the significance of restricting the range of preferences, either by coercion or indoctrination, for attaining political stability;

conversely, it illustrates as well why cultural complexity may produce turmoil in countries experimenting with democracy.[10]

Moreover, even when democratic institutions do not exist on a national level, majority rule may be used in more restrictive domains. It may be employed in local councils, for example, or in key administrative committees when allocating such important resources as licenses, contracts, or foreign exchange. In such settings, the insights about the impact of agendas and other institutional features on political outcomes would of course be relevant.

In general, however, outside of offering an interpretive heuristic or a set of tools for understanding relatively restricted phenomena, positive political analysis proves disappointing as a source of theory for studying governmental behavior in developing countries. The basic conditions that support this analysis – electoral accountability and the existence of well-defined institutions – prevail but ephemerally in less developed societies.

Quo vadimus?

Many of us in the development field were drawn to political economics because we sought an approach that would emphasize choice. We have moved away from the heavily market-oriented approaches from which many initially took guidance. We have also increasingly recognized the way in which political factors – the interests of politicians and the power of state structures – help to determine which material interests can make an impact on collective outcomes. We are frustrated, however, by our inability to adapt many of the tools forged for the study of aggregation to developing areas of the world. In environments relatively bereft of democratic institutions, we find ourselves unable to make strong predictions about how the choices of rational individuals are likely to yield collective outcomes.

In a situation of such seeming adversity, those who work in the development field nevertheless face exciting opportunities. The most significant of our advantages is the broad overlap between problems central to the development field and those relevant to political economy. Normal progress in one field offers the prospect of breakthroughs in the other.

The study of institutions. Much work in contemporary political economy is concerned with institutions. Developing areas of the world have many institutions, particularly in the political arena. I have already stressed the difficulty their changeability creates. What I wish now to stress are the advantages their changeability offers. The very impermanence of political institutions in developing areas underscores the degree to which these institutions are themselves chosen.

One implication is that those studying developing areas face a subject that stands at the very frontier of the field of political economy: the problem of institutional origins. Another is that by working on this problem they can generate results that will themselves feed back into the study of development. More specifically, researchers stand poised to return to the basic foundations of the political economy of development – those that rest on Marxism.

I have argued that for many in the development field the movement toward political economy represented a search for choice theoretic foundations. For many purposes, choices are best analyzed while treating institutions as constraints. But factors that are treated as fixed can be regarded as variable, especially when longer time periods are analyzed. One characteristic that distinguishes the development field from other social science fields is that it analyzes change in the long run. As a consequence, students of development can treat institutions as endogenous. When they do, they open up an exciting topic for research: the relationship between capital and institutions.

Capital is the factor of production that generates intertemporal change. In particular, growth occurs when individuals choose to withhold resources from present consumption to form capital and thereby to create enhanced economic possibilities later. Because capital is intertemporal, the decision to invest is inherently shrouded in uncertainty. Contracts that could foresee all possible contingencies are prohibitively costly to write. Therefore, markets in which people could exchange such contracts and organize optimal investment programs, given their preferences, cannot be formed. A major implication of this insight is that people possess incentives to create institutions to compensate for the poor performance of capital markets. Both those demanding capital and those seeking to invest it have strong incentives to develop institutions that reduce risks and thereby facilitate mutually beneficial investments.

For two reasons, potential investors in developing areas of the world have particularly strong incentives to create new institutions. If developing areas have low capital stocks, the value at the margin of new investments should be high; opportunities yielding a high level of return remain as yet unexploited. Second, capital markets remain poorly developed; property rights are ill-defined or are defined so as to make collateralizing loans difficult; and government regulations limit the pooling of risks on national or international markets. Both those who demand and those who supply capital to developing areas are therefore strongly motivated to develop institutions designed to lower risks.

Macropolitical economy in the field of development

Capital formation is central to development. And, for the reasons just given, those who seek to augment the capital stocks of less developed countries often play major roles in creating institutions. Capital markets therefore become prime sources of nonmarket institutions in developing countries.[11] This line of reasoning represents one of the most productive areas of research in the political economy of development.

Adding to the topic's luster is a profound sense of intellectual closure. Classically, the study of capital has played the central role in the analysis of development, and a principal insight of Marxism is that capital not only determines the productive potential of the forces of production but also adjusts the relations of production. Marxist theory has failed to provide an adequate account of the causal link between institutional and economic analyses. The line of investigation advocated here is exciting precisely because it offers a means of closing that analytic gap.[12]

The politics of Adam Smith. A second topic promises to promote a fertile interchange between development studies and political economy: the study of the political introduction of markets.

Today the World Bank, the International Monetary Fund, and Western bilateral aid agencies promote the use of markets in developing countries. In this they are aided by the burden of debt that many developing countries bear. In order to qualify for further lending, developing nations must adopt economic policies their creditors prescribe. Among the foremost conditions creditors impose on further lending is that Third World governments liberalize their markets. Governments in developing countries are asked to abandon attempts to allocate key resources – food, credit, and foreign exchange, for example – and instead to let market forces allocate them.

In the contemporary developing world, then, the creations of markets are political acts. Just as classical economists and nineteenth-century politicians in Great Britain debated the repeal of the Corn Laws, so too are Third World intellectuals and politicians debating the liberalization of key markets. Political conflict focuses on issues of openness and free trade. Some countries, such as Ghana, appear to have shifted from interventionist policies to policies favoring market forces; in Zambia, by contrast, political reactions against using market prices to allocate foreign exchange led to the termination of relations with international creditors. In some countries, such as in South America, the movement toward markets has led to violence; in others, it has been peacefully achieved.

49

Table 2.1. *Distinctive approaches*

	Postulate 1 Individual is basic analytic unit	Postulate 2 Individuals (including politicians) are rational	Postulate 3 Politics is relatively autonomous	Postulate 4 Individual rationality implies social rationality
Political culture approach	No	No	No	—[a]
Radical political economy	No	Yes	No	No
Decision theoretic approaches	Yes	Yes	No	Yes
Market-oriented approaches	Yes	Yes	No	Yes
Collective action and related approaches	Yes	Yes	No	No
The political economy perspective	Yes	Yes	Yes	No

[a]The approach takes no stand on this issue.

What accounts for the varied political support for markets in less developed countries? Why have political leaders in some countries been able to win popular support for market-based policies whereas interventionist programs prevail in other countries? Why do no political parties in Black Africa champion less government intervention rather than more? Investigating questions such as these would lead to an exploration of the political conditions that allow for the existence of free markets.

Just as the study of capital will lead students of development to the analysis of the Marxian foundations of political economy, so too will the study of the structural readjustment of Third World economies lead them to the analysis of the discipline's Smithian roots.

DISCUSSION

In closing, it might be useful to characterize the political economy approach schematically and to highlight the qualities that differentiate it from other approaches. Our critique of earlier approaches suggests that they can be differentiated by the positions they take on four key postulates.

1. The individual actor is the basic unit of analysis.
2. Individuals, including politicians, are rational.
3. Politics is relatively autonomous; institutions create incentives for politicians.
4. Individual rationality implies social rationality.

Table 2.1 shows stances each approach takes to these four assertions.

I have already identified two frontier topics in the political economy of development. By way of summing up it may be useful to return to the second. A further discussion of the politics of the transition to markets provides a way of highlighting the distinctive properties of the political economy perspective and, in particular, of distinguishing it from the market-oriented approaches with which it is often confounded.

At present a strong demand exists for the strengthening of markets in developing areas of the world. This demand is most forcefully articulated by international agencies such as the World Bank and the International Monetary Fund. It is also articulated by neoclassical development economists, who point to the losses of efficiency and the destruction of incentives brought on by government interference. It is less frequently articulated in developing countries that stand to benefit from market liberalization.

According to conventional economic reasoning, all parties would be better off under free markets, and rational individuals should therefore

51

agree to let the market allocate resources. Market distortions must therefore be caused by politicians who are economically irrational or poorly informed about the laws of economics (see, for example, the contributions in Schultz 1978). Purely for purposes of argument, let us assume that the market-oriented economists are correct. Then they face a dilemma, but one that could be resolved were the problem of economic policy reform analyzed as a problem in political economy. Because of their endorsement of postulate 4, market-oriented economists lack adequate tools to account for Third World governments' opposition to the introduction of markets. The political economy approach finds this behavior less difficult to explain.

According to postulate 3, political institutions stand relatively autonomous from the economy; they therefore create incentives of their own. According to postulate 2, rational politicians will respond to these incentives and may therefore make political choices that are individually rational but economically perverse, as noted in postulate 4.

Armed with these assertions, we can begin to understand why rational politicians favor policies that distort markets. When governments shift prices away from those that would prevail at market equilibrium, they create an imbalance between supply and demand; private sources of supply leave the market, and the good sold rises in value as demand exceeds supply at official prices. The result is that officials who control the market control a good with a new value. They also create the opportunity to ration – to give the good to some and to withhold it from others.

Government intervention in markets thereby creates the capacity to form patron-client networks, or political machines. Through the controlled market, public officials can organize groups of faithful supporters who possess the valued commodity – now rendered scarce by government policy – because of official favor.

We can therefore better understand why politicians may choose strategies of market intervention. The political economy perspective also casts light on the persistence of such policies. In particular, it helps to explain why, even though all individuals may be made better off from the promotion of markets, there may be few organized demands for government withdrawal from them.

Postulate 2 – the assumption of individual rationality – explains in part why this is so. Many individuals, behaving rationally, are averse to risks. Many therefore prefer certain incomes they receive in regulated markets – be they ever so low – to the possibly higher but future (and therefore uncertain) incomes that they would receive in unregulated markets. Postulate 4 also contributes to the explanation. Even if all individuals were certain that they would benefit from a free market, behaving rationally, they might not try to force the government out of the market. They may see benefits to free riding – to letting others pay the costs of political action, while seeking to secure the economic benefits for free.

Why, then, would politicians not intervene to provide the necessary organization? We have already explained why it is rational for politicians to advocate government intervention: Market regulation facilitates the construction of political organizations. When all politicians pursue their individual political interests, however, the costs to society exceed private benefits, and political leaders and their followers may realize that there are better forms of economic management. But – and this is critical – no single politician can alone afford to initiate economic reform. If one politician renounces the apportionment of special benefits, then that politician's rivals would be in a position to gain a political advantage by defending the interests that prospered from special favors. Any politician committed to withdrawing from the market would have to act in concert with others. Such organized withdrawals would be difficult, given the temptation to reap short-run political rewards from protecting those who owe their special fortunes to the protection provided by the *ancien régime*. Once again, as emphasized in postulate 4, there is a disjunction between collective and individual rationality.

Market-oriented reasoning emphasizes the benefits of the market. It stresses individual rationality, and, given the power of the analogy of the hidden hand, it presumes that rational individuals will secure any social outcome that they unanimously prefer.

Political-economic reasoning would also emphasize the benefits of the market and would stress individual rationality. But it finds many reasons – some arising precisely from the rationality of individuals – why markets may not be created. It provides insight into why economic policies, which might enhance the collective welfare, would not be provided politically, even by rational individuals.

CONCLUSION

In political science, a commitment to choice theoretic reasoning is often equated with a commitment to market economics. Indeed, in the early days of rational choice theorizing, the prize seemed to go to those who could make political analysis resemble as much as possible economic analysis (Ilchman and Uphoff 1971). I have therefore ended this chapter by highlighting the distinction between political economy and the use of market-based reasoning, particularly in the field of development.

There is a second reason for ending this chapter in such a manner: to achieve a sense of closure. I began it by shouldering aside the contribution of cultural studies. Now, at the end, I want to return to this scholarly tradition. Having ventured into the field of political economy, scholars have acquired new tools. It may now be time for them, with these tools in hand, to analyze the significance of values and institutions. Who can fail to appreciate the opportunity offered by contemporary game theory to provide a formal structure for kinds of symbolic displays analyzed by Goffman (1959) or Geertz (1983), for example? Work on games of imperfect information offers grounds for analyzing their powerful insights into the subjective side of influence and power. And who can fail to appreciate the significance of models of collective choice for the analysis of such institutions as lineage systems, village councils, or systems of traditional authority? Some scholars have already recognized the value of these tools. One can hope that their contributions represent but a beginning of a new tradition of research into the properties of significant institutions in developing nations (examples would include Wilks 1975; Posner 1980; and Bates 1989).

Nothing I have said in this chapter questions my conviction that the particularities of specific cultures count. Anyone working in other cultures knows that people's beliefs and values matter; so too do the distinctive characteristics of their institutions. What needs to be specified, rather, is the manner in which these factors systematically shape collective outcomes. A major attraction of the theories of choice and human interaction, which lie at the core of contemporary political economy, is that they offer the tools for causally linking values and structures to their social consequences.

In the early years of political economy, rational choice theorists posed as revolutionaries, attacking their sociologically minded brethren. Now it may be time to synthesize these traditions. Because they work in cultures with distinctive beliefs, values, and institutions, students of developing areas may be among those best poised to take this important step.

PART II

Organizations, transactions, and opportunities

3

Bargaining costs, influence costs, and the organization of economic activity

PAUL MILGROM AND JOHN ROBERTS

This chapter is concerned with the economics of organization and management, a relatively new area of study that seeks to analyze the internal structure and workings of economic organizations, the division of activity among these organizations, and the management of relations between them through markets or other higher-level, encompassing organizations.

The dominant approach to this subject is transaction-cost economics, as introduced by Coase (1937, 1960) and developed by several others since, most notably Williamson (1975, 1985). The main tenet of Coase's theory is that economic activities tend to be organized efficiently – that is, so as to maximize the expected total wealth of the parties affected.[1] In this context, two sorts of costs are customarily identified – those of physical production and distribution and those of carrying out necessary exchanges. Because these are typically treated as distinct and separable, the efficiency hypothesis becomes one of transaction-cost minimization: The division of activities among firms and between a firm and the market is determined by whether a particular transaction is most efficiently conducted in a market setting or under centralized authority within a firm.[2]

This approach has two conceptual problems. First, the total costs a firm incurs cannot generally be expressed as the sum of production costs – depending only on the technology and the inputs used – and transaction costs – depending only on the way transactions are organized. In general, these two kinds of costs must be considered together;

We thank Yoram Barzel, Patrick Bolton, John Ferejohn, Victor Goldberg, Ed Lazear, Oliver Williamson, and the editors of this volume for their helpful comments. We also thank the National Science Foundation and the John Simon Guggenheim Foundation for their generous financial support. Much of the work reported here was done while Milgrom held a Ford Visiting Professorship at the University of California, Berkeley, during the 1986–87 academic year.

efficient organization is not simply a matter of minimizing transaction costs.[3] Second, the general theory is too vague to be useful. If an existing institution or arrangement appears to be inefficient, one can always claim that it is simply because the observer has not recognized all the relevant transaction costs. To give the theory more power and to generate more specific predictions, recent developments of transaction-cost economics have focused on identifying the major components of transaction costs and how they affect the efficient form of organization.

Our principal purpose here is to add two elements to this theory. First, we will argue that the crucial costs associated with using markets to carry out transactions (rather than bringing them within a more complex, formal organization) are the costs of bargaining over short-term arrangements between independent economic agents. This accentuation of short-term bargaining costs contrasts with received theory (as presented by Williamson), which emphasizes asset specificity, uncertainty, and frequency of dealings as the key factors. Second, we identify certain costs attached to the centralized, discretionary decision-making power inherent in formal economic organizations such as firms. Particularly important among these are the costs of essentially political activity within the organization, which we call *influence costs:* the losses that arise from individuals within an organization seeking to influence its decisions for their private benefit (and from their perhaps succeeding in doing so) and from the organization's responding to control this behavior. These costs are an important disability of centralized control and help to explain why integrated internal organization does not always supplant market relations between independent entities.

The remainder of this introductory section discusses the firm's role in traditional economic theory, that theory's failure to treat issues of organization and management, and the need to address such issues. The section headed "Transaction-Cost Economics" articulates the received elements of the transaction-cost approach to the economics of organization. The section titled "Critique and Extension of the Received Theory" contains our criticisms of this approach, including our basic arguments for the centrality of bargaining and influence costs. The sections on "Bargaining Costs" and "Costs of Centralized Authority" explore each of these costs in more detail. The section on "Influence Costs in the Public Sector" briefly uses the logic of influence costs to examine some issues of government. The final section contains general conclusions.

Until recently, economists paid little attention to the internal workings of business firms and other economic organizations. In standard microeconomic models, a firm is simply a collection of possible production plans together with a rule for selecting among them. Typical rules include profit or share-value maximization for firms run by the owners of capital, average-wage maximization for labor-managed firms, and surplus maximization for public enterprises. These models allow no explicit role for management activities – the processes by which firms generate and evaluate decision alternatives; formulate, implement, and monitor plans; coordinate distant branch stores, factories, and offices; balance the competing interests of employees, owners, customers, suppliers, and creditors; and motivate them all to work in the general interest. Although these models could include such activities, they are not explicitly represented.[4]

Why have economists clung for so long to such an incomplete account of economic organizations? Historically, economic theory's chief task has been to explain how market economies, with so little centralized direction, could have performed as well as they have. The performance of Western European and North American market economies over the centuries is, by world standards, nothing short of spectacular. Moreover, recent experience with economic development elsewhere in the world confirms the connection between the West's remarkable economic growth and the prevalence of market organization: Recall the success of the market economies of Japan and Singapore, or contrast the recent economic performance of Eastern and Western Europe, of mainland China and Taiwan, or of North and South Korea. The great economic puzzle that the sustained growth and development of market-oriented economies poses is not that firms and other centrally managed organizations can achieve order in their affairs but that markets, with little apparent planning or explicit coordination, can direct available resources to such good effect.

In the two centuries since Adam Smith's original explication of how markets might guide economic activity to serve the public interest, economists have dissected, analyzed, refined, and formalized the theory of markets controlled by impersonal forces – the invisible hand. But even as these economists worked, the economies around them were changing. No longer were firms mostly family affairs with bookkeeping and management operations done at night when the shop was closed. Continuous production processes and specialized equipment came into use, and the very visible hands of engineers, chemists, and professional managers came to control production activities. In the United States, as Chandler (1977) has explained, the growth of the railroads and the telegraph opened national markets and made large-scale factory production economical. This strained the capacity of local suppliers, and so required factory managers to plan more carefully. With this planning came both a greater opportunity and a greater need to consider alternative ways of organizing production. Should an automobile manufacturer make or buy its headlamps, batteries, and body parts? Should it own a network of dealers selling directly to the public, contract with existing distribution companies, or sell to independently owned retailers? Purchasing supplies or hiring services in the market came to be just one organizational alternative for acquiring the necessary inputs for production, assembly, distribution, and sales.

What determines which inputs a firm will acquire by ordinary market exchange and which it will produce itself? What difference does it make whether a firm produces an input itself, has a regular supplier produce it, or buys it on the market from the lowest bidder? The second formulation of the question shifts attention subtly away from the mechanical details of how production is arranged toward a focus on how the relationships between those who carry out the successive stages of production are managed. It suggests that whether production is arranged internally or externally need not determine what equipment will be used or which people will do the work. "Internal" and "external" production are just terms to describe in a very partial way how productive relationships are to be managed.

Economists who study organizations have come to see the market as but one alternative for solving the management problem of coordinating the diverse activities and interests of consumers and firms. Markets can then be fairly evaluated only by comparing them to other means of solving the same problem. A full evaluation cannot be made until a unified theory of management processes has been developed. Without such a theory, economists' recommendations about such bread-and-butter economic questions as whether to regulate monopolies and whether public or private organizations should provide services like education, communication, transportation, and so forth must be regarded as tentative, at best. Economists can no longer ignore the economics of organization and management.

TRANSACTION-COST ECONOMICS

Coase (1937) created transaction-cost economics by shifting the focus on the firm from technological possibilities and the maximization of some market objective to transactions and the management of relationships. *Transact,* as an intransitive verb, means "to do business with; negotiate."[5] *Transaction costs* encompass the costs of deciding, planning, arranging, and negotiating the actions to be taken and the terms of exchange when two or more parties do business; the costs of changing plans, renegotiating terms, and resolving disputes as changing circumstances may require; and the costs of ensuring that parties perform as agreed. Transaction costs also include any losses resulting from inefficient group decisions, plans, arrangements or agreements; inefficient responses to changing circumstances; and imperfect enforcement of agreements. In short, transaction costs include anything that affects the relative performance of different ways of organizing resources and production activities.

As indicated earlier, a central tenet of transaction-cost economics is that production in capitalist, profit-oriented economies will tend to be organized so as to economize on transaction costs. For example, inputs will tend to be acquired in the market rather than produced by the firm when the costs of market transactions are less than those of internal transactions. The tenet does not specify how this tendency to economize on transaction costs arises. Careful planning by especially competent management may sometimes be responsible,[6] as may imitation of successful firms by less successful ones or the growth of efficiently organized firms and the collapse of inefficiently organized ones (Nelson and Winter 1982).

In its general form, the tenet is not an empirical hypothesis: It is too nebulous to be confronted directly with evidence. To make specific predictions from the theory, it is necessary to identify the costs characteristically associated with transacting business in different ways and to discover how circumstances cause these costs to vary.

Oliver Williamson (1985) has proposed one framework within which Coase's theory can be made more specific and operational.[7] Williamson's theory is based on an analysis of the costs of contracting in business relationships. Contracts (explicit or implicit) govern a firm's relationships with its suppliers, employees, customers, creditors, and shareholders. A central premise in Williamson's theory (foreshadowed in Coase's own work) is that any contract that calls for the future delivery of a good or service, the future provision of capital, or the future performance of work must be incomplete. That is, a contract can never specify exactly what actions are to be taken and what payments are to be made in all possible future contingencies. There are several reasons for this. First, parties cannot perfectly anticipate all the possible contingencies that may affect their costs of performing as promised, or even their ability to do so. Second, even for circumstances that can be anticipated, it is often more economical to respond when the need arises rather than to plan in advance for every foreseeable contingency (Lindblom 1959). Third, writing unambiguous contracts is difficult because of the limitations of natural languages (Quine 1960). Drawing up contracts with too many fine distinctions may simply increase the likelihood that emerging events will fall into areas of ambiguity or overlap, leading to disagreements that will have to be resolved after the fact. Finally, enforceable contracts can be made contingent only on information that the parties will share and that courts can verify. They cannot be based on information that only one contracting party will have, even if that information would be necessary for efficient future decisions.

What are the consequences of this incompleteness of contracts? If planning and contracting were complete and costless activities, parties to a contract would, after their initial agreement, act as one. They would determine in advance and in detail the best possible actions for every contingency that might arise, and the contract would specify that those actions be taken and would provide incentives to do so. In reality, because planning and contracting consume real resources and because perfectly explicit and freely enforceable contracts cannot be written, the theory posits that contracting parties content themselves with an agreement that *frames* their relationship — that is, one that fixes general performance expectations, provides procedures to govern decision making in situations where the contract is not explicit, and outlines how to adjudicate disputes when they arise. The differences among simple market contracting, complex contracting, vertical integration, and other ways of organizing transactions lie primarily in the institutions they specify for governing the relationship when circumstances not foreseen in the contract arise.

For the transaction-cost theory to explain the great variety of contracting practices that actually exist, it must identify the critical dimensions that favor one form of contracting over another. According to Williamson (1985, p. 52), "the principal dimensions with respect to which transactions differ are asset specificity, uncertainty, and frequency. The first is the most important and most distinguishes transaction-cost economics from other treatments of economic organization, but the other two play significant roles."

Asset specificity refers to the degree to which an asset's value depends on the continuation of a particular relationship. Consider, for example, a firm that rents a computer system and invests in software and training for the employees who will use the system. If an identical or perfectly compatible computer cannot be rented or purchased from another source, the software and employee training are specialized assets because they would lose much of their value if the firm switched to another computer system. A supplier who acquires specialized dies or locates a plant near a customer's remote factory has similarly invested in specialized assets. Klein, Crawford, and Alchian (1978) have dubbed the profits an investor stands to lose from terminating a particular business relationship "appropriable quasi-rents."[8] Logically, although quasi-rents may exist any time costs have already been sunk, appropriable quasi-rents exist precisely when there are specialized assets.[9]

For concreteness, let us suppose that a supplier invests in specialized assets. The supplier's worry is that a customer might behave opportunistically – that is, might try to force a reduction in future prices, curtail purchases, make unreasonable quality demands, increase the variability of demand and the number of rush orders, or take other actions that would diminish the supplier's margins. Note that none of these concerns would arise if the two had a complete, enforceable contract. Moreover, if the assets were not specialized, these threats would again not be cause for great concern: The supplier would be protected by the option to shift the assets to other uses in which they could command an equal return. However, specialized assets, by definition, cannot be shifted to other uses without loss, so the investor may be forced to accept reduced margins, leading to a substandard return on investment.

Indeed, it has frequently been argued that concerns that the buyer will appropriate quasi-rents may lead the supplier to invest too little in specialized assets.[10] As an illustration of this, Klein, Crawford, and Alchian cite the case of Fisher Body. In the 1920s, Fisher refused to build plants adjacent to the General Motors plants that the company served. The authors argue that Fisher Body quite rightly feared that such plant sites would make the company vulnerable to General Motors' subsequent attempts to force reductions in its margins.

Similarly, a buyer might enjoy quasi-rents that are subject to appropriation by a supplier, or both parties might earn appropriable quasi-rents from their assets. Generally, Klein, Crawford, and Alchian emphasize the importance of *co-specialized assets* – ones that are most valuable when used together. For example, an electricity generating plant at the mouth of a coal mine is co-specialized with the mine. Generally, when different parties own co-specialized assets, at least one party enjoys a flow of appropriable quasi-rents.

One apparent option to mitigate the problem of appropriation of quasi-rents is to make the contract's price and other terms more explicit and rigid and to impose greater penalties for breach of contract. However, this solution is itself costly. Adding rigidity to a contract may reduce the parties' flexibility in responding to future circumstances. Alternatively, if clauses are added to specify in advance more contingencies and the corresponding responses, direct contracting costs rise and the likelihood of ambiguity in the contract's provisions increases.

Uncertainty about what circumstances will prevail when future actions must be taken is the primary factor that makes complete contracting impossible. Greater uncertainty about what future actions will be appropriate makes rigid contracts, which recognize few contingencies, more likely to lead to bad decisions; they are therefore more costly. Flexible contracts, too, entail costs. They are, of necessity, open to different interpretations and thus to effective renegotiation. They therefore do little to reduce the risk that quasi-rents will be appropriated. In this context, Coase's hypothesis is that parties will normally agree on the contractual arrangements in which these costs are minimized.

If opportunities to appropriate quasi-rents from a particular specialized investment arise frequently, then contracting parties may find it economical to craft a specialized governance structure to deal with these temptations. Depending on the nature of the transaction, many alternative structures may be available, and these may vary greatly in their complexity and costs. The simplest are generally worded contracts. These are intended to be interpreted (by the courts, if necessary) in the event of a dispute, but the parties involved in such agreements rely primarily on each others' goodwill and business reputation, standard procedures, and their continuing business relationship to smooth out disagreements without extensive bargaining. When the specialized investments and associated appropriable quasi-rents are not large, as with arrangements to deliver standard commodities at an agreed price, simple contracts may be entirely adequate. In other situations, more careful planning or governance may be needed. Then contracts can be more detailed. For example, they may include price-escalator clauses and clauses indicating penalties for breach of contract or how to deal with specified contingencies.[11] They may specify procedures for selecting and using arbitrators or private judges to substitute for courtroom litigation. Firms can also merge[12] and give executives authority for making decisions. Highly detailed contracts and specialized procedures for making decisions and resolving disputes are expensive to write or design, but the costs of writing and designing are fixed costs that, once sunk, can be applied again and again to similar transactions. Hence, detailed contracts and specialized procedures are most cost-effective when similar transactions are frequently conducted.

As Williamson (1985) states them, the predictions of transaction-cost economics can be summarized as follows: In comparing business relationships that occur in the same legal environment and at the same time, governance structures will be most complex and most finely crafted for transactions with (1) the greatest value of appropriable quasi-rents, (2) the greatest uncertainty about performance conditions, and (3) the greatest frequency.[13] Beyond these, we can add the prediction by Klein, Crawford, and Alchian that co-specialized assets will be co-owned, because co-specialization means that separate ownership exposes one or both parties to appropriation of quasi-rents while the assets' long life means that the frequency condition for the efficiency of specialized governance is met.[14] Finally, we have an observation made by Grossman and Hart (1986). If ownership rights in some assets are not transferrable (for example, an individual's human capital of knowledge, skills, connections, and so on) and if these assets are co-specialized with one or more other assets, then the relative degrees of co-specialization will determine ownership patterns.

CRITIQUE AND EXTENSION OF THE RECEIVED THEORY

Our principal intent in this section is to argue the importance of bargaining costs in market relations and to identify certain costs of centralized decision-making authority.

Received transaction-cost theory emphasizes the implications of the incompleteness of contracts that cover actions to be taken in the uncertain future. However, we will argue that this emphasis is somewhat misplaced. Instead, we will show that the key to evaluating the efficacy of market transactions is the costs of negotiating suitably detailed short-term contracts. If these costs were always zero, then organizing economic activity through market exchange would always be perfectly efficient. On the other hand, when the costs of negotiating periodic exchange agreements are sufficiently high, then regardless of other factors, such as the presence or absence of specialized assets, potentially important savings are to be realized by placing the activity under a central authority, which can quickly settle potentially costly disputes.

To understand these claims we must first understand what we mean by the terms "short-term" and "bargaining costs." When describing contracts "short-term" refers to a period short enough so that all the information that is relevant for current decisions is already available. Short-term contracts, by definition, do not specify how to act in the longer term as new circumstances arise. We interpret "bargaining costs" expansively, just as we did the term "transaction costs," to include all the costs associated with multilateral bargaining, competitive bidding, and other voluntary mechanisms for determining a mutually acceptable agreement. Bargaining costs include not only the wages paid to the bargainers[15] or the opportunity costs of their time, but also the costs of monitoring and enforcing the agreement and any losses from failure to reach the most efficient agreement possible in the most efficient fashion.

With these definitions, having zero short-term bargaining costs means that the bargainers require negligible physical and human resources to reach efficient short-term contracts. (A short-term contract is *efficient* if there is no other feasible *short-term* contract that both parties would prefer.) However, by definition, bargainers cannot commit themselves through a short-term contract to restrict their long-term behavior in any way, even though they may recognize the long-term impacts of their short-term decisions. For example, the parties to a short-term contract may agree on what investments in specialized assets to make this year and who will pay for these, but they cannot commit themselves to behave benignly next year toward the party who, having paid for the investment, has appropriable quasi-rents.

To establish the key role of bargaining costs, suppose that the costs of negotiating short-term contracts were zero. We consider a two-party relationship (such as between a supplier and a customer) for which efficient production demands that the supplier, the customer, or both invest in specialized assets. We assume that the parties meet the standard assumptions of the transaction-cost literature in that each is a risk-neutral, financially unconstrained, expected-wealth-maximizing[16] bargainer. The two also share common beliefs about the relative likelihoods of various future contingencies and both are farsighted in the sense that they understand how their current actions and agreements will affect future bargaining opportunities and behavior. They are also opportunistic in the sense that their behavior at any time does not depend on past unbonded promises or on how past costs and benefits have been shared. Finally, we assume that contracts governing prices and behavior in the distant future are prohibitively costly to write because too many contingencies need to be evaluated and described (that is, there is too much uncertainty), but that contracts governing prices, bonus payments, and the actions to be taken in the near term, over which the relevant conditions are already known, are costless to write.

In general Williamsonian terms, the situation involves opportunistic behavior, imperfect long-term contracting, specialized assets, and uncertainty about the future. According to transaction-cost theorists, these conditions are sufficient to prevent a market arrangement based on a series of short-term contracts from yielding an efficient outcome. Nevertheless, we claim that if the costs of bargaining over short-term arrangements were zero – a condition that is apparently consistent with our other specifications – then the market outcome would be efficient. That is, the actions taken by the parties both in the short run *and in the long run* would *in all contingencies* be identical to those that would have been specified in the "ideal contract" – the efficient (possibly long-term and complete) contract the parties would sign if there were no restrictions at all on contracting.[17]

Bargaining, influence costs, and organization

Before proving this proposition and explaining the argument supporting it and the defect in received theory, we should emphasize two points. First, given our assumptions of risk neutrality and common beliefs, the actions taken under an efficient contract do not depend on the bargaining power of the parties involved: Only the distribution of the fruits of the bargain depend on bargaining power. Conversely, because the parties are risk-neutral, if the actions they take coincide with those that would be specified in the ideal contract, then the arrangement is efficient, regardless of the payments made between the parties. Second, we do not claim that the inability to write complete contracts has no effect on the way the parties' share risks: By their very definition, incomplete contracts imply a limited capacity to make intertemporal or contingent transfers. What *is* unaffected is the set of actions the parties will eventually take and hence the agreement's efficiency.

To establish the proposition, we consider a two-period problem with two parties. (The extension to more parties and periods is straightforward.) Bargaining over first-period actions (x_1 and x_2) and first-period transfers (s_1 and s_2) is costless in the above sense, and, once the second period arrives, it will be costless to bargain over the actions (y_1 and y_2) and transfers (t_1 and t_2) in that period. However, at the first date, no binding agreements can be made about second-period actions and transfers. We assume that net transfers are zero: $t_1 + t_2 = s_1 + s_2 = 0$. Let $V_1(x_1, x_2, y_1, y_2, \mu, \nu, \pi)$ be the payoff (benefits less costs) accruing directly to the first party in the second period. This depends on the actions taken in each period, the resolution of any uncertainty before first-period bargaining (as indicated by μ), any uncertainty resolved after first-period bargaining but before second-period bargaining (ν), and any uncertainty not resolved until after second-period bargaining (π). Define $V_2(x_1, x_2, y_1, y_2, \mu, \nu, \pi)$ similarly as the direct second-period returns to the second party. The presence of x_1 and x_2 as arguments of V_1 and V_2 reflects the possibility that these decisions may be investments with long-term payoffs, and the presence of y_i as an argument of V_j allows for the possibility that the second-period returns (quasi-rents) may be subject to appropriation: The returns to j's first-period actions depend on i's second-period actions. Note that risk neutrality implies the absence of income effects, so first-period transfers do not affect second-period payoffs. Also, note that both μ and ν are known when second-period bargaining occurs and that x_1 and x_2 are already fixed at that point.

By hypothesis, the agreement reached at the second date, given the circumstances $C = (x_1, x_2, \mu, \nu)$ that prevail then, will be efficient; that is, y_1 and y_2 will be chosen to maximize expected total wealth ($E[V_1 + V_2 \mid C]$). Letting $W_i(C) = t_i + E[V_i \mid C]$ be the portion of expected

67

Paul Milgrom and John Roberts

total wealth that accrues to bargainer i, we then have $W_1(C) + W_2(C)$ = $\max_{(y_1, y_2)} E[V_1 + V_2 \mid C]$. (The transfers t_1 and t_2 will depend on the parties' relative bargaining strength, but the optimal, chosen actions $y_1(C)$ and $y_2(C)$ will not.)

At the first date, the parties, being farsighted, will correctly forecast the agreement that would be reached in any circumstances C in the second period. Thus, each will evaluate first-period agreements according to the utility functions $s_1 + E[U_i(x_1, x_2, \mu, \nu) \mid \mu] + E[W_i(C) \mid \mu]$, where $U_i(x_1, x_2, \mu, \nu)$ is the first-period payoff net of transfers to i when the actions taken are x_1 and x_2 and the outcome of the uncertainty is given by μ and ν. Since the short-term agreement reached in the first period is, by hypothesis, efficient, it maximizes the sum of these two valuation functions. With common beliefs, this is equal to $E[U_1 + U_2 + W_1 + W_2 \mid \mu]$. Hence,

$$\max_{x_1, x_2} E[U_1 + U_2 + W_1 + W_2 \mid \mu]$$

$$= \max_{x_1, x_2} E[U_1 + U_2 + \max_{y_1, y_2} E\{V_1 + V_2 \mid C\} \mid \mu]$$

$$= \max_{x_1, x_2, y_1(C), y_2(C)} E[U_1 + U_2 + V_1 + V_2 \mid \mu].$$

But the first expression is the wealth achieved under short-term contracting in the absence of bargaining costs, and the last expression is the wealth that would be achieved under an efficient long-term contract. Their equality means that full efficiency is realized in the absence of short-term bargaining costs.

To illustrate, consider the relationship between Fisher Body (the supplier) and General Motors (the customer) analyzed by Klein, Crawford, and Alchian. Suppose the relationship lasts for two periods. In the first period, the parties reach an agreement about plant site and design (investments in specialized assets, corresponding to x_1 and x_2) and about the share of the cost of constructing the plant each will bear. Such an agreement specifies only the immediate actions the parties will take and how they will be compensated for these. In the second period, the parties negotiate prices, possibly a fixed transfer payment, quality standards, and a delivery schedule (t_1, t_2, y_1, and y_2) in full knowledge of the circumstances then prevailing (e.g., current model year body designs, demands for various models, the costs and availabilities of steel and substitute materials, and so on, modeled in our equations by μ and ν, as well as the previously made investments). By our assumption of costless bargaining, regardless of the first-period agreement, the second-period agreement will be efficient given the conditions that prevail then.

Now consider what would happen if the parties were to agree in the initial period to make the efficient plant site and design decisions.[18] Then, the actions taken in the second period would, in all circumstances, agree with those specified under the hypothetical ideal contract. We therefore conclude that the parties could sign a short-term contract in the first period that would lead to them making efficient decisions in both the first and second periods. Actually, by varying who pays for the initial investment in the plant, all distributions of the fruits of these efficient decisions can be attained. Any contract, therefore, that leads to inefficient decision making can be improved upon for both parties by some contract that leads to efficient decision making. Thus, if the costs of short-term bargaining were zero, the agreement reached would indeed lead to efficient actions.

What, then, was wrong with the argument advanced in the first section of this chapter? Why shouldn't the fear of opportunism by General Motors make Fisher Body unwilling to enter into the arrangement? The answer is that Fisher can be compensated for the risk by having General Motors bear part of the plant's cost. Why, then, shouldn't General Motors fear that Fisher will appropriate its quasi-rents? Because the agreement can call for General Motors to pay for only as much of the plant's earnings as it expects to appropriate in future negotiations. Threats of appropriation are simply distributional threats; they are not threats to efficient action as long as bargaining costs are zero. Among risk-neutral parties with common beliefs and no private information, distributional threats can be compensated by initial cash payments. The efficiency of market arrangements is limited only by the costs of negotiating efficient short-term contracts. This conclusion points to the central importance of bargaining costs in determining the efficiency of market transactions. We shall study the origins and determinants of bargaining costs in the next section.

The preceding analysis relied on the assumptions that all parties are risk-neutral and that they can contract for current actions without restriction. The first of these assumptions is not reasonable when contracting parties are individuals, and the second fails when current actions cannot be precisely monitored. Nevertheless, as Fudenberg, Holmstrom, and Milgrom (1990) have shown, the conclusion that short-term contracts are as good as long-term contracts when no bargaining costs are involved applies equally to situations involving risk-averse bargainers and imperfectly observed actions, provided contractual payments in each period can be made to depend on any information obtained during the period and provided no new information about any period's actions arrives only in later periods.

Our other criticism of early transaction-cost theories concerns their relative silence regarding the source, nature, and magnitude of the costs incurred in nonmarket transactions. Indeed, despite the firm beliefs of many economists that markets often hold great advantages over non-market forms of organization,[19] received transaction-cost theory leaves unclear why market transactions are *ever* to be preferred to nonmarket ones.

Identifying the costs of general nonmarket transactions is a task to be approached with great caution. As Chandler (1962) has documented, business organizations have changed substantially and repeatedly over the past century, and the disabilities (transaction costs) suffered by an older form of organization may be overcome by its replacement. Perhaps wisely, then, transaction-cost theorists for a long time were largely silent about the source and nature of the costs of centralized organization, although they were certainly aware of the problem.[20] Quite recently, however, Williamson (1985) and Grossman and Hart (1986) have addressed explicitly the disabilities of nonmarket organization.

Williamson's treatment of the question of "Why can't a large firm do everything a collection of smaller firms can do, and more?" employs a crucially important idea: the notion of *selective intervention*. Many of the arguments purporting to explain the limits of organization fail when confronted with the policy of replacing previously autonomous units with semiautonomous ones in whose operations and decisions central managers intervene only when uncoordinated or competitively oriented decisions are inefficient. Any adequate explanation of why all economic activity is not brought under central management must confront this possibility.

Grossman and Hart (and Hart and Moore 1988) attempt to deal with this problem with a unified theory that treats the costs and benefits of different forms of organization as being all of a single type. Specifically, they identify asset ownership with the possession of residual control rights over the assets – that is, all rights to the disposition and use of the assets that are not either given away in explicit contracts or claimed by the state. Ownership of a firm is then solely an issue of who retains these residual control rights over the collection of physical assets that Grossman and Hart identify with the firm. Because contracting is necessarily incomplete, such residual rights must exist. Moreover, Grossman and Hart assume that contracts are so incomplete, even in the short term, that parties cannot commit themselves to current actions, so that the analysis we have given does not apply. Under these conditions, the allocation of control rights affects the ability of the parties to appropriate one another's investments and to protect their own investments from appropriation. Thus, just as the costs of a transaction between two independent owner-managed firms arise because each owner-manager's decision making ignores how his or her actions may benefit the other firm's asset values, the cost of integrating two previously independent firms is that the manager who is no longer an asset owner will ignore how his or her actions affect the integrated firm's assets: He or she will no longer manage these assets efficiently.[21]

Williamson's treatment of these issues is also based on incentive arguments. He focuses on why "high-powered", marketlike incentives that replicate residual claimant status are not feasible within a centrally managed organization – that is, he focuses on why selective intervention is not in fact possible. His answer is based on the idea that difficulties of (verifiable) measurement give rise to two moral hazard problems. First, the assets of the acquired stage will not be carefully managed because the manager cannot truly be the residual claimant, given that observation of the manager's actions is imperfect (or, at least, not contemporaneous); that resignation is an option; and that mechanisms for conveying reputations are imperfect. Thus, as in Grossman and Hart, assets will be mismanaged. Second, the returns of the acquired stage will be subject to appropriation via manipulation of the transfer prices and other accounting constructs that the center controls and that are too complex to be subjected to complete contracting. This, too, destroys incentives for proper asset management at the acquired stage.

These arguments have much to recommend them, but their focus on physical assets is too narrow. In particular, Grossman and Hart specifically do not distinguish between an organization with paid employees and one that contracts for labor services with independent suppliers but that owns and retains title to the tools and other physical assets that workers use in production. But what of the many firms, such as computer software development, public accounting, management consulting, and legal services firms or, to a somewhat lesser extent, universities and sports teams, whose only significant assets are the working relationships among their employees? Either the theory is silent in such cases, or it suggests that such organizations should have no bounds on their efficient size because they have no significant assets of the type Grossman and Hart consider.

A second criticism of the Grossman-Hart approach recognizes that incentives are a function of income streams, not just of decision rights, and that residual decision rights do not totally determine income streams when decisions have multidimensional consequences that extend over many periods and are not immediately and perfectly observable. A more satisfactory theory would integrate both factors.[22]

Despite these criticisms, we believe that these incentive arguments have substantial force. Nevertheless, these theories miss an important class of generally identifiable costs of internal organization that do not depend specifically on control of assets. In the section titled "Costs of Centralized Authority," we argue that the crucial distinguishing characteristic of a firm is not the pattern of asset ownership but the substitution of centralized authority for the relatively unfettered negotiations that characterize market transactions. And, we argue, the very existence of this centralized authority is incompatible with a thoroughgoing policy of efficient selective intervention. The authority to intervene inevitably implies the authority to intervene inefficiently. Yet such interventions, even if they are inefficient overall, can be highly beneficial for particular individuals and groups. Thus, either inefficient interventions will be made and resources will be expended to bring them about or to prevent them, or else the authority to intervene must be restricted. This implies that some efficient interventions must be foregone.

BARGAINING COSTS

What are the costs of bargaining? We have defined these to include the opportunity costs of bargainers' time, the costs of monitoring and enforcing an agreement, and any costly delays or failures to reach agreement when efficiency requires that parties cooperate. Our analysis in this section will focus on costly delays and failures to reach agreement. The idea comes easily to economists that when parties in a bargaining situation have all the relevant information, they will agree to an efficient bargain. Nash (1950, 1953) elevated this proposition to an axiom in deriving his famous bargaining solution, and Coase (1960) made it the linchpin of his theory of property rights. Buchanan and Tullock (1962) made the same point in connection with their argument that only costs – inefficiencies – of private bargaining can justify government provision of goods or services:

If the costs of organizing decisions voluntarily should be zero, *all* externalities would be eliminated by voluntary private behavior of individuals regardless of the initial structure of property rights. There would, in this case, be no rational basis for state or collective action beyond the initial minimum delineation of the power of individual disposition over resources. (pp. 47–48)

The evidence supporting this idea, however, is mixed.[23] When experimental subjects are asked to divide a sum of money, say ten dollars, they have little difficulty agreeing to split the sum equally without costly delays or disagreements. But when the thing to be divided is more complicated, so that symmetry does not focus the bargainers' attention on an obvious solution, posturing, haggling, and disagreement is more likely, as each party seeks to create or stake out a reasonable-sounding position that yields a large share of the available rewards.

To get a better idea of how serious these coordination difficulties might be, we turn to the analysis of a bargaining by demands game introduced originally by Nash (1950, 1953). Suppose that two parties have one dollar to divide. We can interpret the dollar as the maximal wealth attainable from exchange between the two parties. For example, it might represent the value a potential buyer puts on an object that is worthless to its current owner. The rules of the bargaining game are as follows. Each of the two parties, A and B, makes a demand, a and b. If the demands are consistent with the available resources – that is, if $a + b$ does not exceed one dollar – then each party gets what it demanded. If the demands are inconsistent with available resources, both parties get a payoff of zero.

If the problem were presented in just this way, the parties would very likely each demand fifty cents, resulting in a 50–50 split. In the terms Schelling (1960) used, the 50–50 split is an obvious *focal point* – a way for the parties to coordinate their demands. However, most real bargaining situations have either no focal points on which to coordinate, or many possible ones, which is just as bad. What should we expect to happen then?

For a game-theoretic analysis, we may ask, what is the full set of noncooperative equilibrium outcomes of this demand game? These outcomes represent patterns of behavior that are consistent with the rational and well-informed pursuit of self-interest on both sides. The answer is that for any pair of positive numbers summing to one dollar *or less,* there is a Nash equilibrium (possibly in mixed strategies[24]) of the demand game at which the players' expected payoffs are precisely those numbers.[25] In particular, there is a Nash equilibrium in which both bargainers demand the whole dollar and, as a result, both receive zero.

This game-theoretic analysis not only captures the familiar idea that the division of the gains from trade may be indeterminate under bilateral monopoly, it also shows that the actual magnitude of the total gains realized may be similarly indeterminate.[26] The bargainers may fail to agree on any efficient solution, and, indeed, the resources that rational parties may squander in jockeying for bargaining position can be as little as zero or as large as the entire potential gains from trade.

Remarkably, the introduction of a minimal amount of competition virtually eliminates the potential for such coordination failures in two-party bargaining. Suppose, for example, that the bargaining situation involves two suppliers and a buyer. In terms of our model, there are now three parties to the bargaining – A, B, and C, who make demands a, b, and c. The demands are compatible if either $a + b$ or $a + c$ is less than one dollar. The rules of the game are as follows. If the buyer's demand is inconsistent with both suppliers' offers, no agreement is reached, and each party receives a payoff of zero. Otherwise, buyer A does business with the supplier making the smaller demand or randomizes if the suppliers' demands are equal. If the buyer and a seller make consistent demands, each receives the amount demanded, and the other supplier gets zero. Almost all the "equilibria" of this "auction" version of the demand game are efficient.[27] Moreover, just as in a competitive market, the buyer receives all the surplus at equilibrium.

Variations on this three-party demand game lead to the same conclusion. For example, suppose that if the demands are consistent, one party gets one dollar minus the other party's demands or, alternatively that the parties split the difference. In each of these games, essentially all of the equilibria lead to the efficient outcome, in which the buyer receives all the surplus. This is a natural result of bidding competition among the suppliers.

These demand games can be interpreted as models of a competitive supply market in isolation. When perfectly competitive suppliers must make simultaneous offers, competition among them reduces the scope for disagreement with the buyer, leading to efficient outcomes. (Clearly, competition among buyers has the same effect.) The two-party demand game, by contrast, illustrates the inefficiencies that may result with a single supplier and purchaser. Specialized assets tend to generate bilateral monopolies which are accompanied by struggles for rents and consequent bargaining inefficiencies. Thus, specialized assets *cause* bargaining costs, which may explain the predictive successes of received transaction-cost theory.[28]

The first class of bargaining costs, then, are coordination failures. They arise in situations where individuals could adopt several different patterns of mutually consistent, self-interested behavior and where market institutions fail to ensure that only efficient patterns actually emerge. Both standard economic theory and transaction-cost theory have typically assumed that, with competitive supply conditions, market mechanisms overcome these coordination problems. The analysis offered in this chapter does not contradict that view. However, recent studies involving detailed models of market institutions for price and quantity determination raise serious doubts about this assumption when multiple goods are involved and more than two parties must agree in order to benefit from exchange (Roberts 1987). In such situations, even when competitive pressures lead to perfectly competitive prices, coordination problems may still be so severe that beneficial exchange completely collapses. Of course, a key task of management is coordinating actions within an organization, so the case in favor of internal organization is strengthened by recognizing the possibility of coordination failures even in a system of competitive markets.

Measurement (information acquisition) costs are a second source of bargaining inefficiencies. Barzel (1982) and Kenney and Klein (1983) emphasize these costs to explain specialized contracting practices and vertical integration. They provide the basis for what has emerged as a second line of transaction-cost analysis – the measurement costs branch, in parallel with the asset specificity branch on which we focused in the previous section of this chapter. The idea is that individuals operating under standard short-term contracts will expend socially excessive amounts of resources to determine the private benefits and costs of an agreement when only its total costs and benefits, and not their distribution, matter for efficiency.

As an example of how measurement costs affect market arrangements, consider the Central Selling Organization (CSO) of De Beers, which in 1980 supplied between 80 and 85 percent of the world market in diamonds.[29] Kenney and Klein (1983) describe the CSO's marketing practices as follows:

Each of the CSO's customers periodically informs the CSO of the kinds and quantities of diamonds it wishes to purchase. The CSO then assembles a single box (or "sight") of diamonds for the customer. Each box contains a number of folded, envelope-like packets called papers. The gems within each paper are similar and correspond to one of the CSO's classifications. The composition of any sight may differ slightly from that specified by the buyer because the supply of diamonds in each category is limited.

Once every five weeks, primarily at the CSO's offices in London, the diamond buyers are invited to inspect their sights. Each box is marked with the buyer's name and a price. A single box may carry a price of up to several million pounds. Each buyer examines his sight before deciding whether to buy. Each buyer may spend as long as he wishes, examining his sight to see that each stone is graded correctly (that is, fits the description marked on each parcel). *There is no negotiation over the price or composition of the sight* [emphasis added]. In rare cases where a buyer claims that a stone has been miscategorized by the CSO, and the sales staff agrees, the sight will be adjusted. If a buyer rejects the sight, he is offered no alternative box. Rejection is extremely rare, however, because buyers who reject the diamonds offered them are deleted from the list of invited customers.

Thus, stones (a) are sorted by De Beers into imperfectly homogeneous categories, (b) to be sold in preselected blocks, (c) to preselected buyers, (d) at non-negotiable prices, with (e) buyers' rejection of the sales offer leading to the withdrawal by De Beers of future invitations to purchase stones. (p. 502)

What accounts for these nonstandard practices? In an ordinary market the buyers and seller would evaluate and haggle over each stone or

75

group of stones. The evaluation process would waste an inordinate amount of resources, and the haggling might even prevent agreement. Each buyer would carefully inspect each rough stone to determine how to cut it to create the largest, most flawless, and most valuable diamond and would use that information to estimate the stone's value. To bargain effectively, the seller must be equally well-informed, but to be so would require a substantial nonproductive investment. If the buyer and seller fail to agree on a price, another buyer would have to make the same evaluation, which would result in a duplication of effort and a waste of resources.

Given De Beers's initial classification of its diamonds, there is little social gain from further refining the allocation of diamonds among buyers. In a traditional market arrangement, customers would evaluate some stones that they will never cut, and the seller, in self-defense, would examine stones more closely than it would otherwise need to do. The De Beers system minimizes these measurement costs, which are attendant to haggling over price, and so represents one possible efficient response.[30]

Notice how the De Beers system moves away from markets and introduces an element of centralization. Haggling is eliminated and the CSO is given authority to allocate the diamonds subject to certain categorization rules. Buyers who refuse their sights thereby terminate their relationships with De Beers. This is analogous to the right employees of any business have when they are unhappy with their wages or jobs; they can quit.

Even the most casual review of markets suggests many circumstances in which presale product evaluation and negotiation by buyers would not help allocate goods more efficiently but would give buyers an edge in bargaining. In such circumstances, alternative arrangements that economize on these costs should be expected. Barzel (1982) uses this idea to explain fruit and vegetable packaging (which discourages product evaluation) and product warranties (which make careful product evaluations less valuable to the buyer, and so reduce measurement activities).[31] Kenney and Klein (1983) use it to explain the packaging of diamonds and the block booking of movies (which prevents theater owners from picking and choosing among new releases and so economizes on measurement costs). The royalties paid to authors of books can be similarly explained. If fixed fees were paid to an author, competing publishers would incur excessive costs in estimating the book's market potential for fear of the "winner's curse," according to which they acquire rights only to those books whose market potential they have overestimated and that other publishers, who have better estimates, spurn. Compensating authors with royalties alleviates the winner's curse by making publisher's payments depend on actual rather than estimated sales.[32] Part of the costs of allowing speculators to trade in a commodity market is that their profits must compensate for their socially unproductive investments in the information that is so essential to them (Hirschleifer 1971). The fact that these last markets are auction markets with little explicit negotiation has little import for our argument.

In general, initial uncertainty about a good's quality coupled with the possibility of resolving this uncertainty at some cost leads bargainers to act on this possibility, thereby increasing the costs of market arrangements. Such diverse arrangements as vertical integration, product warranties, and nonstandard market arrangements may emerge as the parties attempt to economize on these costs.

A third source of bargaining costs, and the one most often emphasized in the recent theoretical literature,[33] is private information about preferences. Unless the parties' valuations of a good being traded are common knowledge, the parties may be delayed in reaching an agreement or may even fail to agree at all, because they may strategically misrepresent the good's value. By insisting, for example, that "it's worth only fifty dollars to me, and I won't pay a penny more," a buyer can hope to get a lower price even though his or her actual valuation of the good may in fact be far greater. But this may prevent trade when the seller's value is relatively high, even though it is less than the buyer's true value. Moreover, given uncertainty about whether trade is efficient, bargaining costs of this form are absolutely inevitable, regardless of the bargaining procedure used (Myerson and Satterthwaite 1983). However, little is presently known about the determinants of these costs.

The role of uncertainty in generating bargaining inefficiencies dovetails nicely with Williamson's analyses, whether the uncertainty is about quality, with both sides initially being symmetrically informed but expending resources to acquire nonproductive information, or about parameters such as individual valuations, where informational asymmetries are inherent.

Our analysis of the sources of bargaining costs has been tentative and preliminary. Yet, it has served more than one valuable purpose. It has reinforced the logic of transaction-cost theory, provided a unifying perspective from which to investigate two previously distinct branches of transaction-cost economics – one based on specialized assets and one on measurement costs – and pointed to a new agenda for bargaining theorists and experimenters.

COSTS OF CENTRALIZED AUTHORITY

Accounts of Western economic growth often emphasize the importance of decentralized economic control rights (North and Thomas 1973). As Rosenberg and Birdzell (1986, p. 24) have recently written:

We have emphasized the part played by innovation in Western growth. The decentralization of authority to make decisions about innovations, together with the resources to effectuate such decisions and to absorb the gains or losses resulting from them, merits similar emphasis as an explanation of Western innovation. This diffusion of authority was interwoven with the development of an essentially autonomous economic sector; with the widespread use of experiment to answer questions of technology, marketing, and organization for which answers could be found in no other way; and with the emergence of great diversity in the West's modes of organizing economic activity.

Thus, Western economic history suggests that centralization stifles innovation. Is this a generalizable proposition? Even if one agrees that guild, church, and feudal authorities squelched experimentation and innovation in medieval Europe and that China's mandarinate, Japan's feudal lords, and Islamic mullahs did the same in their own domains, the historical record does not show that a modern central planner, who has studied the lessons of history, cannot guide an economy to duplicate and improve upon the performance of market economies. Yet the belief that such centralized planning and control stifles innovation is widespread; it even won official credence in the Communist economies of the Soviet Union and Eastern Europe.

Why can't a centrally planned, consciously coordinated system always do at least as well as an unplanned, decentralized one? For many years scholars, failing to find an answer to this question, have boldly (and, we think wrongly) concluded that there is no answer. For example, in his presidential address to the American Economic Association, Frederick Taylor (1929) held that socialist economies can allocate goods as well as capitalist economies because they can duplicate those economies in all their desirable respects:

In the case of a socialist state, the proper method of determining what commodities should be produced would be in outline substantially the same as that just described [for capitalist economies]. That is, the correct general procedure would be this: (1) The state would ensure to the citizen a given money income and (2) the state would authorize the citizen to spend that income as he chose in buying commodities produced by the state – a procedure which would virtually authorize the citizen to dictate just what commodities the economic authorities of the state should produce.

Substantially the same puzzle arises in trying to explain why there are any limits to a firm's size and scope. Thus, economists have asked, "Why, if by organizing one can eliminate certain costs and in fact reduce the cost of production, are there any market transactions at all? Why is not all production carried out by one big firm?"[34] And, "Why can't a large firm do everything that a collection of small firms can do, and more?"[35]

The form of these questions assumes that benign, costless, *selective interventions* of the type Williamson considered are possible. This requires a decision maker with the authority to intervene, the interest in doing so only when appropriate, and the ability to consider and reject interventions without distorting the behavior of others in the organization. We argue that these requirements realistically cannot be met.

We take the view that what most distinguishes any centralized organization is the authority and autonomy of its top decision makers or management – that is, their broad rights to intervene in lower-level decisions and the relative immunity of their decisions from intervention by others.[36] Increases in centralized authority carry with them increases in the discretionary power to intervene. This increased power necessarily has costs that are avoided in more decentralized contexts. From this perspective, the principles that guide a firm's decision whether to manufacture an input (centralized organization) or to buy it from an independent supplier (decentralized organization) can be applied equally well to evaluate the relative productive efficiency of capitalist and socialist economic systems.

Two kinds of costs generally accompany increases in discretionary centralized authority. Both have the same fundamental cause: The very existence of such authority makes possible its inappropriate use. The first kind arises because those with discretionary authority may misuse it directly, on their own initiative. The second arises because others in the organization may attempt to persuade or manipulate those with authority to use it excessively or inappropriately. Inappropriate interventions, the attempts to induce them, and the organization's efforts to control both – all generate costs of increased centralization.

The first source of the costs of centralized, discretionary authority is inappropriate interventions that occur because individuals with increased authority are unable or unwilling to resist interfering where or in ways that they should not. This may happen simply because the individuals feel an imperative to manage – that is, after all, what managers are paid to do! Business people often cite this imperative to intervene as a characteristic and a cost of government bureaucracies: Bureaucrats look for something to do, whether or not their intervention is likely to be helpful. Private managers are presumably not immune to this failure, let alone to believing that their interventions will be beneficial when they are actually unlikely to be. Another possible reason for inappropriate intervention is that individuals in authority may have personal interests in decisions: Will the empty lot next to the apartment building owned by the park commissioner's cousin be converted into a city park? Will the executive's protégé be appointed to replace a retiring division head? For any of these reasons, authority will be exercised more often and in other ways than efficiency alone dictates.

In a related vein are the costs of outright corruption, which is possible only with discretionary centralized authority: The central authority may seek bribes or other favors and may block efficient decisions when bribes are not paid. Or, the authority may favor an inefficient supplier who offers a bribe over a more efficient supplier who does not. Bribery scandals involving public officials are frequently reported, as are cases of sexual harassment with bosses demanding sexual favors from candidates for promotion. Among the legal forms of bribery in the United States are the gifts many companies give to their customers' executives (unless the customer is a government entity). Wherever there is discretionary authority over decisions that people care about, there is a temptation to offer or solicit bribes.

Note that monetary bribes themselves do not necessarily represent an economic inefficiency, because they are but transfers. Rather, the costs of corruption arise first because productive decisions are distorted, either from favoring those who pay bribes or from punishing those who refuse. Secondly, if trust between individuals and faith in the system facilitate economic activity, widespread corruption and bribery may result in further, less direct, but possibly more significant costs.

These costs of discretionary authority depend on flaws in decision makers' incentives, intelligence, or character. Presumably, then, they can be reduced or even eliminated by vesting authority in honest, wise individuals and by giving them incentives to care about organizational performance.[37] However, discretionary authority results in a second kind of cost which is incurred even when the central authority is both incorruptible and intelligent enough not to interfere in operations without good reason. These are what we call *influence costs*.

Influence costs arise first because individuals and groups within the organization expend time, effort, and ingenuity in attempting to affect others' decisions to their benefit and secondly because inefficient decisions result either directly from these influence activities or, less directly, from attempts to prevent or control them.

At first blush, it might seem easy to avoid these costs: Simply have decision makers ignore attempts at influence. If this does not provide a sufficient incentive to deter influence activities, severely punish any such behavior. In some circumstances, this may in fact be possible, and we will assume that organizations follow this policy whenever feasible. However, an essential difficulty exists with such an approach. The policy of ignoring attempts at influence – and, indeed, the policy of selective intervention more generally – is not what macroeconomists call "dynamically consistent" or what game theorists call "subgame perfect." *Ex post,* when relevant information is available and those at lower levels have already taken actions that cannot be reversed, there will be interventions that are now organizationally desirable and that the center will thus want to take. However, recognition of the center's *ex post* incentives will alter the behavior of the organization's members in ways that are organizationally dysfunctional. Thus, the center would like to be able to commit *ex ante* to not making these interventions – that is, to restrict its own discretion. For example, decision makers might want to motivate workers by committing to promote the most productive one. However, after the fact, they would want to renege and promote the worker who, on the basis of training and other credentials, appears best qualified. As long as central decision makers reserve for themselves the right to make selective interventions, commitments are impossible, if only because of the impossibility of complete contracting. Thus, the possibility of attempts at influence will remain and will inevitably exert costs (Milgrom and Roberts 1988a).

One reason influence is inevitable is that decision makers must rely on others for information that is not easily available to them directly. Central office executives are not islands unto themselves; they commonly rely extensively on others for information, suggestions, and analyses to reach decisions.[38] Moreover, the employees affected by a decision are often the very ones executives must rely on. In such circumstances, employees will have strong reasons to try to influence decisions, and their attempts at influence will impose costs on the organization. For example, employees may distort the information they report or withhold information from the central office and from other employees. Candidates for possible promotions may spend valuable time polishing their credentials, thereby establishing their qualifications for the desired assignment at the expense of current performance (Milgrom and Roberts 1988a). Managers, worried about how higher authorities will evaluate their performance, may avoid risky but profitable investments because such investments pose career risks if they turn out badly (Holmstrom 1982). Or, less specifically, employees may simply waste time trying to figure out what issues are on the agenda, how they might be personally affected, and how to shape decisions to their benefit. The loss of productivity from these distortions in the way employees spend their time, report their information, and make their decisions is one category of influence costs. These are costs of discretionary authority because they arise only when an authority exists whose decisions can be influenced.

A second sort of influence cost arises when central authorities make suboptimal decisions because of employees' influence activities, particularly their suppressing or distorting information. In some situations these distortions may be undone by properly accounting for individuals' incentives, and efficient decisions may still be reached (Milgrom and Roberts 1986). However, when these incentives are unclear or when the underlying information is so complex that unscrambling is impossible, decision makers will have to rely on information that they know is incomplete or inaccurate. Consider, for example, the problems of the U.S. Congress in dealing with military appropriations. Congress must rely on the military for information, and it understands that the military may have incentives to distort the information that it provides. But it is impossible for Congress to disentangle interservice rivalries, individual career ambitions, and genuine concerns with national security, all of which motivate particular spending requests. Even if the incentives of those providing the information to distort or suppress it could be determined, the impossible problem of inferring what information they actually have would still remain. In such complex circumstances, decisions must be based on fundamentally incorrect information, and inefficient decisions must be expected.

The incentives to attempt to influence an organization's decisions are, to some extent, endogenous. The costs and benefits of influence activities depend on an organization's information-gathering and decision-making procedures and on its reward systems. Thus, careful organizational design can at least partially control the direct costs of influence activities. For example, Holmstrom and Ricart (1986) have investigated how capital budgeting practices that reward investment and growth per se and establish high internal hurdle rates for investments can help alleviate managers' natural reluctance to undertake risky but profitable investments. Milgrom (1988) and Milgrom and Roberts (1988a) have examined how compensation and promotion policies can be used to make employees more nearly indifferent about company decisions, thereby reducing resistance to change and other organizationally unproductive influence activities.[39] As an alternative to using compensation policies and promotion criteria to control incentives to attempt influence, Milgrom and Roberts also explored limiting communication between decision makers and potentially affected parties and otherwise restricting these parties' involvement in decision making.

Even the very boundaries of the firm can become design variables used to control influence. The widespread practice of spinning off or isolating unprofitable subsidiaries can be partly interpreted in these terms: It is done to prevent the subsidiary's employees and management from imposing large influence costs on the organization through attempts to claim corporate resources to cover their losses and thereby to avoid having to become efficient or to curtail operations.[40] Similarly, a university's policy of requiring its schools to be "tubs on their own bottoms," each individually responsible for its revenues and expenditures (subject to formula payments to or from the central administration), limits influence activities that would amount to raids on other schools' or the university's resources. For example, when universities centrally determine and fund salaries, research support, and teaching loads, faculties have incentives to try to get more for themselves from the center by invoking comparisons with other schools and departments rather than by raising their own resources. Of course, they can (and do) still make the same complaints when financial boundaries exist between schools, but they have less to gain by doing so because resources cannot easily be shifted from the envied to the envious.

Of course, such responses as these bring costs of their own. Worthwhile investments will be foregone, and managers may seek out the wrong investment opportunities; less qualified people will be assigned to key positions; too many valued employees will quit to increase their pay; bad decisions will be made because communication has been restricted and available information is not used; and desirable resource transfers between divisions will not be effected. These costs of employing policies and organizational structures that would be inefficient if influence activities were not a problem are then in themselves a third category of influence costs.

In this context, an important element of organizational design involves trading off these various costs. For example, Japanese firms make use both of wage policies and of organizational rules to facilitate extensive involvement of their employees in decision making without encouraging excessive attempts at influence. Lifetime employment for key decision makers, relatively small wage differentials within age cohorts, relatively low wages for senior executives,[41] and promotions based largely on seniority[42] combine to insulate employees from the effects of the firm's investment and promotion decisions and to make promotion decisions relatively immune to influence.[43]

A central example to test the applicability of these ideas against is the case in which a multidivisional conglomerate buys another firm and resolves to run it as an independent division. For our purposes, a firm is a business organization with a central office that has substantial discretionary authority as well as substantial independence from other discretionary authorities. Expanding the activities carried out within the firm, rather than through the market, increases the range over which centralized discretionary authority may be exercised and, by our logic, should increase the attendant costs. A true conglomerate acquisition is a particularly clean example because there is a clear increase in centralization free of the confounding effects that come from the acquirer's attempts to integrate the acquired firm's assets and operations with its own.

Such acquisitions often fail (Porter 1987), and frequently the acquired division's performance deteriorates. Tenneco's late-1980 acquisition of Houston Oil and Minerals Corporation is illustrative.[44] Although Tenneco (then America's largest conglomerate) had resolved to run Houston as an independent subsidiary, within a year of the acquisition Tenneco lost 34 percent of Houston's management, 25 percent of its explorationists, and 19 percent of its production people. All this made it impossible for Tenneco to maintain Houston as a distinct unit. A Tenneco executive commented on the difficulties occasioned by the acquisition of Houston, which was accustomed to giving large production-related bonuses to key people: "We have to ensure internal equity and apply the same standard of compensation to everyone." Why did this acquisition fail? And why did the executive insist on the need for "equity" and a commonly applied "standard of compensation"?

In an acquisition like that of Houston Oil, the acquired firm's previously independent chief executive is replaced by a division head subordinated to the larger organization's central office. This opens up several new kinds of interventions for the conglomerate chief, each of which carries costs of the kind already described. With new levels of executives having authority, there are greater possibilities for mistaken or self-interested interventions. The opportunities for influence costs to arise also expand. The head of an older division may attempt to influence the chief's new decisions by, for example, demanding that the new division purchase supplies from it. One argument might run that although the old division's prices, based on average costs, make its product unattractive to the new division, internal acquisition still serves the overall firm's interest because marginal production costs are low. Similarly, the head of the new division may play politics in an attempt to influence job assignments, pay, and capital budgeting decisions. These are new and costly uses of executive time that were not incurred in the same form[45] before the firm was acquired. Finally, division heads will expend some resources on defensive influence. For example, the newly acquired division must be prepared to explain why its positions should be filled by promotion from within or why its salaries and bonuses – high compared to those in other divisions – should not be part of the larger organization's general salary pool.

Taken together, the activities just described could consume a major portion of division heads', and central office personnel's time, diverting them from more productive activities. The boundaries between independent firms reduce the possibilities for influence.[46] Consequently, those boundaries reduce influence costs.

In the case of Houston Oil, Tenneco's failure to run Houston as an independent subsidiary can most likely be explained by excessive intervention arising from a combination of mistaken perceptions and influence activities. Tenneco's executives may have seen an opportunity to cut wages or benefits for Houston's generously compensated professional work force, disbelieving Houston's protestations that the results would be disastrous. Or, employees in other divisions may have coveted Houston's compensation package, raising the organization's costs of making an exception for Houston. Either way, the mere existence of an executive with discretionary authority to intervene imposed costs that could have been avoided if Houston had remained separate.

The validity of these arguments depends on our characterization of the firm as a centrally controlled organization considerably free from outside intervention. In capitalist economies, several institutions support executives' having much more extensive control over their firms than do courts or government agencies acting from outside. First, property rights tend to limit government interventions more than executive interventions because property rights over the firm generally reside at the executive level or higher. Thus, a court, a governmental regulatory agency, and a firm's central office can all order a plant that is polluting the environment to cease operations until the problem is fixed, but the central office can also replace the plant manager if it finds that to be the most effective way to do the job. Second, executives generally have better and more fluid information systems than courts or government agencies do. Managers in firms hear most of the important information they need in conversations and meetings where they can query sources informally to resolve ambiguities and acquire needed detail.[47] In contrast, agencies and courts must rely on written reports or adversary proceedings. Finally, executives can deliver incentives directly where they count most – to individual employees – and can tailor the incentives to take the form either of rewards, such as pay increases, bonuses, promotions, or desirable assignments, or of punishments, such as undesirable assignments or layoffs. The incentives courts and government agencies offer consist mostly of threats to collect penalties against the firm's treasury.

Moreover, although some laws explicitly allow discretion to regulators, and others are so vague that the courts have considerable latitude in interpreting them, the role of courts and government agencies is principally to enforce rules. The court or agency must justify its action in terms of the particular rule to be enforced. This procedure denies courts and agencies the degree of fully discretionary authority that a firm's sole proprietor, partners, or senior executives and board can exercise. In fact, this difference of degree is at times so great as to be fairly treated as one of kind.

Still, we do not wish to overstate the extent of centralized authority actually exercised in firms. The most decentralized multidivisional businesses allow division managers considerable autonomy. The holding companies that existed in the United States in the early twentieth century were even more decentralized; their central offices were little more than partial substitutes for capital markets and bankers. However, the authority to intervene, even if not often exercised, still remains and still may exact costs.

Finally, although our argument views firms in a capitalist economy as having considerable autonomy, one should not underestimate the degree of centralized authority present in market economies. Courts do settle contract disputes and interpret the law. Government agencies issue permits, restrain certain business activities, and enforce court orders. Legislatures enact laws to govern contracts, to limit firms' rights to pollute or to engage in dangerous activities, to govern foreign trade, to control the use of land, and to promote societal ends, such as developing the arts or improving the economic status of women and minorities. If our principles are indeed general, then these forms of centralized intervention must be subject to some of the same costs that accompany the creation of centralized executive authority within firms.

INFLUENCE COSTS IN THE PUBLIC SECTOR

Our theory of influence costs dovetails with the theory of rent-seeking behavior. The seminal essays exploring this theory are those by Tullock (1967), Krueger (1974), and Posner (1975), all of which are reprinted in Buchanan, Tollison, and Tullock (1980). The theory holds that government interventions in the economy, whether in the form of tariffs, regulations, the awarding of monopoly franchises, or various attempts to correct market failures, are costly because they create rents and so lead firms and citizens to waste resources attempting to capture those rents. Although this argument has obvious appeal, its presumption that rents lead to inefficiencies only when they result from *government* intervention (as in Buchanan's essay in Buchanan et al. 1980) is, we believe, a mistake. Our general proposition is that *any* centralization of authority, whether in the public or private sector, creates the potential for intervention and so gives rise to costly influence activities and to excessive intervention by the central authority. These costs need to be weighed against the benefits of centralization to determine the efficient extent and locus of authority.[48]

Of course, our theoretical argument that increased centralization leads to increased influence applies with as much force to government and nonprofit organizations as to firms. As an empirical matter, then, we should look for influence activities and their costs in the halls of government as well as in the executive offices of firms. Instances of influence in government are not difficult to find. The frustration of U.S. federal officials who try to manage the nation's affairs in the face of constant attempts at influence was highlighted in recent testimony by former U.S. Secretary of State George Shultz: "Nothing ever gets settled in this town. It's not like running a company or even a university. It's a seething debating society in which the debate never stops, in which people never give up, including me, and that's the atmosphere in which you administer."[49]

The current crisis in tort litigation in the United States provides a second illustration of the importance of influence costs in government. The crisis has arisen in part from the increasing frequency with which novel legal arguments win. In effect, courts increasingly act like discretionary authorities, and litigants incur costs in their efforts to capture newly appropriable sums. The costs of this litigation, which diverts some of the nation's finest minds into largely nonproductive activities and causes talented corporate executives to devote much of their time to defending and avoiding lawsuits, are enormous. The offsetting gains, in improved justice, for example, are much harder to estimate. Limits on damage awards, which are puzzling in standard economic theory,[50] are easily understood as a device to reduce influence costs.

The importance for encouraging economic development of limiting government's discretionary authority is clear in the economic history of Western Europe. Rosenberg and Birdzell (1986, p. 113) have identified these limits as among the key factors that encouraged the development of trade and early capitalism:

Some of the institutional innovations reduced the risks of trade, either political or commercial. Among them were a legal system designed to give predictable, rather than discretionary, decisions; the introduction of bills of exchange, which facilitated the transfer of money and provided the credit need for commercial transactions; the rise of an insurance market; and the change of governmental revenue systems from discretionary expropriation to systematic taxation – a change closely linked to the development of the institution of private property.

Constitutional checks on governmental power that limit both what interventions can be made and who can make them thus reduce the costs of centralized authority. The improved economic efficiency that can accompany constitutional limitations on state power can be spectacular, as in the case of the gains that followed the Glorious Revolution in England (North and Weingast 1987). Similar limitations enforced within private organizations presumably have similar effects. For example, union contracts that govern layoffs and job assignments or antidiscrimination laws may improve efficiency by restricting managerial discretion.

Of course, rules themselves must be decided upon – either centrally or through bargaining; presumably their general applicability renders the stakes large. However, to the extent that rules can be set up well in advance of their application, so that their *predictable* distributional consequences are small, then the bargaining and influence costs incurred in rule making may be small relative to the potential gains. For this to be true, constitutional change must be a difficult and slow process or must require near unanimity among the affected parties.

SUMMARY AND CONCLUSIONS

We have examined the organization of economic activity under the hypothesis that capitalist economic institutions are organized so as to minimize the sum of the costs of resources used in production and the costs of managing the necessary transactions. The costs of negotiating short-term contracts emerged as the distinctive costs of traditional market transactions. An analysis of the determinants of these bargaining costs indicates that two leading theories, one attributing transaction costs primarily to specialized assets and the other attributing them primarily to measurement costs, could both be subsumed under the bargaining cost approach.

The costs associated with nonmarket forms of organization have received less attention in the existing literature, but must be assessed to identify when market organization is more economical than internal procurement. As a first step, we argued that transactions within firms in a capitalist economy are characterized by greater centralization of authority than market-mediated transactions. Indeed, top management's autonomy and discretion and lower management's lesser autonomy are the firm's principal defining characteristics.

Bargaining, influence costs, and organization

Whenever a central authority, whether a governmental unit or an executive in a firm, has discretion to intervene, certain identifiable costs are incurred. These include (1) a tendency for the authority to intervene excessively, both because intervening is that authority's job and because the authority may have a personal interest (licit or illicit, but in either case differing from the organization's interests) in certain decisions; (2) increased time devoted to influence activities and a corresponding reduction in organizational productivity, as interested parties seek to have the authority intervene in particular ways or to adopt their favored alternatives; (3) poorer decision making resulting from the distortion of information associated with influence activities; and (4) a loss of efficiency as the organization adapts its structure and policies to control influence activities and their costs.

We believe that these ideas about influence cost are important in analyzing organizations. For example, they might be used to examine issues of corporate control, financial structure, bankruptcy, proxy fights, and takeovers. Moreover, because influence activities are essentially political and because the theory applies equally to public and private organizations, we believe that it may also prove valuable in the more general study of political economy.

4

Corporate culture and economic theory

DAVID M. KREPS

INTRODUCTION

In this chapter, I explore how an economic theorist might explain or model a concept such as corporate culture. While the theoretical construction that is given is far from inclusive (which is to say that many aspects of corporate culture are not covered), I conclude that economic theory is moving in the direction of what seems a reasonable story. But before that story can be considered told, we must employ tools that are currently missing from the economist's tool kit. In particular, we require a framework for dealing with the unforeseen.

I can give two explanations for why I present this topic. The first concerns how economists (and those weaned on the economic paradigm) deal with the topic of business strategy. If we take Porter (or Caves or Spence) as the prototype, business strategy could roughly be called applied industrial organization. The firm and its capabilities are

This work was prepared in 1984 for presentation to the Second Mitsubishi Bank Foundation Conference on Technology and Business Strategy. It subsequently appeared in Japanese in *Technological Innovation and Business Strategy,* M. Tsuchiya (ed.), Nippon Keizai Shimbunsha Press, Tokyo, 1986, and appears here in English with the kind permission of the previous publishers. The chapter surveys the current state of research and is, of course, quite dated now. But, with the kind permission of the current editors, it appears now much as it was written in 1984, except that references have been updated where appropriate and punctuation and English have been made more correct. In a very brief postscript, following the appendix, I engage in a bit of updating and revisionist thinking. And, in one place in the text, where it is too painful to reread what I wrote, I alert the reader that something more on this issue will be said in the postscript.

I have benefited from discussion with too many colleagues to give a comprehensive list, but two individuals must be cited for particularly helpful ideas: Jose Scheinkman, concerning the overlapping generations model, and Bengt Holmstrom for stressing to me the important distinction between observability and verifiability. The financial assistance of the National Science Foundation (Grants SES–8006407 and SES–8408468), the Sloan Foundation, and the Mitsubishi Bank Foundation are all gratefully acknowledged.

more or less taken as givens, and one looks at the tangible characteristics of an industry to explain profitability. It sometimes seems, in this approach, that there are good industries (or segments of industries) and bad: Find yourself in a bad industry (low entry barriers, many substitutes, powerful customers and suppliers, many and surly competitors), and you can do nothing except get out at the first opportunity. Now, this is assuredly a caricature of the Porter approach. The size of entry barriers, relations with suppliers/customers, and, especially, competitive discipline within an industry are all at least partially endogenous. Bad industries can sometimes be made good, and (perhaps a more accurate rendering of Porter) good niches can be found or formed even in bad industries.

This approach carries with it a powerful legacy from textbook microeconomics: The firm is an exogenously specified cost function or production possibilities set, and market structures (also exogenous) determine how it will fare. The actual purpose of the firm qua organization is not considered. This is rather strange, for if one has an economic mind-set, one must believe that the firm itself performs some economic (efficiency-promoting) function. From there it is a short step to consider as part, perhaps the largest part, of successful strategy those actions designed to increase the firm's organizational efficiency.[1] But since textbook economics doesn't explain firms qua organizations, it comes up empty as a discipline for analyzing this part of strategy.

Of course, disciplines other than economics deal with organizational efficiency or effectiveness. One could simply assert that Porter's approach is incomplete, to be supplemented or, better, taken concurrently with other disciplines and approaches. The dangers here are that prescriptions from the economic approach may interact negatively with organizational efficiency in specific cases and that individuals trained in one approach may ignore the other. In order to reduce these dangers, it seems a good idea to develop a theory that addresses issues of organizational efficiency in the language of economics and then to integrate it with Porter-style analysis.

When I say that economics has not come to grips with issues of implementation, I mean standard textbook economics. I believe that the foundations for such analysis have been and are being laid. There are the obvious and very visible contributors: Williamson and his colleagues. But I believe that "higher" theorists (which, in economics, means more mathematical) dealing in such topics as agency theory, the theory of repeated games and reputation, and (less formally) the theory of focal points in noncooperative games should also be counted.

This, then, gives rise to my second and primary reason for writing this chapter. I think economists are moving in a profitable direction, and I want to present the outlines of the theory that is developing. I hope in so doing to interest readers in further developments.

With my objectives stated, I can describe the nature of this chapter. With significant exceptions, no new theory is being presented here. What little is new is undeveloped – it constitutes conjecture and little else. This chapter is meant to be expositional and exploratory and, perhaps, just a bit synthetic: I want to sketch out the pieces of the theory that have been developed, to connect them (as they are connected in my mind), and to conjecture as to what is missing. (Needless to say, what is missing largely coincides with my current research agenda.) I have tried as much as possible to stay away from technical details; sometimes, however, this has been impossible to avoid, and I apologize.

This chapter sprawls somewhat, but I have in mind a very definite plot that ties things together. At the risk of completely losing the reader, let me give here an outline of the plot. It has three fundamental building blocks. The first is that in many transactions, in particular ongoing ones, contingencies typically arise that were unforeseen at the time of the transaction itself. Many transactions will potentially be too costly to undertake if the participants cannot rely on efficient and equitable adaptation to those unforeseen contingencies. Note that such reliance will necessarily involve blind faith; if we cannot foresee a contingency, we cannot know in advance that we can efficiently and equitably meet it. (For those who find the notion of an unforeseen contingency unpalatable, we could equally well imagine how costly it is to specify how every contingency will be met.)

Transactions can be characterized by the adjudication processes that meet unforeseen contingencies. In particular, some transactions will be hierarchical in that one party will have much more authority in saying what adaptation will take place. The firm (or other organization) is meant in this theory to play the canonical role of the authoritative party: When I am employed by a firm, I accept within broad limits the firm's right, as expressed by my superior, to specify how my time will be spent as contingencies arise. Or, to take another example, when students attend a university, they accept the university's right, through its administrators, to spell out the terms of the commodity students have bought.[2]

If employees or students are to grant such authority to a firm or university, they must believe that it will be used fairly. What is the source of this faith? It is that the firm and university are characterized by their reputations. The way an organization adapts to an unforeseen contingency can add to or detract from that reputation, with consequences for the amount of faith future employees or students will have.

This faith is the glue that permits mutually beneficial transactions to take place, transactions that would otherwise not be made because of their costs. The organization, or, more precisely, those in the organization who have decision-making authority, will have an interest in preserving or even promoting a good reputation to allow for future beneficial transactions. Thus, workers or students can trust the organization to act equitably in its own interest to protect its valuable reputation. Note that the organization must be an ongoing entity here: If ever it loses its incentive to protect its reputation, an incentive derived from the incentive to undertake future beneficial transactions, then it can no longer be trusted, and the hierarchical transaction will fall apart.[3]

With these three blocks in place, we come to corporate culture. In order for a reputation to have an effect, both sides involved in a transaction must *ex ante* have some idea of the meaning of appropriate or equitable fulfillment of the contract. Potential future trading partners must be able to observe fulfillment (or lack of) by the hierarchically superior party. These things are necessary; otherwise the hierarchically superior party's reputation turns on nothing. When we speak of adaptation to unforeseen contingencies, however, we cannot specify *ex ante* how those contingencies will be met. We can at best give some sort of principle or rule that has wide (preferably universal) applicability and that is simple enough to be interpreted by all concerned. In the language of game theory, unforeseen contingencies are best met by the sort of principle that underlies what Schelling (1960) calls a focal point. The organization will be characterized by the principle it selects. It will (optimally) try to promote understanding of that principle in the minds of its hierarchical inferiors. In order to protect its reputation for applying the principle in all cases, it will apply the principle even when its application might not be optimal in the short run. It will apply the principle even in areas where it serves no direct organizational objective, if doing so helps preserve or clarify the principle. Because decision-making authority in a firm is diffuse, those who make decisions in the firm's name will be judged by their diligence in applying and embracing the principle. In this light, I interpret corporate culture as partly the principle itself (or, more realistically, the interrelated principles that the organization employs) and partly the means by which the principle is communicated to hierarchical inferiors (so they can monitor its application) and hierarchical superiors (so they can apply it faithfully). It says how things are done, and how they are meant to be done in the organization. Because it will be designed through time to meet unforeseen contingencies as they arise, it will be the product of

93

evolution inside the organization and will be influenced by the organization's history.

This, very roughly, is the economic theory of corporate culture that I wish to lay out. As noted earlier, this theory captures at most one facet of corporate culture. The economic paradigm also contains explanations that rely on the screening function of internal cultures. Outside of the economic paradigm, at least so far as I can see, are explanations that rely on concepts such as need for affiliation and other things that I know nothing about. I don't mean to advance the theory as all-inclusive; rather, it fits in well with recent advances in the economic theory.

Rather than proceeding with the theory as already outlined, I will first exposit those pieces of the story that are in the extant literature and then go on to pieces that are missing or underdeveloped. This will make the basic plot harder to understand, but if readers can keep this plot in mind it will make it easier to see how several strands in economic theory interrelate. Since underlying this plot is the basic need to render efficient otherwise inefficient transactions, I begin with a section on the basic transactions theory of Coase and Williamson. I give here as well the standard criticism of Williamson: He analyzes why (and when) market-based transactions are costly but insufficiently justifies his assumption that when market-based transactions are costly, hierarchy-based transactions are not equally (or more) costly.

Next, in the section on Grossman and Hart, I discuss a recent paper by those authors (1986) that gives an example of an adjudication process for dealing with unforeseen (or, more precisely, uncontracted-for) contingencies. In their model the authority to decide to employ capital rests with the legal owners of the capital. The authors use this, together with an inability to contract for certain contingencies, to explain particular patterns of ownership for particular transactions. This is not quite the theory I will later employ – authority in hierarchical transactions is typically much less tangibly based than in something like ownership – but it provides a reference point for the type of theory I am suggesting.

In the next section, the parts of game theory that are needed to discuss reputation are put in place and are used to make a first pass at a theory of the firm. The section begins by reviewing repeated games, the folk theorem, and implicit contracts, and then recasts the folk theorem into a story of reputation.

Finally, I give a simple parable that shows how something as intangible as a reputation could become an economic good – one that economic actors would invest in and, when the time comes, sell. This gives us a rather pat explanation for what a firm is: an intangible asset car-

rying a reputation that is beneficial for efficient transactions, confer-
ring that reputation upon whoever currently owns the asset.

The theory developed in the section on reputation will seem rather
disconnected from notions such as corporate culture, or even from the
concept of a hierarchical transaction. But in later sections, I will use
the reputation construction to move in the direction of these ideas. The
first step is to make the basic reputation construction encompass transactions that are hierarchical in the sense already given. This is the subject of the section titled "Hierarchical Transactions." Also in this
section, we refine a point made in the previous section: Reputations for
behaving in a particular way work more efficiently the more deviations
from that behavior are observable.

Through the section on hierarchical transactions, we will work
within the standard framework of neoclassical microeconomics. The
theory developed in the sections on reputation and hierarchical transactions plays entirely within the usual rules of economic theory. As a
consequence of this, however, it does not provide a very good case for
its own importance. A stronger case emerges if one considers the possibility of contingencies arising that parties to a particular transaction
have not *ex ante* thought through, either because they were *ex ante*
unimaginable or because it is simply too costly to think through all
possible contingencies. The section on unforeseen contingencies that
follows also speculates as to how a (useful) formal theory of this sort
of unforeseen contingencies might develop. Then, the section on focal
points takes a brief excursion into Schelling's (1960) very underdeveloped area of game theory. This concept of focal points will play an
important role in the theory finally constructed in the section titled
"Corporate Culture."

In this last-mentioned section, the various pieces are assembled into
an economic theory of the role of corporate culture. More precisely,
the outlines of such a theory, together with some conjectures as to
where that theory might lead, are given. It is my hope that the theory
will be in line with the well-developed theories reported in earlier sections and that readers will see that the final steps, while not yet accomplished, are not excessively difficult to traverse. Concluding remarks
and questions are given in the final section.

WILLIAMSON, TRANSACTION COSTS, AND
THE THEORY OF THE FIRM

Following in the footsteps of Coase (1937), Simon (1965), and Arrow
(1974), among others, Williamson and his students have been developing a theory of what hierarchical organizations such as firms

accomplish. Williamson states this theory most fully in his 1975 book; his more recent work and a very good summary statement can be found in his 1981 article.

The heart of the theory is the concept of transaction costs. For parties to consummate a transaction or an exchange they must expend resources other than those contained in the terms of the transaction. Among these transaction costs are resources expended to spell out in advance the terms of the transaction, so that each side knows what it is getting, and resources expended to enforce the terms of the transaction. Textbook economic theory, which calls forth images of the exchange of one physical good for a second or of one physical good for money, tends to treat transaction costs as being near enough to zero to be ignored. Costs can, however, be substantial in more complex transactions, such as those in which one party sells labor to the other, in which the good sold has hidden qualities or in which one side must sink resources in preparing for the transaction before the other side fulfills its part of the bargain. In deciding whether to undertake a transaction, both parties must weigh the benefits they will accrue, net of the cost of transacting. Transactions that give the parties positive benefits gross of transaction costs (which, according to textbook economics, would therefore take place) may not give benefits sufficient to cover the transaction costs and so will not take place.

The organizational structure the transaction takes place within can affect transaction costs. An exchange in the marketplace may be more or less costly than the same exchange in a hierarchical organization. Holding benefits constant, a transaction will tend to occur within whatever infrastructure minimizes its cost. When transactions take place in firms, the presumption (and direction for analysis) should be that the transactions are less costly within the firm than they would be in the marketplace.

That, very briefly, is the basic theory that Coase advanced (1937) and that Williamson extended and elaborated on. The study of markets and other organizations that transactions take place in becomes a study of the relative transaction costs within those organizations. Note well the type of firm in this analysis: The firm is like individual agents in textbook economics, which finds its highest expression in general equilibrium theory (see Debreu 1959, Arrow and Hahn 1971). The firm transacts with other firms and with individuals in the market. Agents have utility functions, firms have a profit motive; agents have consumption sets, firms have production possibility sets. But in transaction-cost economics, firms are more like markets – both are arenas within which individuals can transact. Indeed, we might think of firms as marketplaces, contrasting them with other marketplaces, such as the stock exchanges, within all of which transactions take place.

Williamson goes on to study five factors that make transactions relatively more costly. He divides these factors into two categories – those that pertain to the transaction itself and those that pertain to the parties to the transaction. The transaction itself can be described according to its complexity, which includes the amount of uncertainty that the transaction bears, especially uncertainty about future contingencies; according to the thinness of the transaction, or the number of alternative trading partners involved in it; and according to the extent of impacted information in it, information some but not all parties to the transaction possess. The transacting parties may be more or less opportunistic, in that they pursue selfish interests in a guileful manner. They may also be limitedly rational, in that it is costly and sometimes impossible for them to carry out all the computations required to find a truly optimal course of action or to elaborate and think through all contingencies that might bear on the transaction. Relatively greater complexity and/or thinness and/or impacted information, joined with relatively greater guile and/or relatively more limited rationality, will raise transaction costs.

Williamson goes on to analyze particular scenarios in which transaction costs are high, suggesting that in these cases there is a clear case for organizing the transaction in a hierarchy rather than in a traditional marketplace. Examples drawn from Williamson (1981) include vertical integration, when costs need to be sunk in transaction-specific capital before the transaction is actually executed, and franchising, when the quality of the good sold depends in part on services a salesperson delivers.

Williamson builds quite a substantial case in these and other instances for large transaction costs in market-mediated transactions. He is less convincing in arguing that transacting through a hierarchical organization lessens transaction costs. This is a frequent criticism of his work: He explicitly recognizes that transacting through a hierarchical framework incurs costs (what he sometimes refers to as the costs of bureaucracy), but he doesn't say enough about how they would differ from market-mediated transaction costs. Increasing the five factors cited will mainly increase market-mediated transaction costs. There is little reason, though, to think that these factors will not simultaneously increase (and perhaps by more) hierarchy-mediated transaction costs. Therefore we cannot, without a leap of faith, expect to see more hierarchical mediation and less market mediation in transactions with large levels of Williamson's five factors. This is not to say that

David M. Kreps

we do not see this; casual empiricism suggests that we do, and over-whelmingly so. But the argument why this is so has not been completely made (please see the postscript).

GROSSMAN AND HART AND THE RESIDUAL RIGHTS
CONFERRED BY OWNERSHIP

One hinge on which the argument could turn is the legally mandated default clauses in contracts. Grossman and Hart make such an argument in a recent article (1986). They give a story for Williamson's vertical integration due to transaction-specific capital. Roughly put, they argue that contracts that would be optimal under vertical disintegration and a market transaction cannot be written, while contracts that would be more efficient in an integrated setting can be. The key to their argument is the notion of residual rights; owners of capital equipment own the right to use that capital as they see fit, subject to the specific contractual arrangements that have been made. If certain contingent contracts cannot be made (because they are costly to make or enforce), then the second-best arrangement between an upstream and a downstream entity might well be one where the residual rights associated with capital ownership are concentrated in one hand. Grossman and Hart suppose that detailed contingent contracts cannot be made and thus that ownership (and the residual rights thereby entailed) changes the space of feasible contracts (a "contract" here means all clauses, including unwritable ones that are nonetheless created by a pattern of ownership). In such a case, they show that certain ownership patterns for physical capital might be more efficient than others.

Besides providing an interesting analysis, Grossman and Hart point us in what I believe is the right direction to pursue. Williamson, following Coase, wishes to make the transaction the unit of analysis; Grossman and Hart do so with a vengeance. Indeed, taking Grossman and Hart at their word, one might expect a much more active market in physical capital: As the particular transaction for which that capital is employed changes, ownership of the capital (optimally) changes as well. That is, the authors explain ownership patterns for a particular transaction but not the permanence or stability of that pattern, which marks the modern corporation. (Of course, Grossman and Hart can easily defend themselves on two grounds: Insofar as other identical or even similar transactions follow the one being analyzed, the optimal ownership arrangement might be quite stable. And markets for physical capital will have severe moral hazard and adverse-selection problems.)

98

My point is that Grossman and Hart study the requirements for a particular (ideal) transaction and the way various institutional arrangements approximate those requirements. Theirs is not a theory of the firm per se; rather, they entitle their work "The Costs and Benefits of Ownership." At the level of their analysis, capital ownership by single entrepreneurs is as likely a consequence as is ownership by an entity with a firm's legal status. One can begin with their analysis and, using other pieces, build a theory of why firms exist.[4] But their specific concern is with transaction efficiency. The tie to the theory of the firm comes from the observation that conditions conducive for efficiency in the sorts of transactions the authors examine (concentrated ownership of capital) correlate with conditions in which one finds "firms" (efficient sharing of risk).

This leads to a second (niggling) criticism of Williamson: He tries too hard to dichotomize directly the market and the firm. It will prove more fruitful, I think, to characterize particular sorts of transactions and to then correlate the characteristics that lead to efficient transacting with firms/markets. Drawing a clean line between firms and markets will not prove possible; cleaner lines can be drawn if the transaction is the unit of analysis.

As outlined in the introduction, I develop in this chapter a dichotomy in transactions that correlates well with the distinction between firms and markets. I will also attempt to explain the source of the correlation. The dichotomy is between hierarchical transactions and, for lack of a better name, specified transactions. Roughly, in a specified transaction all terms are spelled out in advance. In a hierarchical transaction, certain terms are left unspecified; what is specified is that one of the two parties has, within broad limits, the contractual right to specify how the contract will be fulfilled. There is, to be sure, less than a perfect dichotomy here, for one can think of many other variations – for example, transactions with *ex ante* unspecified clauses, with *ex post* fulfillment determined by negotiation and requiring unanimous consent; or where the authority to determine *ex post* fulfillment is split among the parties. Here I will concentrate on arrangements where one party has the authority to determine *ex post* fulfillment, comparing this with cases where there is no need for such authority. (This notion is far from original to me; see, for example, Simon 1951.)

Note that Grossman and Hart's residual rights from ownership are very much of this flavor. They assume that the contract cannot provide for the use of the capital in certain contingencies and that the owner of the capital has the right to decide on how those contingencies will be met. The difference between their analysis and the one developed here is that they assume that ownership confers this authority and that thus

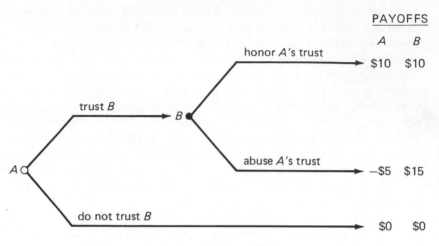

Figure 4.1. The trust game

the efficient placement of this authority determines the pattern of ownership. In what follows, ownership will not determine who retains hierarchical authority. Instead, we will attempt to use the notion of reputation to endogenize the determination of (efficient) authority. (This particular endogenization will provide the raison d'être for the firm – the source of correlation between firms and hierarchical transactions, and, eventually, the role of corporate culture.) But still, the similarity is more important than the difference; they, as we, concentrate on explicit contracts that are incomplete descriptions of the transactional relationship and on how those contracts might be completed as circumstances arise.

REPUTATION AND THE ROLE OF FIRMS

We leave for the time being transaction costs and hierarchical transactions in order to supply another of the three pieces from which the theory will be constructed – the theory of reputations that emerges from noncooperative game theory.

Repeated games, the folk theorem, and implicit contracts

Consider an individual, A, who is playing the following game against some second party, B. First A must choose whether or not to trust B. If A elects not to trust B, then both A and B get nothing. If A elects to trust B, B is made aware of this and has the option either to honor that trust or to abuse it. If *A* trusts *B,* and *B* chooses to honor that trust, both get $10. But if *A* trusts *B* and *B* chooses to abuse that trust, *B* gets $15 and *A* loses $5. A diagram of this game is given in Figure 4.1.

This is a one-sided version of the well-known prisoners' dilemma game. The salient feature of this game is that, played once and with no considerations other than those in the previous paragraph, *A* would not willingly trust *B*. For if *A* does so, then *B* must choose between honor, which nets $10, and abuse, which nets $15. Absent other considerations, *B* will choose $15. So trust will lead *A* to pay $5, and *A* is better off without trust. Of course, this makes both worse off than they would be if *A* had chosen trust and *B* honor – in the language of economics, it is an inefficient outcome. But it is the unique equilibrium outcome of this game, played once and played noncooperatively (that is, if we assume that individuals are motivated only by the monetary payoffs involved – part of our qualification "absent other considerations" – and if we assume that they have no opportunity to sign a binding and enforceable contract – more of the qualification – then this outcome is the unique self-enforcing outcome of this game).

This is meant to represent the archetypal transaction with some element of moral hazard. *A,* say, must sink some resources into preparing for a transaction with *B,* who can (at personal gain) take advantage of *A*'s position to an extent that makes the entire thing unworthwhile for *A.*

"Absent other considerations" can now be examined. One thing that the two transacting parties might do is to sign at the outset a contract that binds *B* to honor. Note that *ex ante* each will willingly sign such a contract as long as it is enforceable, because without it each will net nothing. But such a contract's execution may be costly. *B* will have an incentive to violate the contract once *A* has sunk resources. So some enforcement mechanism must be provided; this could also be costly. These are typical examples of Coase/Williamsonian transaction costs. If they are sufficiently great – if, for example, enforcement costs are greater than $20, or if the contract cannot be enforced because courts cannot distinguish between honor and abuse – then this otherwise mutually beneficial transaction will be foregone, the victim of transaction costs that are too high.

Now suppose that *A* and *B* are involved in this situation not once but repeatedly. Specifically, suppose that after each round of play, there is a 90 percent chance that they will play at least once more and a 10 percent chance that this (current) round will be the last. Suppose, for simplicity, that both want to maximize their winnings (less losses) from the sequence of plays. (If you wish, you can discount those winnings, but then the product of this continuation probability times the discount

101

factor plays the role of the 90 percent in what follows.) Now the analysis changes dramatically. A could, for example, say to B, "I will begin by trusting you, hoping that you will honor that trust. Indeed, I will continue to trust you as long as you do not abuse that trust. But if ever you abuse that trust, I will never again trust you." If B hears and believes this statement, B will indeed honor the trust. The following becomes the relevant calculation: Abuse in any round will increase the payoff in that round by $5. But weighed against that is the fact that the payoff will be nothing in all subsequent rounds (if any). There is a 90 percent chance of at least one more round, and if honor is chosen in that round, then in the next round at least $10 will be obtained, so the expected profits in the future from honor in this round outweigh the immediate gain of $5 from abuse.

Note that B must always have some substantial stake in the future if this is to work. If, say, there is only a 10 percent chance of a continuation of the game or if, say, A only chooses to trust B 10 percent of the time, then the calculation will come out the other way: B should (optimally) take the money and run.

This sort of result is the subject of the so-called folk theorem of noncooperative game theory. It is called the folk theorem because it has been well-known for so long, and no one has the presumption to claim to have originated it. (Actually, there are many versions of the folk theorem. The earliest ones concern games that are infinitely repeated with probability one and for which an average-payoff-per-round objective function is used. For a version appropriate to the discounted game we have posed, see Fudenberg and Maskin 1986.) Roughly, the folk theorem states that we can sustain feasible expected payoffs as noncooperative equilibrium payoffs for players that are sufficiently above the worst that others can inflict on them. The term "feasible" means that there must be some way to play the game and get those expected payoffs; for example, since the most in present value either player can get is $150 ($15/.1), we can't sustain an equilibrium for the game in which each side nets an expected $10,000. The term "sufficiently" has to do with the discount factor and with the most players can get in the short run by defecting from the arrangement. The bigger the discount factor (the smaller the probability of continuing for another round at least), the greater must be the payoffs to be sustained as an equilibrium; and the greater the possible short-run gains, the greater must be the payoffs to be sustained. One mechanism for sustaining such payoffs as equilibria is in our example. Each player says to the other, "As long as you stick to the arrangement that gets us the payoffs we are aiming for, we will continue to cooperate. But if you try to take short-run advantage, you will be punished." As long as the punishment (including at least the loss of subsequent cooperation) looms large enough relative to the gains from cooperation (the source of the qualifier "sufficiently"), neither will want to defect from the arrangement, which will become self-enforcing.

Note well what has been accomplished here. We began with a transaction that, on the face of it, looked beneficial to both sides. To assure that one side does not take advantage of the other, we argued that transaction costs would need to be expended on writing and enforcing a contract. Should that contract prove too expensive or even impossible to write or to enforce, then the transaction might not take place at all (it must be beneficial net of transaction costs). But by repeating the situation (with sufficiently high probability), we are able to avoid transaction costs entirely; the trust-honor arrangement is self-enforcing.

There are three problems with this result:

1. It says how trust-honor might emerge as an equilibrium outcome, but it allows for many other equilibria as well and doesn't offer any guidance as to which we will see. For example, in the game we began with, B might say to A, "I intend to honor your trust two out of three times and to abuse it once every three, as long as you continue to trust me. But if ever you choose not to trust me, then I will abuse your trust every time I get the opportunity." If A accepts such a declaration, A's best response is to trust B and take lumps every third round. The two $10 prizes outweigh (even with the 10 percent chance of the game ending at any moment) the $5 loss A sustains every third time. The point is that each player has many feasible expected payoffs sufficiently above the maximin point of zero that can sustain an equilibrium. The theory doesn't say which will emerge; it just says that the repeated character of the situation makes them possible outcomes.

Indeed, the folk theorem requires that a person repeat this encounter over and over against the same opponent. Williamson might argue that this transaction thinness actually increases transaction costs; he certainly lists thinness as one of the cost-increasing qualities of a transaction. We see something of this arising from the richness of the equilibrium set: We can get many efficient arrangements once we repeat the encounter, but the two participants might then expend time and resources bargaining over which arrangement they will in fact follow. Having arrived at an agreement, they might expend further resources to guarantee somehow that neither side subsequently tries to renegotiate. Perhaps the cleanest way to think of the power of repetitions is to imagine that many parties of each type fall into two-party arrangements; a market-determined agreement is reached through supply and demand for partners. That is, the equilibrium reached between A and B is determined by their opportunities with other trading partners. We have the thickness needed to avoid Williamson's problems with thin markets. At the same time, repetition allows partners to trade efficiently without fixing on paper (or needing to enforce) the market-determined terms of trade. (The astute reader will see a problem in this argument: If *B* has many alternative trading partners, why not abuse a current trading partner and then find another? Somehow, abuse must have deleterious future consequences or the entire construction falls apart. This anticipates what will happen in the next subsection, so we leave the reader to guess the answer that will be supplied.)

2. Suppose that we modify things ever so slightly as follows: We will play the game over and over, just as before, with a 90 percent chance each time of proceeding with another round. But should it ever be reached, the game will definitely terminate on round one hundred million. It seems unlikely that this will have much effect on the way the game is played (in experimental situations, it doesn't), but the theory suggests otherwise: If we do reach round one hundred million, then trust, if given, will surely be abused. There is at this point no future to be traded off against the current benefit from abusing trust. Thus, in round one hundred million, if reached, *A* should offer no trust. But then if *A* offers trust in round 99,999,999, it is sure to be abused: There is no point in *B* honoring it, because it will not be offered in the last round. Thus, trust will not be offered in round 99,999,999. And so on – the whole thing unravels from the back.

This problem, noted first by Selten (1978) and called (in a slightly different context) the chain-store paradox, can be resolved theoretically, at the cost of complicating the analysis. This is not an appropriate forum to discuss what ensues, but the basic idea runs as follows: Suppose that, at the outset, there is a small (say, one in a thousand) chance that *B* is the type of person who on moral grounds would never abuse trust. *B* knows, of course, whether he or she is of this type, but *A* is unsure. This small change is enough to restore for most of the game the trust-honor outcome.[5] Indeed, we get the same result if, say, *A* is sure that an opponent is not this sort of person and *B* knows that *A* knows this and *A* knows that *B* knows this. But *B* is a little unsure that *A* knows that *B* knows that *A* knows that *B* is not of this type. This can be modeled formally, and it is enough to get us back to the trust-honor outcome, as long as a large but finite number of rounds are left to go. (For the basics of the approach, see Kreps, Milgrom, Roberts, and Wilson 1982 and Kreps and Wilson 1982. This approach can help with the problem (1) of too many equilibrium outcomes, but it does not solve the problem entirely; see Fudenberg and Maskin 1986.)

3. Suppose that *A* cannot observe directly whether *B* chooses to honor or abuse *A*'s trust. Instead, what *A* sees is simply a payoff from

this round. Suppose that A's payoffs are not quite what we have discussed: If A trusts B and B honors that trust, then A's payoff is normally distributed with mean \$10 and variance \$1, whereas trust followed by abuse nets A a payoff that is normally distributed with mean \$–5 and variance \$1. Suppose A makes the speech that we began this section with: A will trust B as long as that trust is met with honor. A trusts B in the first round, and then A receives a payoff of \$–4. If A complains that this trust has been abused, B could reply (indignantly) that this is not the case; that A was simply unlucky. And, after all, this is a possible (but unlikely) outcome. What does A do? Carry out the threat and close off all possibilities of future cooperation? Or modify the threat to punish B (by choosing not to trust) for a long but finite length of time? And, if the second, for how long? And what should trigger this punishment?

The point is that when one player cannot observe directly that the agreement is being carried out, and when this player can only rely on noisy, indirect observations, the problem of finding self-enforcing arrangements is vastly more complicated. Some loss will necessarily result from the efficient arrangements, because some punishment will be required in any arrangement: If A never punishes B, then B will optimally respond by always abusing A's trust. To be a viable mechanism when there is noise, punishment must be used at least occasionally. In deciding when and how much to punish B, A must consider that the quicker or more severe the punishment, the more will be lost during punishment. But the slower and less severe the punishment, the more incentive B will have to take advantage of A by abusing trust. (For a formal analysis of this type of situation, see Green and Porter 1984.)

Repetition allows for the possibility of self-enforcing implicit contracts. We needn't write down the terms of the contract, nor need we provide an enforcement mechanism for it. But because enforcement is by punishment when the contract is broken, we must be able to observe compliance. As we become less and less able to observe compliance, we become less and less able to use this device at all.

Let me throw in a remark at this point that foreshadows later developments: When we say that compliance must be observable, we naturally suppose that we understand what "compliance" means. In simple toy problems like the one under discussion, this is not a very strong supposition, except for the problem of knowing which of the many equilibria constitutes the implicit contract. But when we turn to the real world, in which circumstances arise that no one initially foresaw or in which so many circumstances arise that it would be too costly to think through what compliance would mean in all of them, knowing what the contract calls for is problematic at best. The contract may be implicit, but that doesn't mean it is vague; the clearer it is, the better for monitoring compliance. Correspondingly, such contracts will be written in ways that give the best chance for observing compliance. Absolute clarity will not be possible in real settings, limiting the ability of participants to monitor compliance and, hence, the ability of this sort of arrangement to get us to efficient outcomes.

Reputation

In the game in the preceding section two participants engaged in a transaction repeatedly. This would seem to limit the game's applicability, because many transactions between individuals do not recur much or even occur only once. So it seems sensible to ask, to what extent must the participants to the transaction endure as trading partners?

Suppose that, instead of having one individual offer trust and a second honor or abuse that trust, we had a sequence of individuals A who must choose whether or not to trust a single trading partner B. For the sake of exposition, let us call the sequence of individuals $A_1, A_2, \ldots$ Let us make the following formal assumptions: A_1 must decide whether or not to trust B, and then (if trusted) B must choose to honor or abuse that trust, with payoffs to the two as before. Then, with 90 percent probability, B faces the same situation with A_2. And so on.

A moment's reflection should convince you that the following arrangement is self-enforcing. Party B carries a reputation from past behavior. For simplicity, we will suppose that B begins with an unsullied reputation, and B's reputation is irrevocably sullied if ever B abuses trust. Any A will trust B if B has an unsullied reputation, and A will refuse to trust B if B's reputation is sullied. Then B will always honor trust, and all As will (in sequence) put their trust in B. This is just like the self-enforcing agreement of the previous section, except here we see that only B must be enduring, *as long as* B's *opportunities in later rounds can be tied to behavior in earlier rounds.*

There are two parts to this statement. First, B's behavior, not A's posed the original problem in getting to the efficient transaction, so in this case only B must endure. Compare this with the situation in which A and B are both at risk in the transaction. For example, suppose A and B were engaged in the well-known prisoners' dilemma. In this game, A and B must simultaneously and without binding contracts each choose whether to cooperate or take advantage of the other. If they both cooperate, both get, say, $5. If one cooperates and the other takes advantage, the one cooperating loses $1 and the one taking advantage makes $7. If both take advantage, neither wins nor loses anything. Played noncooperatively and only once, both sides will choose to take advantage: Each does better doing so, regardless of what the other does. This leads to an inefficient outcome where neither makes any money, compared with the $5 that each can make if each cooperates. If we repeat this, however, with there always being a, say, 90 percent chance of playing at least one more time, then cooperation can emerge as an equilibrium outcome. (Each side will cooperate as long as the other does and threatens, say, never to again cooperate if the opponent takes advantage.) The point is that in this case both sides must endure. If one side played a sequence of opponents, each of whom played only once, then the opponents would always take advantage, and the one enduring side would have no reason to do otherwise. Whether it is enough to have only one side enduring (as it is in our model transaction) depends on the nature of the specific transaction.

Second, there must be a mechanism that ties *B*'s opportunities in future rounds to past behavior. It is critical to our story that the *A*s are able to observe *B*'s past actions and that they condition their behavior on *B*'s actions. If either condition is not met, then *B*'s incentive to honor trust in any particular round disappears and, therefore, so does the incentive of the *A*s to give trust.

Note our use of "reputation" to describe what transpires in this situation. *B* has a reputation built up from past encounters, and the *A*s consider that reputation when deciding whether to trust *B*. The nature of the reputation is quite circular – it works because it works: *B* guards a reputation because it influences future trading opportunities; it has this influence because *B* guards it.

In this game, some caveats must be observed.

1. Just as before, many reputations would work. *B*, for example, might have the reputation of abusing trust randomly, with, say, a probability of one-third each time. If any particular *A* feels there is a one-third chance that trust will be abused, that *A* is still willing to trust *B*. Of course, such a reputation will allow *B* to make greater profits. In general, we would expect that, in a situation where there are many long-lived *B*s, competition among them would limit the extent to which they can take advantage of the *A*s they deal with. This fleshes out the point made earlier concerning competition between *B*s. Whether or not the *A*s are long- or short-lived, we can imagine that they can, in any round, select from among a number of alternative *B* trading partners, selecting the *B* that has the best general reputation for trust. The *B*s will then compete for *A*s through their reputation. When a single *B* is the only possible trading partner for the *A*s, then the economics of the situation suggests that this *B* will take maximal advantage of his or her power, just as any monopolist would.

David M. Kreps

2. This story about reputations depends critically on there being no last round. As before, more complex models can get around this problem.

3. Reputations must be based on observables in order to work. Ambiguity and uncertainty cause problems. This point is best made by considering the reputation previously described above in point 1: B abuses trust with probability one-third in any particular round. Before, with only one A and one B, B could abuse trust every third round, threatening to abuse trust every time if A didn't trust every time (suffering every third). It would be easy for A to monitor compliance with this arrangement, because there is no uncertainty about what B will do in any single round. But this won't work at all if one B faces a sequence of As. Threatening to abuse trust every third round would only result in every third A deciding not to trust. Each A must have a sufficiently large probability that trust will be honored. Hence, B can only do something like abuse trust each round with probability one-third.

But if B tries to build such a reputation, how do the As know whether B is living up to the deal? Suppose that, as is possible but unlikely, B abuses trust ten times in a row. Should the As conclude that B is no longer living up to a reputation? At some point the As must punish B for too much abuse, otherwise B will (optimally) abuse trust every time. But how severe should that punishment be? When should it be triggered, and how long should it last? These are difficult questions, and when real-world ambiguity is added to the game, they become questions that might never get sorted out. This is getting us closer to a theory of the type of reputation that might be expected – better to use a reputation that is easier to monitor. (Note that B could abuse trust based on some *ex post* observable random number. For example, B could abuse trust if the closing stock price of AT&T, on a day after trust is offered or not but before B must choose to honor or abuse trust, is an even multiple of one dollar, or a dollar plus one-eighth, or a dollar plus two-eights. Because it is *ex post* observable whether B follows this rule, we have perfect ability to monitor, and no loss in efficiency from punishment periods is required.)

Firms

In the previous section we made the As short-lived, as long as B endured. But what if the Bs were also short-lived? For concreteness, suppose that at discrete dates $t = 1, 2, \ldots$ we have an A_t and a B_t who might engage in the transaction described. Absent binding contracts or some other costly contrivance, the transaction seems unlikely to take place. A_t cannot trust B_t *because* B_t has no incentive to do other than

108

Corporate culture and economic theory

abuse trust. We are almost out of business, but with one change we can resurrect our constructions. We suppose that B_t lives for two dates, at t and at $t+1$. At date t, B_t engages in the potential transaction with A_t; at date $t+1$, B_t retires to Florida and lives off savings. Also, we suppose that B_t comes endowed in period t with some resources, perhaps the fruits of labor early in period t.

Now consider the following arrangement: In this society there is a partnership called B Associates. At date t (prior to the transaction between A_t and B_t), B Associates is owned by B_{t-1}, who is about to move to Florida. For a price, B_{t-1} will sell a position in B Associates to B_t, who would purchase it out of preexisting resources.

Why would B_t pay anything for this place? Suppose that B Associates has a reputation for never abusing trust. A_t claims to be ready and willing to trust B_t, if B_t is a member of B Associates but not otherwise. Then B_t will certainly be willing to pay something to B_{t-1}, in order to have the opportunity to undertake the transaction with A_t.

Why should A_t trust B_t if B_t purchases a place in B Associates and not otherwise? Suppose that the As have a somewhat more complex decision rule: They will trust a member of B Associates as long as no previous member has ever abused the trust of some previous A. In other words, a member of B Associates will be trusted as long as the company's reputation is unsullied. Then B_t, having purchased a place in B Associates and having received the trust of A_t, must make the following calculations: The trust of A_t can be abused, which will net $15 today. But then the reputation of B Associates will be sullied, and B_{t+1} will pay nothing tomorrow for a place in it. On the other hand, honoring the trust of A_t will net only $10 today, but it will preserve the association's reputation, an asset that can be sold to B_{t+1}. The proceeds from that sale can be used to finance retirement in Florida. As long as the value of that asset is enough greater than five dollars so that its discounted value to B_t at date t exceeds $5, B_t will, having purchased a place in the association, optimally honor the trust of A_t. And A_t, realizing this, will happily trust B_t if B Associates is unsullied.

There is perhaps less to this argument than meets the eye initially. Suppose, for example, that the market price of a place in B Associates is $9. (We'll justify this as the approximate value in a second.) Then buying a place and protecting its reputation will probably be a good deal for the Bs. Not to buy will net nothing, because the corresponding A will not grant trust. To buy and then abuse trust nets $6 today ($15 from dealings with A, less the $9 purchase price) and nothing tomorrow. To buy and then honor trust nets $1 today and $9 tomorrow. Assuming a discount rate of 0.9 between the two dates, the last course is optimal, with net present value $9.10. (Hence the $9 price for a

109

David M. Kreps

place; assuming competition for places, we would have an equilibrium with a slightly higher price or a slightly greater discount rate.)

Now suppose that instead of this elaborate construction we allowed *B*s to make the following contract with *A*s: B_t posts a bond of nine dollars at date t if A_t gives trust, a bond that is forfeit if B_t abuses that trust. But if B_t honors the trust given, then B_t gets back the posted bond (perhaps with interest?) in period $t + 1$. It is hardly surprising that such contracts, if they can be written and enforced, will lead to the trust-honor outcome. From a mathematical point of view, this is all that the invention of *B* Associates has done for us. Although they are mathematically similar, the two arrangements work differently. With the bonding arrangement, even in this simple setting, we must have some agency that enforces the forfeiture of the bond. Courts would be natural candidates. That is, the two parties could write up a contract with the bonding provision, giving them recourse to the courts if the contract provisions are not fulfilled. But the drafting and (if necessary) subsequent enforcement of the contract might be costly. Such costs need to be weighed against the benefits accrued from the transaction. Indeed, because enforcement must occur after the transaction is completed, it may not be in the interests of A_t *ex post* to go to court if B_t fails to fulfill the contract. A_t certainly would want B_t to believe that he or she will in fact go to the courts, but it isn't clear that this is altogether believable. What does A_t gain *ex post* for expending time and money? If the threat to go to court is not credible, then the bonding arrangement won't work at all. (A simple cure, it would seem, is to stipulate in the contract that the bond is forfeited to *B*.)

Another problem, more nettlesome and more fundamental to what will follow, arises if honor is observable but not verifiable. The distinction here is important. *A* and *B* and others as well may be able to observe whether *B* honors *A*'s trust, but to substantiate this in a court of law is quite another thing. Verification or substantiation will be required if we are to have the courts as an enforcement agency, and this verification may be very costly or even impossible. If the costs of verification rise above the value to either party of any effective bond that can be posted, or if verification is simply impossible, a bonding scheme would not work.

With *B* Associates, however, the arrangement is self-enforcing as long as the *A*s can observe whether trust has been abused or not. It needn't be verified in court; no third party need be employed at all to enforce the agreement. If future *A*s simply refuse to transact with a sullied *B* Associates, then any *B*'s honoring of trust is enforced by self-interest – namely interest in recovering the full value of the asset originally purchased.

110

This very simple example gives our first cut at a theory of the firm. The firm is a wholly intangible object in this theory – a reputation bearer. It exists so that short-term transactors can be made sufficiently enduring to permit efficiencies borne of reputation or enduring relationships. Two things are necessary in this simple story: Reputation or enduring relationships must have some role to play, and the entity or entities that make decisions in the firm's name must have some vested interest in the firm's continuing to have a good reputation. It is crucial to our story that B_t lives beyond the association with B Associates and that the good name of B Associates represents to B_t a valuable asset to be (self-interestedly) preserved in order to sell later. But given these two requirements, we can see a potential role for an entirely intangible name.

Of course, in building a case for the use of B Associates, we have looked at a setting that ignores some of the major disadvantages of this sort of arrangement. The reputation construction is decidedly fragile: If reputation works only because it works, then it could fall apart without much difficulty. In real life, these risks will appear as substantial costs of undertaking transactions in this way. We don't see such costs here because our model is insufficiently rich to capture them. Still, these costs do exist; and it would not be unreasonable to conclude that the case for firms and other organizations we have made so far is hardly convincing.

HIERARCHICAL TRANSACTIONS

Consider the following elaboration on the simple game between A and B. For concreteness, we will adopt a version of the game with a sequence of As (labeled, where necessary, $A_1, A_2, \dots$), and a single, enduring B. But what follows can be adapted to the other two scenarios as well.

In this elaboration, A_t may hire B to perform some task that requires B's expertise. It is unclear at the outset how hard B will have to work to accomplish this task. We suppose that the task is either *easy* or *difficult*, each with probability one-half. The difficulty of the task is irrelevant to A_t in determining his or her value for it. A_t simply values it at $9 if it is adequately accomplished and A_t can tell whether or not it has been adequately accomplished *ex post*. The difficulty is relevant to B: If it is easy, a $3 compensation is adequate to B; if it is hard, a $13 compensation is required. A bargaining problem between the two parties must be solved here, but that bargaining problem is not germane to my point. So I will assume that for some reason the equilibrium arrangement gives B a $3 compensation if the job is easy and $13 if it is hard, as long as this arrangement can be enforced. Also, I assume that this equilibrium generates positive surplus for *B*, for reasons that will become apparent later.

We assume that *ex ante A* doesn't know how hard the job is. Imagine that the two could sign and enforce the following contract: *A* pays *B* $3 if the job is easy and $13 if it is hard, with no payment paid to *B* if the job is inadequately done. Then, assuming that the no-payment clause gives *B* the incentive to do an adequate job, *A* nets $9 in benefit against an *expected* payment of $8, making this a worthwhile transaction for *A*.

Now suppose that this contract cannot be enforced. Specifically, we assume that its provisions are observable but not verifiable. The distinction here is just as before: *ex post* both sides can observe the difficulty of the task and whether the task was adequately performed. But offering adequate proof of either thing in the courts is impossible.

If both *A* and *B* deal once only, this will kill the precise transaction already described. Indeed, the transaction will be killed even if we can enforce adequacy of performance. This is so because we cannot enforce payment – *A* will always want to pay the lesser amount, and *B* will want to collect the greater amount. How is the payment amount to be determined and enforced if we cannot enforce clauses contingent on the job's difficulty? (If it is possible to enforce such a contingent contract, we would still need to reckon in the cost of enforcement.) Seemingly, we must have a payment that is not contingent on the job's difficulty. Now if *B* is risk-neutral this might allow another transaction to take place: The two agree that *B* will be paid $8 regardless of the difficulty of the task, which is the same to *B* as the contingent payment. But the entire transaction may be rendered infeasible if *B* is risk-averse. The certain payment required to get *B* to undertake the task may then exceed the $9 value that *A* places on it. (We could, by elaborating the situation still further, get other reasons that lack of contingent fees would make the transaction impossible. For example, we could suppose that *A* ascribes a higher value to a more difficult task, give *A* the ability at some cost to ascertain the difficulty of the task *ex ante*, and then put the usual adverse selection argument to work.)

But we are concerned here not with one *A* and one *B* but rather with a *B* who might perform this service for a sequence of *A*s. Then we can get the contingent fee arrangement, even supposing that adequacy of performance is observable but not verifiable. That observability is sufficient to ensure adequate performance is our old story: Future *A*s may refuse to deal with *B* if ever *B* fails to perform adequately. (Of course, *B* must derive enough positive surplus from this transaction so that benefits from future transactions outweigh any present benefits from inadequate performance.) But a similar construction will yield the contingent fee structure. Imagine that A_t and B sign a contract that leaves payment unspecified and at the discretion of B, subject to a limit of $13. That is, A_t agrees *ex ante* to pay any bill B submits up to that limit. As adopt the following rule in deciding whether to transact with B: They will enter into transactions only if B has never gouged a former client; that is, if B has always charged $3 when the task was easy and $13 when it was hard. Because we are assuming that difficulty is observable, the As have sufficient data to adopt such a rule. If the value to B of future transactions exceeds the immediate $10 extra to be had by gouging a customer, this arrangement is self-enforcing.

In a mathematical sense, there is absolutely nothing new here. If we simply reinterpret *honor* to mean *to perform adequately and to bill appropriately* and *abuse* (now multifaceted) to mean to *do anything else*, then we are noting that sufficient potential gains from future trade, combined with As who observe and react to what B does in the right way, suffice to get the trust-honor outcome. The new twist is that we see how, in certain circumstances, trust could involve agreeing *ex ante* to obey dictates from the other party that are *ex ante* unspecified, awaiting the resolution of some uncertainty. In this sense, trust can encompass transactions that are hierarchical, where one party grants to the other the right to specify *ex post* just what the contract in fact calls for (always within limitations).

Even though mathematically there is nothing novel here, the reinterpretation in terms of hierarchical transactions and the connection between such transactions and reputation is key. We often see contracts that are *ex ante* quite vague about what will happen as contingencies arise. These contracts often include adjudication procedures. There may be specified recourse to independent arbitration of some form or another. Further negotiation may be called for (without specification as to what will happen if those negotiations fail to come to an agreement). In a large number of cases, discretion is left to one party or the other (always within broad limits). I contend that such transactions are characteristic of hierarchies; at some point, the hierarchically superior party, either explicitly or implicitly, has the right to direct the inferior party. Why would anyone ever willingly enter into such a contract in the inferior position? It might be because the worst that could happen is good enough so that the transaction, even on those terms, is worthwhile. But when the superior party has a reputation to protect or enhance, a reputation that turns on how that party exercises authority, then the inferior party need not presume the worst. That party can count on the superior party to live up to an implicit contract in his or her own interests.

113

The notion of a hierarchical transaction and the connection with reputation goes back to Simon (1951). He makes clear the distinction between this sort of transaction and the usual exchange of goods for money that is the basis of standard economic theory. He argues that hierarchical transactions are particularly prevalent in employment relationships. Beginning with a transaction in which A presumes the worst (or, rather, that B will act solely for short-run interests), Simon shows that in such cases the authority that A willingly grants to B can be quite small. Then he argues, just as we have done, that this authority can be enlarged (or the compensation demanded by A decreased) in cases where A and B may wish to repeat the transaction over time, with B implicitly threatened by suspension of the transaction for abuses of hierarchical authority.

Of course, in this particular explanation for hierarchical transaction, authority *must* rest with a long-lived party. Suppose that A is long-lived, participating in this transaction with a sequence of Bs. If there is no problem in enforcing adequate performance, then the proper hierarchical form could have A paying whatever is appropriate, with each B agreeing *ex ante* to let A determine what is appropriate (no less than $3). (What if adequate performance is not enforceable? With a small enough discount rate, we could even have A's payment of whatever is appropriate be zero in cases involving inadequate performance.)

In the story just told, it seems crucial that the task's difficulty be observable. What would happen if we changed the story so that this is not so? Note well that this unobservability need only be on the part of future As; they and not the current A must be able to monitor compliance with the implicit contract. Again, we know the answer from the previous section: Some inefficiencies will enter, but all is not necessarily lost. If, say, the difficulty of the task cannot be observed, then B could claim to follow the billing rule already explained but will have to be watched carefully and punished (by withholding transactions) occasionally. The As can ascertain whether B is indeed charging $3 around half the time, according to the billing rule described. If there is a history of too many $13 charges, then the As can (for a while) refuse to transact with B. Note that it is crucial that B be punished occasionally. We cannot arrange things so that punishment is avoided altogether, for that would mean accepting without question any bill B submits. B would then charge $13 every time. There is no way to avoid some loss of efficiency when the As are unable to observe the task's difficulty. But lack of observability needn't completely prevent a transaction.

Considerations of observability will play a large role in what is to follow, so let me make this point one more time in a different way.

114

Imagine that the task's difficulty is indeed unobservable, but concrete signs are observable that imperfectly indicate whether the job was difficult. To be precise, suppose that each job either does or does not require calculus. Of the difficult jobs, 97.5 percent require calculus, and 2.5 percent don't. Of the easy jobs, 20 percent require calculus, while the other 80 percent don't. If it is observable whether calculus is required for the job but not whether the job is difficult, then it might well be better to base payment on whether the job required calculus than on whether the job was really difficult. That is, we can, using the reputation construction, have a self-enforcing arrangement in which the bill is $13 if the job requires calculus and $3 otherwise, even if the requirement to use calculus is observable but not verifiable. This may not be the first-best arrangement; that will be the one for which payment is based directly on the job's difficulty. But to try to base the bill directly on difficulty runs us into inefficiencies that exist because the job's difficulty is unobservable. It may be better to contract implicitly on some contingency that is clearly observable but that is not the ideal contingency to base the arrangement on, because what is lost in moving away from the ideal contingent contract may be regained from the greater efficiency of the reputation arrangement. (In the spirit of results by Holmstrom [1979], it is natural to conjecture that the most efficient implicit contract will not be based solely on the observable contingency. In the simple example we have described, one can show that this is so. But I am unaware of any general result in this direction.)

A concrete example of this phenomenon may be helpful in understanding it. In the United States, it is a commonplace observation that doctors run too many tests on patients in order to protect themselves from malpractice suits. The phrase "too many" presumably means that more tests are given than are necessary, given the doctor's information. But it is hard to observe *(ex post)* whether a doctor's subjective *ex ante* judgments were professional. It is far easier to observe whether the doctor followed some pattern of generally accepted practice that allows for few subjective options. That such a clearly laid-out pattern of practice is suboptimal relative to the (first-best) application of subjective judgment is obvious. But it is also irrelevant to any reasonable analysis of the problem: We have to consider the full equilibrium implications of having doctors rely more on subjective judgments. (So that no one gets upset, I am not suggesting that what we see in the United States is the most efficient feasible arrangement; I haven't thought about it nearly enough to have an informed opinion. But the simplistic argument that one often hears is incomplete, ignoring as it does the costs of monitoring, enforcement, and so on.) Another, quite similar example, comes from the accounting profession, where accounts are kept according to Generally Accepted Accounting Principles, even when those practices might not be the most informative for the particular accounts being kept.[6]

UNFORESEEN CONTINGENCIES

We have now reached the point where orthodox economic theory will be abandoned because it lacks the two final ingredients of the stew being concocted. Before we head off into less orthodox waters, let me offer the following summary of where we've been.

In transactions where one side must trust the other, the reputation of the trusted party can be a powerful tool for avoiding the transaction costs of specifying and enforcing the terms of the transaction. Indeed, when the contingencies upon which the terms are based are observable but not verifiable, reputation may be the only way to effect the transaction. Reputation works as follows: The trusted party will honor that trust because to abuse it would preclude or substantially limit opportunities to engage in future valuable transactions. Such a reputation arrangement can work even when the reputation rests in a wholly intangible entity (the firm), as long as those who make decisions or take actions in the entity's name have a stake in preserving its reputation. Among the types of contracts to which this pertains are those that are hierarchical, where the contract calls *ex ante* for one party to decide *ex post* how the contract will be fulfilled, with the second party agreeing *ex ante* to abide by the first party's dictates, within broad limitations. Finally, this arrangement works best when the actions of the trusted party are based on contingencies observable to all concerned; reputation based on unobservable contingencies is not impossible, but it will always involve some degree of inefficiency. Put another way, the best reputation, from the point of view of effecting the type of arrangement we are talking about, is one that is clear-cut and easy to monitor.

All of these conclusions have been derived from orthodox economic theory. But the examples so far discussed present a fairly weak case for the importance of this theory. Too much seems to rest on the distinction between observable and verifiable contingencies. How many of those are there, and how important are they in real-life transactions?

I contend that there are many such contingencies and that they are very important, if we stretch this theory to include unforeseen contingencies. An unforeseen contingency is a set of circumstances that *ex ante* the parties to the transaction had not considered. Unforeseen contingencies need not be unimaginable: Individuals may simply be unwilling *ex ante* to spend time thinking through all possibilities, on the grounds that it is too time-consuming and expensive to do so. Or it

116

Corporate culture and economic theory

could be that the circumstances really are *ex ante* unimaginable. From the point of view of our development, either interpretation is fine.

Before adding unforeseen contingencies to our analysis of transactions, consider briefly how individuals act when faced with unforeseen contingencies. Introspection suggests that while a particular contingency may be unforeseen, provision for it is not completely impossible. While the exact circumstances of future contingencies may be unimaginable (or too costly to think through), aspects of those contingencies can be anticipated. I contend that unforeseen contingencies follow patterns. At least, I, and, I suspect, others, act as if this is so. Accordingly, my provisions for the unforeseen are somewhat evolutionary. I examine what has happened that was surprising in the recent and sometimes distant past, and I provide for roughly similar contingencies.

Formal models of behavior such as this are easy to produce. Imagine, for example, that I have at my disposal several possible remedies in varying amounts, remedies that may or may not be applicable to a wide range of circumstances. Simple examples are cash and fire extinguishers. Holding these remedies at the ready is expensive: Cash on hand doesn't earn interest, and fire extinguishers are costly. The amount of each remedy that I keep on hand is related to how useful I suspect it will be. Insofar as I can anticipate relatively greater need for a remedy in a particular circumstance, I will adjust my holdings upward. (For example, having just bought a house, I am holding relatively more cash in my checking account to meet the numerous small expenses that I discover.) But I will also be guided by the relative usefulness of the various remedies in the recent past. (In the month that has elapsed since I bought the house, I have discovered that I need to keep more cash in my checking account than I had originally anticipated was necessary.) If there is indeed a stationary pattern to unforeseen contingencies, then in the long run I will wind up holding correct levels of the remedies. If, as seems more likely, there is a pattern that is not stationary but that has secular trends, then although I may not achieve the best levels of remedy holdings, I will still be better off by paying attention to recent events than not.

I meander concerning how individuals (or at least how I) act in the face of the unforeseen because economic theory does not provide an accepted model of behavior. One knows the appropriate model for, say, decision making under uncertainty, from the axiomatic development by von Neumann and Morgenstern, Savage, and others. But there is no corresponding standard model of decision making through time when there are unforeseen contingencies.

Although there is nothing to my knowledge written on the subject, it might be instructive to speculate on what a standard model of choice

117

with unforeseen contingencies might look like. The usual models of choice under uncertainty, of which Savage's theory (1954) is the exemplar, presume that individuals can foresee all conceivable future contingencies; they are uncertain only over which contingencies will develop. Or rather, the standard model posits that individuals act as if that were so at any point in time. This could continue to be so for choice at any single point in time, but with one major change: One of the fundamental pieces of the standard model is the state space – the set of all conceivable future contingencies. This is a given in the model; in the usual interpretation this piece of the model is objectively fixed, not a part of an individual's behavior. But if there are unforeseen contingencies and if individuals attempt at any point to make provision for them, then one might better regard the state space in an individual's model as part of the subjective inputs the individual provides. That is, just as in the standard model the individual's choice behavior reveals probability assessments and utility function, so in a model with unforeseen contingencies might subjective choice behavior reveal the individual's conception of what the future might hold. In such a model, it would then become important to speak of how the individual's state space (and probability assessments and utility function) evolves through time: I have a strong bias toward models in which past surprises are taken as guides to what the future might hold. More precisely, such a model would generate behavior in which provision for future contingencies is positively influenced by what would have been useful in the past; this evolutionary behavior will be modeled by corresponding evolution in the individual's state space and probability assessments. These are no more than speculations, but I do wish to indicate the importance that will be attached to the evolution of behavior: The past, and especially past surprises, will guide how individuals prepare for future surprises.

A model of dynamic choice behavior when there are unforeseen contingencies is an essential precursor to a solid theory of transactions in the face of unforeseen contingencies. As I do not have and do not know of the former, it is somewhat dangerous to speculate on the latter. But I will try, nonetheless. Unforeseen contingencies make explicit and complete contracting impossible. How can we provide *ex ante* for contingencies that *ex ante* we cannot anticipate? Yet many transactions live so long that unforeseen contingencies must be met. An especially good example is that of individuals seeking employment. In many cases, individuals commit themselves to more than a day's or a week's work. Individuals will develop human capital peculiar to a particular firm, and the employment relationship will be relatively more efficient if it continues for many years in the future. Insofar as this is so, it is impossible for workers and the firm to specify everything the workers will do during their employment. Future contingencies are extraordinarily complex, involved, and even unimaginable. Consider also the contract between students and a university. *Ex ante,* students have little idea what courses they will want to take, when they will want to take them, and so forth. There is no possibility of enumerating and providing for the myriad contingencies that could arise.

In such transactions, the workers and the firm, and students and the university, agree *ex ante* not so much on what will be done in each particular contingency as they do on the procedure by which future contingencies will be met. The workers and students have certain rights that cannot be violated by the firm and the university. They have the right to terminate the relationship at will, but workers and students usually agree at the outset that, in the face of unforeseen contingencies, adaptation to those contingencies will be at the discretion of a boss or dean. That is, the adaptation process is hierarchical, in just the sense of the last section. (This can be qualified in important ways when workers or students have a body representing their interests – a labor union or student union, for example.)

Why will workers and students enter into such arrangements? What protection do they get? It is that the firm or university develops and maintains a reputation for how it meets unforeseen contingencies by the way in which it actually meets those contingencies. How the contingencies will be met is not verifiable, at least not in the sense that workers or students could take a firm or university to court and enforce a violated implicit contract. But the meeting of the contingencies is observable *ex post;* others can see what the firm or university did and decide whether to enter into similar transactions with either.

Of course, our previous qualifications to the reputation construction continue to hold. The firm or university does not make decisions: Boss *B* or Dean *B* does so in the organization's name. These people must have some real stake in maintaining their organization's good reputation. Most crucially, the meeting of unforeseen contingencies must conform to some pattern or rule that is observable – that is, the organization's reputation must be for something. This is especially problematic in the case of unforeseen contingencies. Once they arise, we may know what they are, but how do we know that they have been met as they are supposed to be met? Because the contingencies are unforeseen, we cannot specify in advance how to meet all possible contingencies and then observe that advance specifications have been fulfilled. We are in a situation somewhat more analogous to that where the meeting of future contingencies is not perfectly observable, with

119

David M. Kreps

an attendant loss in efficiency. At best, participants will have a rough sense as to general principles with which unforeseen contingencies will be met, and they will have to gauge the extent to which those principles have been honestly applied. To discuss further such principles, we need to return one final time to the tool box of economic theory.

FOCAL POINTS

Consider the following relatively simple game. Here are eleven letters, A, B, C, D, H, K, L, M, N, P, S. Assigned to each letter is a number of points, between 1 and 100. I won't tell you what assignments the letters have, except to tell you that N is assigned the highest number of points (100) and K the least (1). I ask you and another person, unknown to you, to pick simultaneously and independently a subset of these letters. Your list must have the letter S on it, and your opponent's must have the letter B. Each of you is aware of the requirement imposed on the other. Otherwise, you are free to pick as many or as few letters as you want. We will compare lists and make payments to each of you as follows: For any letter on one list and not on the other, the person listing that letter wins as many dollars as that letter has points. For any letter appearing on both lists, both players must forfeit twice the number of dollars as that letter has points. If the two lists precisely partition the set of letters so that each letter appears in only one list, prizes will be tripled.

Before going further, what list of letters would you submit? If you were assigned the letter B instead of S, what list would you submit?

Notice that this game has a vast number of equilibria – two lists of letters, one for each player, such that neither player would wish to change his or her list unless the other person did so. Namely *any* of the 512 partitions of the nine other letters constitutes an equilibrium. Yet I am fairly confident that many readers came up with the list L, M, N, P, S. And, putting yourselves in the role of the player assigned letter B, you thought of the list A, B, C, D, H, and perhaps K. The rule is simple: alphabetical order. One player takes the first five letters, the other player takes the last five. The letter K is problematic, because there are eleven letters. But many of you may have replicated the following argument: The player with the end of the alphabet is getting N, which is the best letter to have, and K is worth only one dollar, so why not let the other person have it?

Note that the rule applied here is wholly dependent on context. I have played a very similar game with Stanford MBA students and Harvard undergraduates that comes to a very different solution. I tell them

120

Corporate culture and economic theory

I have a list of eleven U.S. cities, namely Atlanta, Boston, Chicago, Dallas, Houston, Kansas City, Los Angeles, Miami, New York, Philadelphia, and San Francisco. Each city has been assigned a number of points reflecting its relative importance to commerce, trade, and the arts in the United States, with New York the highest at 100 points and Kansas City the lowest at 1. Two students unknown to each other, one from Harvard and the other from Stanford, are to list simultaneously and independently some subset of the cities, with the Harvard participant required to list Boston and the Stanford participant required to list San Francisco. The game continues as before.

Before reading on, how would you proceed if you had the Stanford role? If you had the Harvard role?

In a surprisingly large number of cases (my rough estimate is 75 percent), Harvard people select Atlanta, Boston, Chicago, Miami, New York, and Philadelphia, while Stanford people take the complement Dallas, Houston, Kansas City, Los Angeles, and San Francisco. When asked why, the usual response referred to which side of the Mississippi River the city is on – Harvard gets everything east of the Mississippi, Stanford everything west. (Kansas City causes problems for individuals unschooled in geography. Miami also sometimes causes problems, when people use Sunbelt/Snowbelt division as the principle for their selections, although the joint presence of Atlanta, which belongs to the Sunbelt, and Miami, usually causes students to reject this principle because of the unequal numbers of Snowbelt and Sunbelt cities. Substituting Detroit for either Atlanta or Miami is a good way to make the Sunbelt principle live in at least some minds, and substituting Detroit for Dallas definitely favors it. Putting either Minneapolis/St. Paul or New Orleans into the list causes great confusion. Foreign students resent this game *ex ante* – they seem to know what the nature of the principle applied will be without knowing just what the principle will be or how to apply it, and they are quick to point out how unfair this is to them.)

These are examples of focal points. This concept, derived from Schelling (1960), refers (roughly) to some principle or rule individuals use naturally to select a mode of behavior in a situation with many possible equilibrium behaviors. (More precisely, the focal point is the equilibrium suggested by some focal principle.) Schelling's discussion is informal but persuasive; he is able to cite many games like these two in which, somehow, most participants know what to do. He finds that most focal points can be characterized by simple qualitative principles. Symmetry is a powerful focal principle, when it can be applied. When one principle singles out a unique equilibrium and other principles do not give a clear-cut answer, the first tends to be applied; uniqueness is

David M. Kreps

a fairly powerful principle. Often the focal point seems a product of culture. For example, the use of the Mississippi River to divide the eleven cities occurs with astonishing frequency to Americans; non-Americans rarely if ever come up with that means of division.

The notion of a focal point is well outside orthodox economic theory. No formal work I am aware of addresses the concept. (I suspect that psychologists have something quite substantial to tell economists on this score, and I am looking forward to getting references from readers of this book.) So, again, reliance on casual introspection seems in order.

One point the game examples just described make is that in any particular situation many focal points may be applied. The individual, trying to decide between them, will look for which one fits best. Which is most suggested by context? (A geographical rule seems more appropriate to cities than does an alphabetical rule. One wonders if an American student who knows that his opponent is from overseas and is relatively unschooled in U.S. geography then focuses on the alphabetical rule?) Which does least violence to other principles? (For example, the presence of both Atlanta and Miami in the list of cities makes application of the Sunbelt principle problematic, since it violates badly the equal division principle. But if I took away Dallas and added Detroit, then the Mississippi River principle would give a seven-to-four division, and, I expect, the Sunbelt principle would get somewhat more play, especially because it lumps New York into a group of five and Kansas City into a group of six.) A choice of a principle to apply must be made, and the choice is usually far from capricious.

Second, it seems to me that focal points arise in part because of evolutionary fitness. A good, useful focal principle in a particular situation will tend to have had successful wide applicability in similar past situations for the individual using it. This will tend to favor principles that are more universal or broader and, of course, that are clearer in a particular context.

A related point, supported by experimental evidence, is that focal points can be learned – and quite quickly. Roth and Schoumaker (1983) have conducted the following experiment. Two individuals play a game in which they bargain over 100 chips. The bargaining procedure is simple: Each simultaneously and independently proposes a number of chips that he or she would like to have. Let the two initial bids be x_A and x_B. If these bids are compatible in the sense that $x_A + x_B \leq 100$, then each gets the number of chips asked for. If the sum of the bids exceeds 100, then each is asked to concede or stick to the initial bid. Those who concede get 100 less the number of chips originally

122

requested by their opponents. If one sticks and the other concedes, the one who sticks gets his or her original bid. If both stick, then both get no chips. These chips are then redeemed: If a player has won n chips, that player is given an $n/100$ chance at winning a monetary prize. The first player's prize is $10, while the second's is $40. Both players are told all this, and both are told that the other is being told. Insofar as is practical, all the above is made common knowledge between the players. Bidding and conceding/sticking are done via computer; communication between the two players is strictly limited. Players participate in this game not once but repeatedly; they are told before each round how well their opponent has done (in terms of chips) in previous rounds.

As a formal game, the bidding situation described has many equilibria. For any number between 0 and 100, if one player is going to ask for and then stick to that number of chips, the second's best response is to ask for and stick to 100 minus that number. That is, there are 101 pure strategy equilibria here. Moreover, there are two somewhat natural focal points: Split the chips 50–50, or split the chips so that each player has the same expected value, that is, 80 chips to the first player and 20 chips to the second. (Another focal point, perhaps to economists only, is the efficient outcome where one player gets all the chips.) In previous experiments, Roth found that the second (80–20) focal point seems to predominate in the population he tested (students at the University of Illinois).

Roth and Schoumaker add a new wrinkle. Unbeknownst to the participants, in their first ten or so rounds of play, they are matched against a computer. In some cases the computer is programmed to insist on the 50–50 split of chips (or, when the computer is the $10 player, to accede to this split); in other cases the computer is programmed to insist on or accede to the 80–20 split. After this training period, players are matched against each other with predictable results: Those whose training has equipped them to come to exact agreement stay at that agreement. Those whose training leads to inconsistent demands (one demanding 50 and the other 80) tend not to come to any agreement. Those whose training leads them to leave chips on the table (one asks for 20 and the other for 50) tend to head for one of the two focal points after a while. (Interested readers should consult the paper, which I am abridging with abandon here.)

The point is clear: Focal points are in part the product of experience. They can be taught through repeated application. It is a heroic leap from this experiment to the evolutionary process we have already conjectured, but, having made the conjecture, I can now finally throw it into the stew and emerge with corporate culture.

David M. Kreps

CORPORATE CULTURE

Recall where we were in the main development before detouring into the subject of focal points: Unforeseen contingencies provide both a golden opportunity for the reputation/hierarchical transaction construction to take life and provide a problem for that construction. The problem is that the reputation argument turned on the ability of future potential trading partners to observe and monitor their degree of compliance with the implicit contract they have with current trading partners. Current trading partners could enter into a hierarchical transaction in the inferior position with equanimity because each could trust the other to carry out the implicit contract in her or his own interests, to protect their reputations and safeguard future beneficial transactions. But the implicit contract is more than implicit in the face of unforeseen contingencies. Practically by definition, it cannot be clear *ex ante* precisely what is called for in a contingency that *ex ante* has not been foreseen. So on what might a reputation turn?

It is not logically impossible for the reputation construction to work without flaw. What is needed is (i) the ability, after observing a particular contingency, to know what should be done and (ii) a belief *ex ante* by the hierarchical inferiors that application of what should be done will be good enough to warrant undertaking the transaction. Truly unambiguous and universal rules could be imagined that could be applied *ex post* to any contingency that arises, and as long as test (ii) above is passed we meet all of the requirements for the reputation construction with such rules. (More elaborate, real-life adjudication procedures have this flavor. For example, the (legal) hierarchical superior may seek third-party mediation in the case of any disputes and have a reputation for always abiding by the recommendations of the mediator.)

But it seems unlikely that unambiguous and universal rules exist, at least in most situations. Or rather, it is unclear that such rules will exist that at the same time will pass test (ii). (An unambiguous and universal rule is: "I decide according to my whims." But this will probably inspire trust insufficient to pass test [ii].) Because every contingency that arises must be dealt with somehow (which is to say that the rule actually applied must be universal), one should expect ambiguity. The hierarchical inferiors, and, more importantly, the population of potential future hierarchical inferiors, will sometimes be uncertain that the rule is being followed. By analogy with formal work on reputation based on unobservable or partially observable behavior, we expect some loss of efficiency.

Yet, as in the formal literature, some loss need not mean complete loss. One might doubt whether, in the face of unforeseen contingencies,

124

there can ever be a rule the application of which is sufficiently unambiguous and sufficiently advantageous to the hierarchical inferior to permit the reputation construction to live at all. But, again arguing by analogy, I contend that the literature on focal points indicates that such rules or principles can in fact exist. Faced with a competitive situation that one has never imagined before, a situation with many equilibrium actions that could be taken, one is often able to see how to proceed, applying a general principle. Indeed, this is so even if one is aware of only the slightest details of one's fellow players and if one must identify on one's own what principle is appropriate. It would seem that this is more likely to be true in cases where the fellow player has a long track record of applying a particular principle in similar but not quite identical situations.

Moreover, features that make for a good focal principle ought to make for a good rule to base the implicit contract/reputation on. *Ex post* unambiguity, as long as test (ii) is passed, is the *sine qua non*.[7] Note in this regard that a quite effective scheme might be to exclude purposely some contingencies from the rule. That is, the rule is to act in some specified manner (or according to some principle) in most cases, but it is not meant to be applied in a few others. Here it will only be necessary that we can agree, *ex post,* that a particular contingency was one in which the rule was meant to be applied. "We do XYZ as long as it makes sense" can be quite effective as long as it makes sense most of the time and everyone can agree on cases where it doesn't.

Enter corporate culture. Let us consider first the organization as a single decision-making entity or as a sequence of decision-making entities who, when they have decision-making authority, have that authority all to themselves. This entity's problem is to identify a rule that permits relatively efficient transactions to take place and on which a viable reputation can be based and then to communicate that rule to current and potential future trading partners. In the preceding formal analysis, we supposed a particular equilibrium, giving passing mention of the problem of multiplicity. In real life, communication becomes much more of a problem, especially where the rule is to some extent abstract. The communication of this principle is crucial: Potential trading partners are judging our decision-making entity on its faithful application of the principle, it is clearly important that the entity let others know just what is the principle. Especially in a world with private information, the entity will want to have a principle tailored to it. Perhaps more importantly, the principle, if communicated well, can be used effectively as a screening device, warning off potential trading partners for whom the arrangement will not be good.

As in most communication problems of this kind, the simpler the message being sent and the more internally consistent it is, the easier it will be to communicate. By analogy with focal principles, simplicity and consistency will be virtues in application. As readers no doubt guessed long ago, I wish to identify corporate culture with the principle and with the means by which the principle is communicated. My (limited) understanding of corporate culture is that it accomplishes just what the principle should – it gives hierarchical inferiors an idea *ex ante* how the organization will react to circumstances as they arise; in a strong sense, it gives identity to the organization.

More than this, corporate culture communicates an organization's identity to hierarchical superiors. Firms and other large organizations do not have a single decision maker but instead have many individuals who make decisions in the organization's name. Even if we suppose that these individuals all have internalized as their objective functions the common good of the organization, it will be hard for them, in the face of circumstances they hadn't foreseen, to know how to proceed. Costly communication will render infeasible completely centralized decision making, yet it will be advantageous to have some consistency and coordination in the decentralized decisions of the many *B*s in the organization. Corporate culture plays a role here by establishing general principles that should be applied (in the hope that application of that principle will lead to relatively high levels of coordination). But it is more than merely a coordinating device: It is especially useful in coordinating the exercise of the organization's hierarchical authority. If the organization is to have a reputation in its hierarchical transactions, it must be consistent in exercising hierarchical authority. Thus, the organization has a crucial task: to communicate the general decision rule it applies to all those who undertake the actual application. The culture inside the organization will do this as well – it will communicate the principle to all concerned.

Corporate culture also provides a means of measuring the performance of hierarchical superiors. In many organizations, individuals have not fully internalized the common good – they are concerned with their own welfare. Thus, an organization must monitor and control individual performance. If individuals within an organization who exercise hierarchical authority are supposed to exercise that authority according to some clear principle, then it becomes easier *ex post* to monitor their performance. (This is simply another variation on our *ex post* observability story.) Hence, in the usual fashion, efficiency can be increased by monitoring adherence to the principle (culture). Violation of the culture generates direct negative externalities insofar as it weakens the organization's overall reputation. Rewarding good outcomes

126

that involve violations of the culture generates negative externalities indirectly through the chain: This weakens individual incentives to follow the principle and thus increases (potentially) the costs of monitoring and control.[8]

This, then, is how economic theory (or rather an economic theorist) might try to explain the phenomenon of corporate culture. It clearly gives corporate culture an economic role to play; indeed, the role is part and parcel of the organization's role. As such, design and maintenance of the culture is crucial to efficient organization. If strategy consists of finding economic opportunities and then maintaining and protecting them, this puts corporate culture in the center of strategy.

The theory (if something so incomplete and bare-boned can be dignified with that title) given here may indicate that corporate culture can be rendered in economic terms, but it would be a good deal nicer if that rendering suggested some consequences. I close by giving a few suggested consequences, although readers will quickly discern that I pay more attention to intuition than to any theoretical constructs. (Perhaps it would be more honest to call what follows my wish list for this theory, things I would like to derive from a fully developed theory.) I will also point out conclusions that are not borne out by any of the formal constructs that I have reported here, but that I think ought to be obtainable.

1. Consistency and simplicity being virtues, the culture/principle will reign even when it is not first best. There are three parts to this hypothesis. First, as part of the communication process, the culture will be taken into areas where it serves no direct purpose except to communicate or reinforce itself. This seems outside the realm of economic theory, which does not have good models of the difficulties encountered in real-life communication. One possibility suggested by Roth and Schoumaker, which can be modeled formally, would be to regard application in irrelevant areas as training for others – that is, to communicate the principle, we administer it repeatedly so that others learn it. This does, however, raise the question, why not engage in direct communication instead? (Or we could spin an allied economics story by discussing the use of culture as a screen, a device to select from among potential transaction partners those individuals who are most appropriate to the transaction desired.)

Second, contingencies will arise in which the principle will not be in the best interests of the two immediate parties involved, yet it will still be applied for the benefit of third parties in order to ensure a general reputation for applying the principle. This follows directly from the formal constructions discussed in the chapter.

127

David M. Kreps

Third, cases may arise in which everyone concerned understands that the principle is inefficient, yet still it will be applied. This will come about in cases where the basis of a reputation is a belief that faithful application of the principle per se is valuable to a hierarchical superior. To provide formal justification for this, we would have to use the reputation arguments that turn on incomplete information, such as in Kreps, Milgrom, Roberts, and Wilson (1982). We have refrained from giving details on this literature, and this is no time to begin, so simply note that a key to this argument is that something may be in everyone's best interests and everyone may know that this is so, but still it may not be done if, say, not everyone is aware that everyone knows that it is in everyone's best interests. In formal terms, it may not be common knowledge.

2. In general, it will be crucially important to align culture with the sorts of contingencies that are likely to arise. There are planted axioms here: Unforeseen contingencies in a particular enterprise do follow patterns. Even though one cannot think through the contingencies, one might be able to predict what principle will be good at meeting them. Principles are better or worse depending on how they adapt to the contingencies that do arise. At this level, this observation has little substance. But there is something potentially substantial here: One can expect difficulties when an organization's mission changes, because reputations grow and die hard (that is, reputations are assets fairly specialized and immutable once created). The theory presented earlier is completely inadequate to provide a reason that this would be so. There is nothing to prevent reputation from having secular trends or discontinuities, as long as everyone understands what is expected of B in every situation and B fulfills those expectations. In order to derive formally the desired rigidity in reputations, it again seems necessary to access the incomplete information construction of reputation, with an appeal to simplicity in the initial conjectures of the As concerning what motivates B. (This last remark is likely to be incomprehensible to readers unfamiliar with the reputation and incomplete information literature.)

(As long as I am putting in remarks incomprehensible to all but the cognoscenti, let me add another: Note that a story based on personal quirks of the Bs is not going to fly in the context of the story of B Associates unless we believe that becoming a member of B Associates changes B_t's preferences or if we make the characteristics of the various B_t's exchangeable or something similar or if we embellish the story by supposing that B Associates, as part of its economic function, screens potential partners. Any of these would get us the probability of a persistent quirk that is necessary to make the incomplete information construction fly. And the last, which is my favorite, also gets us another screening role for corporate culture.)

3. What will corporate culture (or the principle) be based on, and how can we expect it to evolve? I have stressed the evolutionary character of beliefs about unforeseen contingencies and focal principles. Insofar as the principle is meant to provide an adaptation to unforeseen contingencies and is to be based on something like a focal principle, I would expect the similar evolutionary adaptation. Of course, I have no theoretical models to back this up with, and it is a conclusion to which I would like to add caveats. Suppose one could argue convincingly that reputation is somewhat rigid and immutable once in place. Then, one would conclude that the early history of an organization is likely to play a decisive role in the formation of that organization's culture/principle. It is then that the organizational reputation is largely formed, for better or worse. Because the culture will form at least in part in response to unforeseen contingencies that do arise, the nature of an organization will be strongly influenced by early happenstance.

Suppose moreover that interrelated parts of a particular reputation/principle all live or die together. That is, trust of an organization (and its adherence to its various implicit contracts) is not perfectly divisible – violation of one implicit contract raises doubts about the commitment to others. (This could be derived theoretically using the reputations and incomplete information technology by controlling the probability assessments held *ex ante* about managers. The details, though, seem complex, for the same reasons that make the incomplete information story harder to tell. Then the evolution of the organizational culture/principle will be episodic and discontinuous. Events that cause some portion of the contracts to be violated (or that give greater opportunity to break those contracts) will tend to be accompanied by redefinition of the entire culture/set of principles.

4. Since I suggested as subtitle for this paper "The Economics of the Focus Strategy," let me now make that connection. The theory sketched in this chapter has a natural extension into considerations of the optimal size of an organization, when we recast that as the optimal span of the implicit contract. Of course, insofar as an implicit contract permits greater transactional efficiency, an expansion in the span of the contract will be beneficial. But weighed against this is the problem that as the span of the contract is increased, the range of contingencies that the contract must cover also must increase. Either it will then be harder for participants to determine *ex post* whether the contract was applied faithfully or the contract will be applied to contingencies for which it is not suited. Let me take an analogy. If your opponent in the eleven cities game is an individual, *B*, who plays games like this often,

and *B* has a reputation for using rivers or mountain ranges to divide the cities, then *following* play of the eleven cities game, you would have no problem in checking whether *B* is living up to this reputation by using the Mississippi River to divide the cities. But suppose *B* also plays other games using the alphabet as the focal principle and still others using other principles. In playing the eleven cities game, *B* uses the principle, among the many applicable ones, that gives the best advantage. Since *B* did have a number of choices, it would be hard to say that *B* did not live up to his or her end of the deal, which is quite ambiguous. But it is equally true that, in playing with *B*, you might get the feeling that his or her selection of rule is not entirely random. Or imagine that *B* faces a vast array of games where sets must be divided and always uses a geographical rule to divide the set. When dividing sets of fruits, *B* divides according to where they grow; for books, according to where their authors reside; and so on. The problem with such an opponent is that geographical division will be hard to apply to a wide range of division games. *B*'s principle is not ambiguous, but it is appropriate only to some of the possible games.

The point is simple: Wider scope, in the sense of more types of contingencies that must be dealt with, can be dealt with in one of two ways. One could employ a wider range of principles/contracts, but then one may increase ambiguity about how any single contingency should be handled. Increased ambiguity is bad for maintaining reputations. Alternatively, one can keep (in a larger and larger span) the same quite clear focal principle/implicit contract/corporate culture. But then as the span or type of contingencies encountered increases, that principle/contract/culture is being applied in contingencies to which it will be less and less appropriate. At some point, the benefits from widening the scope of the organization are outweighed by the inefficiencies engendered, and we will have a natural place to break between organizations.

Of course, transactions will need to take place across the break points. But these can be transactions undertaken under a different implicit contract – the contract of the impersonal marketplace, for example, where *caveat emptor* rules. Where we have formal, recognized breaks, it will be easiest to have a change in the contract. Included here are formal breaks inside a legal entity – different divisions in a single corporation (cf. Williamson and the M-form hypothesis), or "plants within a plant" (see Skinner 1974), and so on.

From this perspective, the focus strategy becomes a strategy of reducing the range of contingencies with which the implicit contract must deal, in order to deal better – less ambiguously – with those that are met.

Corporate culture and economic theory

5. In this chapter we have kept to cases in which one party A is short-lived and a second B is either long-lived or has vested interests in the reputation of a long-lived entity. Accordingly, any hierarchical transacting places hierarchical authority in B. This is but one arrangement that could be found. A second, quite prevalent arrangement is where As as well have vested interests in a second long-lived entity, and A_t deals with B_t through their two (respective) organizations. Examples are two corporations with an enduring relationship, and a labor union and a corporation. In such cases, transactions would not need to be hierarchical – rather, it would seem that the two parties could deal on equal terms. We would expect to see more transactions in which neither dictates what is done in the face of an unforeseen contingency, but where the two deal with these contingencies as they arise. (More hierarchical authority would rest with one of the parties, *ceteris paribus*, the easier it was to observe that the decisions of that party live up to an implicit contract.)

Since the range of possible implicit contracts is thus increased, one expects an increase in efficiency with such bilateral long lived relationships. It would also seem likely that, when compared with the situation in which only the Bs are organized, the case of bilateral organization would increase the share of surplus garnered by the As, at least in cases where Bs in the transaction are not perfectly competitive. In the case of labor unions as the A organization and firms as the B, these conclusions are borne out empirically (see Brown and Medoff 1978).

CONCLUDING REMARKS AND QUESTIONS

I hope that this chapter has been able to communicate to a wide range of social scientists answers to the questions: How might an economist explain the role of corporate culture? How does that explanation tie in to extant economic theory? What pieces of theory are missing, and what might they look like when put in place? As I imagine is the case with most disciplines, economists tend to be intellectual imperialists, trying to render everything into their own terms of reference. This, then, has been an exercise in imperialism.

I have little doubt that this is a useful exercise for economic theorists. Until recently, we have had very little to say of any substance concerning the role of organizations. The theory outlined here is full of lacunae, and it is far from all-encompassing. But, following from a number of quite active areas of research, it does give a definite role to organization and culture within the organization. In so doing it helps to think (in terms of economics) about the role of organization/culture in strategy. (To readers who are economists: Is this so?)

131

David M. Kreps

The questions I wish to leave noneconomists with (and have your answers to) are: Does this "theory" hold together? From your perspectives, what is missing, and what is wrong? Is this imperialism of any value to social scientists other than economic theorists? Are the economic terms of discourse helpful in thinking about these questions?

APPENDIX

I provide here a simple formal model of some of the ideas discussed in the chapter. Consider the situation where A must decide whether to contract with B to perform a task that is either *easy* or *difficult*, each with probability $\frac{1}{2}$. A values performance of this task at $9 and is risk-neutral. B is risk-averse, and the utility B derives from performing the task and being paid for it depends on the task's difficulty and the amount paid. We give B's von Neumann-Morgenstern utility as a function of the amount paid and the task's difficulty (for several values of the amount paid) in tabular form. (You can check that these numbers are consistent with utility functions that are concave in dollar amounts.)

Table 4.1. *Utilities for B for certain payment and task difficulty combinations*

	Payment to B					
	$3	$3.40	$8	$9	$12.50	$13
Easy Task	2	2.32	4	4.3	4.9125	5
Difficult	−16	−15	−6	−4.4	1.2	2

We will assume that B can obtain utility equal to zero in any period when not allowed to perform this task for A. Moreover, we assume that B's marginal utility for money when the task is difficult and payment is $13 equals the marginal utility for money when the task is easy and payment is $3. (This is consistent with the numbers given in the table.)

We will not be explicit for a while as to which version of the story we are telling – a story with one A and one B or one B and a sequence of As or a sequence of each type and B Associates – for any of these the calculations to follow will work. (For the sake of definiteness, we will speak in terms of the first of these three stories.) Also, we will speak in terms of an infinite horizon version of the story, with a per-period discount rate, rather than in terms of a probability of continuing. Of

132

course, the mathematics works precisely the same for the continuation probability version of the story.

Note first that if we cannot make a contract contingent on the task's difficulty at all, then A and B cannot strike a deal. (This would pertain if, say, they played only once, there was nothing like B Associates, and the task's difficulty was not verifiable.) For then B's payment would have to be certain. A is willing to pay no more than $9 and B's expected utility with a sure payment of $9 is less than zero, which is B's reservation utility level. (We assume B must accept or reject the task prior to learning how difficult it is. If the difficulty is observable *ex ante*, then B can always take the task when it is easy.)

The base case: observable difficulty in a repeated setting

If the task difficulty is observable and we have a long-lived B concerned with reputation, then the reputation construction works. Suppose the pair agree that B will submit a bill of no more than $13 after the task is done (and they know how difficult it was), with the implicit understanding that the bill will be $3 if the task is easy and $13 if hard. This gives B a per-period expected utility of 2. Moreover, if B will be forestalled from any further work of this type by gouging A in any period (that is, if A will never deal with B again if B does gouge A once), then by gouging (charging $13 for an easy task) nets B utility of 5 this period and zero ever after. This is as opposed to (at least) utility of 2 stretching out into the future, which, with a discount factor of 0.9, has a present utility value of 20. Thus B does better not gouging, and A can trust B not to do so, giving A an expected gain of $1.

One further point on this case: Our statement earlier on the equality of B's marginal utilities, combined with A's risk neutrality, makes this particular contingent (implicit) contract efficient. There is no way to make B better off without making A worse off, and vice versa. This is not to say that this is the only efficient arrangement. By lowering payments, keeping the marginal utilities equal, we will decrease the expected utility of B and increase the expected payoff to A. Raising both payoffs will do the reverse. These increases can continue until A's expected value from this arrangement hits zero – at the point where the expected payment is $9. On the other side, the decreases in the two payments must stop *before* we reach an expected utility level of zero per period for B, because at zero utility, B will not keep to the equilibrium. The constraint for decreases in B's payments comes at the point where, faced with an easy job, B would prefer to charge the higher amount and have no further dealings of this sort to continuing with the implicit contract.

133

David M. Kreps

Unobservable difficulty

Now imagine that only B can discern the difficulty of the task. A cannot determine how hard the task was either *ex post* or *ex ante*. A certainly would never *always* agree to pay any bill that B submits; for then B would *always* submit a bill of $13, which leaves A with an expected loss of $4 per period. A *must* "punish" B if A thinks B is engaged in gouging. A could employ many complex strategies to do this, choosing behavior based on past bills submitted by B. But, to keep matters simple, we will look at a strategy with a particularly simple form. *Whenever B submits a bill of $13, A will refuse to trust B for the subsequent n periods.* (To make this part of a perfect Nash equilibrium, we will suppose as well that B will gouge A if ever A fails to carry out on this threat, and A will refuse to deal with B ever again in the same instance.)

How will B react to A's strategy? Let v denote B's expected utility from following an optimal strategy in response to A's strategy. Then when the task is easy, B has a choice of either submitting a bill of $3, which will net expected utility $2 + .9v$, or submitting a bill of $13, which will net expected utility $5 + .9^{n+1}v$. Note the difference in the discount factors. We assumed that B nets zero in the n periods it will take to get A to trust once again. Similarly, when the task is hard, B has a choice of submitting the bill of $13 which nets $2 + .9^{n+1}v$, and submitting a bill of $3, which nets utility $-16 + .9v$.

Let us suppose that B submits the correct bill, namely $3 when the task is easy and $13 when it is hard. Then the functional equation that defines v is

$$v = .5(2 + .9v) + .5(2 + .9^{n+1}v),$$

where the first term on the right-hand side is the utility derived if the task is easy, and the second is the utility derived if the task is hard. Solving for v, this gives

$$v = \frac{2}{1 - (.45 + .5 \times .9^{n+1})}.$$

For this v, in order to verify that submitting the correct bill is a best response by B, we must verify that

$$2 + .9v > 5 + .9^{n+1}v \quad \text{and} \quad 2 + .9^{n+1}v > -16 + .9v,$$
$$\text{or} \quad 18 > .9(1 - .9^n)v > 3.$$

As n increases, v decreases (because punishment which follows every $13 bill — that is, after every hard task — lasts longer). But for low values of n, the inequality $2 + .9v > 5 + .9^{n+1}v$ is violated, which simply means that if punishment is not substantial enough, B will always submit a $13 bill. Both A and B have it in their interests to make n as low as possible, consistent with inducing B to submit the correct bill, because both lose during a punishment period. We look, then, for the least n such that the needed inequality holds. This turns out to be $n = 11$, with $v = 4.89$. (It should be noted that for all $n > 11$ we also have equilibria, but the equilibria for larger n are Pareto-inferior to the equilibrium with $n = 11$.)

How well does A do in this equilibrium? The functional equation for u, the expected (discounted) monetary value to A (when we are not in a punishment period), is

$$u = 1 + .5 \times .9u + .5 \times .9^{12}u,$$

this being the expected monetary value from the immediate period ($1) plus the discounted average continuation expected monetary value — if the task is easy, u discounted one period; if the task is difficult, u discounted by twelve periods. This is $u = 2.45$, as compared to the $10 expected discounted present value that A receives without the observability problem. That is, both A and B get approximately 25 percent of their best-expected discounted monetary value/utility when there are problems of observability and we use this equilibrium.

By giving A the ability to use a slightly more complex strategy, we can push up these values a bit. If A punishes B for eleven periods, then B has a strict incentive to send the correct bill. That is, the punishment above is more strict than need be. We could lessen the punishment by having A, say, punish B for eleven periods with probability .99 each time that B submits a bill of $13. Let me be quite precise about this. I mean to assume that A randomizes, and this randomization is observable to B. Suppose, for instance, that there is a month between B's submission of a bill and the next time A must decide whether to contract with B, and in this interim period the government issues, say, a monthly report on the level of M1. A then announces the following strategy: Following the submission of a bill of $13, A will look up the next report on the level of M1; specifically, A will look at the third and fourth significant digits of that report. If the third and fourth digits are, respectively, 1 and 7, A will continue to deal with B; if the two digits are anything else, A will refrain for eleven periods. Note well that B can monitor A's compliance with this randomization procedure (and, for those technically minded, we will work out strategies following any defection so this becomes a perfect Nash equilibrium).

Does this weaker punishment give B appropriate incentives? Let me generalize slightly and consider the following strategy by A. Following submission of a \$13 bill, A will (publicly) randomize so there is a probability p that A will withhold business from B for n periods and a probability $1 - p$ that A will go on trusting B (until the next time A gets a bill of \$13). Then to ensure that submission of the correct bill is B's best response, we must check that

$$2 + .9v \geq 5 + .9(1 - p)v + .9^{n+1}pv,$$

where v, as before, is the value of following the correct bill strategy. This inequality simply ensures that, when the task is easy, submitting the correct bill does at least as well as submitting the incorrect, inflated bill. (There is a second inequality to check – that punishment is not so severe that B will submit a bill of \$3 even when the task is difficult. We'll refrain from explicitly doing this calculation in what follows.) And v will be given by the functional equation

$$v = 2 + (.5 + .5(1 - p)).9v + .5p(.9^{n+1})v.$$

If we call $\delta = .9(1 - .9^n)p$, the functional equation and the inequality become

$$v = \frac{2}{.1 + .5\delta} \quad \text{and} \quad 3 \leq \delta v,$$

respectively. Solving for the largest v that satisfies the inequality yields $v = 5$ and $\delta = .6$. (Readers should not be misled by the fact that both v and the utility of \$13 when the task is easy are 5; this is a coincidence. Indeed, as we lower the utility of \$13 when the task is easy, we will raise the value of the game to B, since lesser punishment is necessary.)

Similar calculations will yield that the expected discounted monetary value to A of using a strategy with a p and n as above is a simple function of δ, namely $1/(.1 + .5\delta)$, so for any p and n combination that yields $\delta = .6$ (just large enough to keep B honest), the value to A is \$2.50.

All this was based on the hypothesis that A could play an observable randomized strategy (in determining whether to start a punishment period). Suppose that A cannot do this. A always has the ability to randomize, but we suppose now that B cannot be given proof that A has carried out an intended randomization. This will raise problems for the equilibria above. If we tried to implement the *precise* $\delta = .6$ equilibrium above, then p cannot be zero or one. And then, once a bill of \$13 is submitted, as long as B is submitting correct bills, it is in the interests of A to go on trusting B. If the randomization cannot be observed (and penalties cannot be enforced if A fails to follow through), then A will have an incentive to *pretend* that the randomization came out in favor of further trust. This then destroys the equilibrium.

We can get an equilibrium with a p different from one, but it has an unfortunate property. We do this by (i) supposing that δ is set so that, given an easy task, B is indifferent between submitting bills of \$3 and of \$13, and by (ii) having B randomize between these two bills in a way that makes A indifferent between triggering punishment (in the face of a \$13 bill) and continuing to trust B. Assuming that u is the game's value to A, requirement (ii) is $.9u = .9^{n+1}u$. Of course, this has a single solution (for $n \neq 1$, which must be so to induce correct billing by B) – namely, $u = 0$. This simple set of strategies yields an equilibrium only when the value to A is driven to zero. This does not raise the value of the game to B, who must be indifferent between gouging and not, and so the same functional equation defines v (as a function of δ).

This scenario pertains only to the simple strategies given here. Since B is having problems with observability, we might consider an A-like strategy for B – say, gouge with high probability for a while if A accepts a \$13 bill. To compute such an equilibrium gets quite tedious, however, so we'll leave this notion here.

Observability of randomization is not, of course, a problem when A is not randomizing. We always have at our disposal the $n = 11$, $p = 1$ equilibrium originally given. (A comment is irresistible here, but readers who are getting a bit lost should skip to the next paragraph: Note the sense in which this *pure strategy* equilibrium is really the limit of the sort of equilibrium suggested in the preceding paragraph. A is not supposed to accept a bill of \$13 and proceed blithely on. What keeps A to this is the supposed out-of-equilibrium behavior by B: Should A accept a bill of \$13 and not begin a punishment period, B responds by gouging perpetually. This is clearly the limit of a strategy of A accepting a \$13 bill, then, with positive probability, gouging for some length of time.)

We have assumed that A follows a simple type of strategy, and we've derived from that equilibria that give B up to an expected utility of 5 and A an expected (overall) payment of \$2.50. Are there equilibria, involving more complex sorts of strategies, in which B can do better

137

David M. Kreps

than this, without having *A* do worse? (Of course, we can make *B* better off in equilibrium at the expense of *A* by raising the levels of each payment.) In other words, is this an efficient equilibrium?

We will not attempt here to answer this question. But it is worthwhile to note that, in principle, the question is answerable. The techniques that are necessary (more or less) are given by Abreu, Pearce, and Stachetti (1987).

Using imperfect signals

This analysis presumes that the *A*'s could not observe the task's difficulty and that payment can be based on nothing else of relevance. Now consider the possibility of there being an imperfect signal that payment could be based on. Namely, suppose that each task either did or didn't require calculus. Easy tasks require calculus with probability 0.2, and hard tasks require calculus with probability 0.975. It is observable *(ex post)* whether the task really did require calculus. Even though this is observable, we assume it is not verifiable. With the usual construction we can have a scheme in which *B* is given the authority to submit any bill up to $13; *B* bills A_t that amount if the task required calculus and $3 if it didn't. Or, rather, we can make this an equilibrium as long as both sides have an incentive to participate in this scheme and as long as *B* hasn't the incentive to submit a higher bill when the task didn't require calculus.

To check that this is an equilibrium, note first that it results in the following round by round: With probability 0.1, the task is easy and the task required calculus, giving *B* utility 5. With probability 0.4, the task is easy and no calculus is required; *B*'s utility is 2. With probability 0.4875, the task is difficult and calculus is required; the bill is $13 and utility 2. With probability .0125 the task is difficult and calculus wasn't required – a bill of $3 and utility −16. In each round, then, the expected bill is $8.875 – enough to keep *A* interested in the arrangement. And *B*'s expected utility in each round is 2.075. This gives *B* a present value of 20.75 in keeping to the scheme. And so *B* will be willing to submit the correct bids: The crucial computation is what happens if the task is difficult and calculus is not required. If *B* tries to gouge *A* by submitting a bill of $13, *B* gets utility 2 today and (assuming punishment forever) zero thereafter. Submitting the correct bill nets −16 today and a (discounted) .9 × 20.75 = 18.675 in the future. Hence *B* slightly prefers to stick to the arrangement.

Is this an efficient equilibrium among all those that base payments solely on whether calculus is or isn't needed? No. Recall the assumption about marginal utilities of money to *B*; this told us that bills of $3

138

and $13 gave an efficient arrangement when the task's difficulty was observable. But now, when the task's difficulty is unobservable, unless the marginal utilities to B of money at $13 when the task is easy and at $3 when it is hard are equal (and equal to the other two marginal utilities), we will not have a second-best scheme. Assuming concavity of B's utility function, these margins will not equate given the values in Table 4.1. So we do better for B, holding A's expected value constant, if we simultaneously increase the smaller payment and decrease the larger payment in such a way that the expected value of the payment stays fixed, up until the point where the conditional expected marginal utilities (conditional on the task requiring calculus or not) are equated. This, note, will not upset the equilibrium, because B will be *more* inclined to follow the equilibrium in the one case where it matters – where calculus is not required but the job is hard. (The other constraint, that B will not wish to upset the arrangement by charging the greater amount when the job is easy and calculus is not required, is not binding.)

How does this compare with the equilibria we computed without the use of calculus? B is certainly better off: an expected utility of 20.75, versus 5 before. But the A's are worse off; they make a bare $0.125 per round in expectation, versus $0.25 on average that they got before. Happily, we can make both sides better off as follows.

Lower the payment that B receives when calculus is required to $12.50 and raise the payment when it is not to $3.40. This gives an expected payment of $8.74625 per period – just better than before. It gives B an expected utility of 18.1675 per period, certainly better than before. And it is an equilibrium: The constraint to check is that B doesn't want to break up the deal when a hard job comes along that doesn't require calculus. By breaking up the deal, B charges $12.50, for utility level 1.2 this round and zero thereafter. By sticking to the deal, B must swallow a utility of -15 this round, plus a continuation value of 18.1675. Discounting the continuation value appropriately, B's net for keeping to the arrangement is 1.35, and B will keep on.

In the construction just made, we barely made A better off than if we had ignored the imperfect calculus signal. Note that B is much better off than in the equilibrium where we ignored calculus and depended on punishments – a utility of 18 or so versus one of 5. It would have seemed that we could borrow more of that surplus from B in order to make A better off. But this is an illusion. B's utility *must* be kept fairly high in the calculus-dependent equilibrium so that, faced with a hard job that does not require calculus, B will swallow that large dose of negative utility. It is a very severe constraint to keep B happy enough to swallow that dose.

139

The constraint gets no easier as the odds of a hard job that doesn't need calculus fall to zero. As long as this has positive probability of happening and we wish to keep B honest in these circumstances, B must be getting a large continuation level of utility. Note the discontinuity here: When the probability of this is zero, we don't need to worry about this constraint; then the binding constraint is that B must be willing to settle for the lower payment when there is an easy job that doesn't require calculus.

This suggests that, given this imperfect signal, we might well do better to stop trying to satisfy this constraint. Instead of breaking cooperation forever if B charges the high amount when calculus is not required, A will stop dealing with B for a few periods. This punishment will be enough to keep B from charging the higher amount for an easy job that doesn't require calculus, but it will be insufficient to keep B from charging that amount for a hard job that doesn't require calculus. That is, in the equilibrium, B will be expected to charge the higher amount for hard jobs that don't require calculus, paying for this privilege with a loss of work for a few periods. And even though this payment will be worthwhile when the job is hard, it will be too much to pay when the job is easy (and calculus is not needed).

Specifically, suppose that the two enter into the following arrangement. The bills will be B's choice of $12.50 or $3.00. A bill of $12.50 will be considered warranted if calculus was indeed required, and A will enter into the agreement again in the next period. A bill of $3.00 is always happily accepted by A – and the agreement will again ensue in the next period. But a bill of $12.50 when calculus is not required will be considered unwarranted, and A will refuse to deal with B for three periods thereafter.

In the equilibrium, B will set the bill at $12.50 whenever calculus is required *or* the job is hard. B will bill $3.00 only for easy jobs that don't require calculus. In this case, one can work out the expected utility for B in any period when the two deal. It is the solution to

$$v = .1 \times (4.9125 + .9v) + .4 \times (2 + .9v) + .4875 \times (1.2 + .9v) + .0125 \times (1.2 + .9^4 v),$$

which is $v = 18.35296$. To ensure that this is an equilibrium, we must ensure that B is willing to charge the lesser amount for an easy job that doesn't require calculus: Charging the lesser amount nets utility $2 + .9v = 17.718$, while charging the greater amount nets utility $4.9125 + .9^4 v = 16.95$, and we see that B will go along. Note that B is doing better here than in the equilibrium we computed just earlier.

Corporate culture and economic theory

A does better, on average, as well. In any round in which there is a contract, *A* expects to pay $8.70 for a net of $.30. Now in approximately .0375 of the rounds, *A* will get zero, since *A* is punishing *B*. But, if you work out the exact expected present value to *A* of this scheme, you come up with $2.91, which is more than before.

This, of course, doesn't demonstrate that an efficient contract that can be obtained through strict adherence to the calculus signal is worse than some equilibrium that allows *B* to put in some unwarranted charge some of the time, at the cost of punishment. In the case of this problem, I am fairly well convinced, however, that this will be so, at least as long as *B* is not risk-neutral. (My conjectured proof requires that two randomizations be publicly observable *ex post* – *A*'s randomization to determine whether to enforce punishment and *B*'s randomization to determine whether to defect from strict adherence.) I conjecture as well that a very general proposition of this sort can be derived, but this will have to await another essay.

POSTSCRIPT – 1988

In the four or so years that have passed since I wrote "Corporate Culture," there has been a fair amount of energy devoted to some of the themes surveyed there. Even given the normal publication lag, it would be unfortunate not to pay some attention to those themes. At the same time, it is amusing to reread the last line of the introduction: "readers will see that the final steps, while not accomplished, are not excessively difficult to traverse." As some of those final steps are barely closer to fulfillment now than then, either I misestimated their difficulty or their inherent interest. I think the former is more likely to be true.

The one point at which, in rereading the chapter, I winced so hard that I felt compelled to signal that I would say something more is where I criticized Williamson for having little to say about the relative advantages and disadvantages of internal organization. (Hereafter, I will use his term and call it unified governance.) I would have profited enormously in writing this chapter from a close reading of Williamson (1985) and, especially in this instance, in reading Chapter 6, on the inefficiencies of unified governance. To recast slightly what Williamson has to say there, when one moves from market governance to unified governance, one trades one set of inefficiencies for another, as the nature of what is exchanged changes. In market governance, a decision maker deals with others only to purchase the outputs derived from their labors. When we move to unified governance, the single decision maker can command the use of all the capital, but now that person

141

must employ the labor services of those he or she earlier dealt with only for the output of their labor. The high-powered market-based incentives for labor are replaced by lower-powered internal incentives. Why are market-based incentives more high-powered? Williamson gives a number of specific reasons, many of which come down to the fact that it is hard in some cases to preserve *ex post* in internal organization the *ex ante* incentives that one has. To say more will take us too deeply into a whole new subject, except to say that Williamson (1985) answers my initial criticism rather substantially. Moreover, Williamson's more verbal theorizing on this point has been met by a number of more mathematical contributions, most notably by Holmstrom (1982) on the general issues of career concerns and by Milgrom (1986) and Milgrom and Roberts (1987) on quasi-rents and influence activities within organizations. (See also the treatment of these issues in the chapter by Milgrom and Roberts in this volume.) Note well that these papers all speak to the diseconomies of unified governance, whereas I was criticizing transaction-cost economics for not being explicit about unified governance's relative economies. (The chapter by Milgrom and Roberts in this volume looks at both sides of this picture.) But this is a case where analysis of one side makes clear the other.

Another point on which I would have benefited from a close reading of Williamson concerns the dichotomy I draw between traditional and hierarchical transactions. There is hardly a dichotomy here. Williamson (Chapter 3) adds to this stark picture bilateral and trilateral relational transactions and, of course, unified governance. Having concentrated my own attention on hierarchical transactions, I might accuse him of not paying enough attention to that form of governance. But it is clear that the picture is much richer than the naive reader of this chapter might come to believe.

This chapter is also severely unbalanced in the role it gives to reputation as the sole raison d'être for the firm. I did wish to stress that role, because I think it connects the firm and its culture, but I don't mean to dismiss other reasons for having firmlike organizations. Beyond the one paper in the chapter that I do cite (i.e., Grossman and Hart 1986), there has been a substantial amount of work recently on those other reasons and especially work on reasons related to the inability to write complete contingent contracts. The very excellent survey by Holmstrom and Tirole (1987) should be consulted for a more balanced view of the subject than one gets here.

There have been some substantial advances on the technical fronts associated with the ideas of the section on reputation. In particular, the technology appropriate for dealing with noisy observables in the folk theorem (and in related agency problems) has been substantially advanced by Abreu, Pearce, and Stachetti (1987), by Fudenberg, Holmstrom, and Milgrom (1987), by Fudenberg and Maskin (1986), and by Holmstrom and Milgrom (1987), among others. Also, the variation on the folk theorem appropriate for the case where there is one long-lived party and several short-lived ones is worked out in Fudenberg, Kreps, and Maskin (1987).

There has been relatively little (or no) formal development of the ideas associated with focal points and with unforeseen contingencies. Regarding focal points, only Crawford and Haller (1987) comes to mind as a really innovative approach to the subject, although Fudenberg and Kreps (1988) will have a bit to say about the evolution of something that will share some of the characteristics of a focal point.

By comparison, bounded rationality has been rather a growth area in economic theory recently; there has been, for example, a great deal of work concerning modeling players as machines (finite state automata or Turing machines), and somewhat more on measures of complexity of strategies for supporting supergame equilibria. But these approaches have not, I think, led us in directions that will help with the problems encountered in this chapter, and I will not, in consequence, bother with references. Unforeseen contingencies have not otherwise arisen in the formal literature to my knowledge, and so on that subject, four years after it was originally promised, I can do nothing more than at long last offer for the reader's enjoyment Kreps (1988).

5

Amenity potential, indivisibilities, and political competition

HAROLD DEMSETZ

My concern here is with a central debate in modern political economy—the degree to which constituency interests are accurately represented by democratic institutions. Those on one side of this debate believe that legislators accurately represent constituency interests. Such representation may not lead to the policy the median voter most prefers because special interest groups carry more political weight than would be proportionate to the number of voters who are members of them. But, just as wealthy people secure larger shares of private sector output than poor people do, so organized groups secure larger shares of public sector output. In this sense, voter sovereignty prevails in politics as effectively as consumer sovereignty prevails in markets. From this perspective, their constituencies effectively control legislators (Becker 1983; Peltzman 1984, 1985).

Those on the other side of the debate believe that legislators exercise significant freedom from the preferences of their constituencies and that they exercise this through political behavior that deviates from behavior that would serve their constituencies. Presumably, deviations favor legislators' ideological preferences, not those of constituencies. Because this view sees that the interests of constituencies diverge from the behavior of legislators, it relies on the proposition that agency cost in politics is important enough to allow legislators to retain office even when they substitute their own political preferences for their constituencies' interests (see Kalt and Zupan 1984, in press).

This discussion has had its conceptual and theoretical moments, but it has relied heavily on empirical studies of voting records. These studies try to determine if a legislator's voting performance can be explained by indexes of the economic interests of residents of the

Members of workshops at the University of Chicago and the University of Southern California provided useful comments. Claire Freidland helped acquire and analyze data.

legislator's state or congressional district. Thus, residents, or voters, are taken to be the relevant constituency to judge these opposing views by.

I argue here the plausibility of a third position: that legislators underrepresent constituency interests, as that term has been commonly used in this debate, and this misrepresentation need not arise from agency cost. This position differs from the first partly in the way it draws distinctions between constituencies. The first position fails to attach importance to, or even to note, an *internal* constituency – that of a legislator's political party. Those who believe that legislators fairly represent constituency interests write as if they consider constituencies to be external to organized politics. The voters and special interest groups of this external constituency are to political organizations what consumers are to business firms: They are served by suppliers but are not analytically meaningful members of the supplying organizations. There is good reason to treat consumers as external to the firm, but there are at least two reasons not to treat members of political parties this way: the large differences (1) between the amenity potentials of political and business organizations and (2) between the divisibilities of the respective outputs of political and business organizations.[1]

Now, in a formal sense, the view being offered here is consistent with the first view, for it portrays legislators as responsive to constituency interests. Yet this third view leads to substantially different predictions about legislators' behavior than does one that sees all relevant consumers of political output as external to political organization. It does so because political parties respond to their constituencies much as they respond to special interest groups – out of proportion to the numbers of people in these groups. If our interest is in understanding political outcomes rather than in formal definitions, we err in not accounting for the preferences of internal constituencies. So as to distinguish this third view from the agency problem, I assume that agency cost is zero. Of course, this does not imply that agency cost is irrelevant to political processes. Legislators can misrepresent the interests of external *and* internal constituencies if agency cost is significant, but I have nothing to say here about this aspect of political behavior.

POLITICAL PARTIES

The following discussion does little justice to differences between parties, to the complexity of any given party, to the varied histories of parties, or to changes in the importance of parties in recent years. In the United States, the Republican and Democratic parties are not the same as the Socialist and Libertarian parties, and none of these is identical to the many other parties that have appeared on, and disappeared from, the American scene. Moreover, U.S. political parties undoubtedly differ in important respects from those found in other countries. These differences are not unimportant to what I have to say, but my knowledge of political parties is too limited to make much of them here.

Nonetheless, even though the differences between political parties are largely ignored here, note should be taken of some of them. Historically, the two major U.S. parties have been more similar than have major parties in Great Britain, France, and Germany. The U.S. parties tend much more to seek support from the same population. The origins of parties in different countries also differ. In Great Britain, for example, some older parties originated in Parliament itself. These parliamentary groupings justified themselves by the need to put together a working parliamentary majority. They did not meaningfully extend their activities beyond Parliament, nor did they purport to represent large populations. Newer British parties, such as the Labour Party, originated largely outside Parliament and have always purported to speak for large outside constituencies. Some parties exist largely to pursue single issues, such as the monetizing of silver or the taxing of land rent, while others pursue wholesale reorganization of society, such as various communist parties around the world. In the United States, to a greater extent than elsewhere, Democrats and Republicans seek support from large numbers of people without much regard to class, income, or ideals, and they purport to represent political concerns that have wide appeal in the loosely connected groups that comprise these masses.

It is not easy to provide a clear, concise definition of the membership of a political party. It is much easier to conceive of the boundaries of a typical business firm than of a typical political party (although someone familiar with the emerging theory of the firm might not think so). Perhaps economists may be indulged in being ambiguous in defining political institutions. What I mean by a political party is what I suppose most people mean – an organization of people who cooperate on a continuing basis to campaign for political office and to influence political preferences. These people devote time, energy, and capital to the party either because it offers prospects for office or because of the policies it favors. By this definition, voters are not members of a political party, because they do not give to it much time, energy, or capital. Employees of political parties, such as typists, are also not members of these parties, because they have no serious concern about policies. Those formally outside a party who nonetheless provide continuing intellectual or financial support to it because they favor its policies are more significantly members of the internal constituency than are voters or the party's unconcerned laborers.

Amenity potential and political competition

The analogy

Just as economists assume that the functions of department stores are to search the world for goods, certify their quality, and make them available to consumers, so they view the functions of political parties to be to search for and certify candidates and issues and to market them to "shopping" voters and special interest groups.[2] A political party's success and survival depend, according to economists, on whether voters choose its output, much as a department store's success depends on buyer preferences. There is much truth in this view of political parties. Political scientists also believe that searching for and marketing candidates and issues are basic functions of political parties, but to them parties also serve additional roles. Important among these are forming opinions, giving direction to their partisans' beliefs, and organizing large numbers of partisans. These activities suggest that parties do more than simply give voters slates of candidates and issues. Even so, there is an analogy between the activities of political parties and of business firms. Firms organize their work forces, if not their prospective buyers, and they rely on advertising to bring buyers to their products and services.

A subtle aspect of political parties raises some doubt about the accuracy of this analogy: the degree to which those working for a firm or party care about the output mix it produces. Owners, workers, and managers of the typical business firm care about maximizing profit and incomes. Which product will maximize these is not terribly relevant to the firm. Members of political parties often do care about the positions and candidates their parties choose. The leaders of a political party and its workers and supporters derive satisfaction directly from their party's goals, programs, and candidates. In a typical business firm, the equivalent personnel derive little direct utility from the good the firm produces, although they may be concerned about the output mix if human capital is highly specific to some outputs and not to others. The distinction I seek to make is partly quantitative and partly qualitative. Quantitatively, I am asserting that a political party's internal constituency is more concerned about output mix than is a typical firm's labor force. Qualitatively, I am asserting that in a typical firm the concern for product mix is really a concern about employability, not about product mix per se, whereas for a political party's internal constituency the product mix directly confers utility. Firms and workers stand ready to supply consumers, whether they are governments seeking napalm, private citizens seeking food and housing, or either seeking narcotics. Plenty of workers and managers are willing to produce goods that they themselves do not wish to consume or that they

147

do not think others should consume. The buyer is sovereign, and the buyer is part of the firm's external constituency to a greater extent than is true for political parties. I begin my critique of the analogy between parties and firms by focusing on this difference. In economic jargon, the difference is found in the objective functions of people in these institutions seek to maximize.

Profit and utility maximization

According to economists, the typical business firm seeks only to maximize profit, employing inputs and producing goods for that reason only. This view assumes that owners maximize utility by using the firm to maximize profit and then by spending this profit at home. Consumption, therefore, can presumably be carried on more efficiently at home than at work. Some firms' objective functions can differ somewhat in this respect. Nontypical firms, such as newspapers and not-for-profit organizations, produce goods and services that are laden with what might be called amenity potential (Demsetz and Lehn 1985). For these firms, outputs contribute directly to their owners' utility.

Owners of newspapers, for example, may run them partly or primarily to satisfy their desire to reform opinions. They derive psychic utility directly from producing editorial opinions and reporting news that serves this desire, and they are willing to accept reduced profits if they can change opinions sufficiently. (Whether or not profit must be sacrificed depends on whether readers purchase newspapers for their political content or for such things as advertising, sports, or comics.) Gratification of such desires through control of the firm constitutes on-the-job consumption for owners. Such situations suggest that some consumption is carried on more efficiently in the workplace, by altering the nature of the product, than it is at home. This premise also operates in not-for-profit firms, although special tax treatment also encourages this form of organization.[3]

If the value a firm's owner gains by producing amenity-laden products is counted as profit, one could say that the owner also maximizes profit. Similarly, if the utility gained by spending profit at home is counted, a firm's owner can be viewed as a utility maximizer. The distinction between our two types of firms, therefore, is found not in the degree to which their behavior is rational or is maximizing. The distinction is also not in consumer sovereignty if we count owners as consumers when they alter the product mix of their firm to raise the utility they derive from being owners. The distinction is found in the way owners of these two types of firms organize resources and choose products to pursue their goals rationally. If a product is rich in amenity potential, the owner's preferences must be taken into account to understand the mix of goods produced and the firm's organization. The objective function of political parties is like that of firms with high amenity potential. Indeed, the amenity potential of political parties plausibly even exceeds that of firms like newspapers.

A political party's output consists of programs and candidates. These are chosen partly to win elections. Consistent with this desire, the perceived political desires of voters and external special interest groups play an important role in the party's selection of programs and candidates. But political parties also select candidates and issues because of their appeal to *internal* constituencies. Although the preferences of individual members of this internal constituency are not equally weighted, they count for more than an equal number of members of the diffuse external constituency (see Peltzman 1984). The political preferences of the party's leaders, members, and supporters influence its output mix.

The internal constituency's preferences are, of course, traded off to secure contributions (see Congleton 1989) and to win office (just as firms producing amenity-laden goods do not completely ignore considerations of profit). But it would be mistaken to suppose that preferences are traded off to the degree required to maximize the probability of winning office. The external constituency's desires are given much weight, but the internal constituency is likely to accept a somewhat reduced probability of winning office if it derives from policies and candidates that cater to its amenity demands.

It follows that the maximand of the political party is a function of the probability of winning office, the probability of accomplishing goals its internal constituency desires, if it wins, and the probability of accomplishing these goals even if it loses. These probabilities often move in opposite directions. A party that holds stubbornly to issues and candidates dear to its internal constituency reduces its probability of winning office. Yet it may, by doing so, increase the probability of implementing desired programs if it wins office or influences the policies of other parties more likely to win. The notion of electoral victory implicit here treats success in today's election as weightier than success in a future election. A party's catering to its internal constituency therefore may be viewed as its acceptance of a reduced probability of immediate victory in order to increase the probability of a later victory. But even with no greater expectation of victory in the future a party may accept reduced chances of victory today if a stand on principle pleases its internal constituency.

Not all parties attach the same weight to these probabilities. When ideology or a single political program, such as a tax on land rent, are

149

important for them, parties will be less exclusively concerned with winning the vote of external constituencies. The Socialist and Libertarian parties in the United States, for example, are less willing to compromise their ideologies to win office than are the Democratic and Republican parties. Indeed, the weights a political organization gives to these probabilities reveal how important internal constituency preferences are to it. The personal political preferences of members and supporters of ideological parties weigh importantly in determining issues and candidates. The Democratic and Republican parties are more like typical for-profit firms. They attach high values to getting votes and obtaining office. Consequently, they heed external constituencies more than do ideological or single-issue parties. But even the major U.S. parties offer voters regulation, welfare, and income distribution programs that partially reflect their respective internal constituencies' political preferences. Their political programs are laden with more amenity potential than the products of typical business firms are.

This is not to allege that political parties have greater agency problems than business firms do. The alleged deviation between votes elected representatives actually cast and votes that reflect the interests of representatives' constituencies has been treated by others (for example, Kalt and Zupan 1984) as a consequence of agency cost. In this view, voters separate such legislators from their offices in the next election unless high agency cost makes it difficult for them to monitor and punish such behavior. Agency cost protects self-indulgent representatives from the wrath of voters, and the larger this cost, the more prevalent is such self-indulgence. Agency cost may in fact be high, and, as others have argued, this may explain some aspects of representatives' voting behavior. But high amenity potential is not the equivalent of high agency cost.

Amenity potential affects a party's choice of programs and candidates even if voters can discipline a party that turns out programs and candidates different from those they favor. Catering to the political preferences of its internal constituency is likely to reduce the probability of the party's winning at the polls, but neither agency cost nor shirking are necessarily relevant to whether the party continues such behavior. To the extent that agency cost is higher for external than for internal constituencies, as it is likely to be, it many prolong and strengthen the influence of internal constituencies by reducing the probability that their tastes will result in election losses. Higher agency cost may therefore heighten amenity potential's impact, but it is not necessary for there to be an impact. The high amenity potential of political parties simply requires them to favor internal over external constituencies more so than they would if election victories were all they sought. (However, see the following discussion of the impact of amenity potential on a party's cost of obtaining victory.)

This relative weighting of the preferences of internal and external constituencies may continue in the face of reduced probabilities of winning elections because a party's viability is not completely dependent on success at the polls. If a party can attract funds and work from those who share its political preferences, it can survive for a long time without notable election success. However, the probability that such a party will win elections is not driven to zero by such behavior. A world in which information is costly is a world in which surprises are likely to occur. Voter sentiment is not so easily forecast, and candidates' viability and acceptability for office are never certain. Even if success at the polls were negligible, a minority party could influence events and so may be worth the energy and resources its principals and supporters supply. Two closely matched major parties behave differently when confronted by a minority party attractive to some potential voters. At the least, a political party may survive simply to give its internal constituency a platform from which to express its political ideas.

High amenity potential thus leaves the survival of political parties less dependent on their pleasing external constituencies than is the survival of typical business firms. A firm must continue to satisfy customers if it is to attract funds and other resources from suppliers. It usually has no significant internal constituency to subsidize its efforts, because those internal to the firm derive no direct utility from what the firm produces, although a few firms may offer their owners enough amenity potential to get them to continue supporting them from their private funds in the face of continuing losses.

The role of collective consumption

The indivisibility of important elements of political programs differentiates parties and business firms. An election yields policies and officeholders. Many of these policies, and the competence of officeholders, necessarily affect all citizens. In defense, foreign policy, and a variety of other areas, political workers cannot consume any political products other than those an election provides. In this respect, they are not like employees of General Foods, who can consume General Mills's products while working hard for General Foods. Unless political workers can reside in one political district and work in another, they have little choice about indivisible political outputs after the dust of an election has settled; they must consume these outputs whether or not they like them.

151

This means that political workers with political preferences are unlikely to be indifferent to the programs of the political parties they work for. If their parties win, workers must consume the parties' politics. Therefore, they are unlikely to work as hard for a party whose programs they disagree with as they are for one whose programs they endorse. Divisibility of goods in markets breaks this nexus between consumption preferences and job productivity. Executives or employees of General Foods can work hard to reduce General Mills's market share, but they are unlikely to reduce it to zero. They can continue to consume their rival's products because both product lines can be produced simultaneously. This separation between work effort and consumption cannot be duplicated when people work for political parties. Only one indivisible set of programs can be available at any given time.

As a consequence of this, workers and employees will be matched differently in political organizations and in businesses. There will be a higher correlation between the political preferences of party workers and the programs of the parties they work for. It also follows that labor will be available at lower wages to more popular political parties, although this effect is reduced by free riders. The greater the divergence between the programs a party offers and those party members desire, measured by outputs both indivisible and of concern to members, the lower will be worker productivity and/or the higher must be explicit compensation.

The relationship between a typical business firm and its employees differs from this. Employees and suppliers of other inputs to firms that produce amenity-laden goods, such as missionary newspapers, can consume goods other than those these firms produce. Business firms, even fledgling ones, secure funds because their backers expect them to succeed, not because backers want to consume their products. Product divisibility makes this independence between consumption and production possible.

This link between inputs and outputs is not irrelevant to the difference between the objective criteria political parties use and those business firms use. A business firm's adoption of a criterion for maximizing profit is facilitated by its workers' indifference to the output mix the firm produces. An alteration in output mix, in and of itself, should not cause employees to demand higher wages to maintain the same productivity. A change in a party's political program forces it to recruit different workers or to raise the wages it pays.

The combination of high amenity potential and product indivisibility implies that political leaders, workers, and financial supporters, who share common ideological beliefs, are less likely to join in a common political effort if they believe the party can make political changes easily. Compared to typical business firms, political parties, especially ideologically oriented ones, can more easily attract inner constituencies if they adopt organizations that make changing goals and programs more, rather than less, difficult. Both firms and parties have difficulty instilling confidence in their team members because agreements are necessarily incomplete or imperfectly policed. The difference lies in the types of expectations that need to be bolstered. Internal constituencies of political parties need to be reassured about output mix. For typical firms, the expectations requiring buttressing are mainly of continued employment, wages, and working conditions, although those whose talents are specific to products gain confidence from assurances about the types of goods to be produced. Except for this last case, workers are seldom concerned about the nature of the firm's output.

THE TYPICAL PARTY AND THE WINNING PROGRAM

To this point, I have been discussing typical parties. One might conclude from this discussion that external constituencies are not as likely to be satisfied in politics as in markets. This conclusion seems plausible enough from the arguments already presented. A typical firm attempts rather exclusively to cater to consumers because it does not confront significant amenity potential or serious product indivisibilities. Its owners can maximize utility by maximizing profit – which means, in general, attempting to give consumers what they want. A political party caters to its internal constituency as well as to voters. The more weight it attaches to the preferences of its internal constituency, the less likely it is to offer voters the programs they most prefer. However, what a political party offers is not identical to what the political process offers.

Political parties that actually win office surely satisfy the wants of larger external constituencies better than do parties that fail to win. Even if no party were to change the programs its internal constituency prefers, elections would favor the party whose internal constituency's political preferences come closest to matching those of voters. Voters can get what they want from parties whose internal constituencies are fairly representative of them, even though because of amenity potential and indivisibilities parties give less than full attention to voter wants. The equilibrium governments or winning parties move toward may accord well enough with a model in which parties seek only to get elected by designing their programs and selecting their candidates exclusively to please voters. (Of course, neither external nor internal constituencies are so homogeneous in preferences as this discussion pretends.)

153

Given that no specific party functions according to this model, parties will be more likely to function this way if entry into politics is open than if it is not. If the internal constituencies of all existing parties are atypical relative to the external constituency, party programs may not match voter preferences. Of course, in competing to win office, parties will attempt to satisfy voter preferences, but the interests of external constituencies are not served as much as they would be by a complete satisfaction of voter preferences. If entry is open, new parties with internal constituencies more representative of voter preferences are likely to arise. Voter preferences will be more likely to reign in politics if new parties can form easily. If they cannot form, there will more likely be a big disparity between the programs and candidates voters want and those they get. Because amenity potential is not high for a typical business firm and because products generally can be divided for consumption, entry conditions are not as important in the marketplace for delivering to consumers the products they want. A monopoly will sell goods at a higher price to consumers, but its owners are best served by producing products that they believe the external constituency – potential buyers – want.[4]

The issue of whether political competition satisfies voter preferences is more complex than is commonly understood. Calvert (1985) examines the validity of the median voter model's equilibrium if candidates are issue-oriented rather than victory-oriented and if voter preferences are uncertain. The political outcome may differ somewhat from the median voter model's equilibrium under these circumstances, but Calvert demonstrates that for single issues, if candidates' policy preferences do not differ much from those of the median voter and if uncertainty about voter preferences is not large, the difference between the political outcome and the outcome the median voter model predicts is small. Calvert's demonstration is based on a two-candidate game in which the candidates and the median voter differ in policy preferences. Calvert does not allow for new candidates, but open entry would attract candidates oriented toward victory or ones whose policy preferences, if they were policy-oriented, are those of the median voter (in which case, I suppose, they would be median voters). These new entrants would have a higher probability of winning than those whose policy preferences differ from those of the median voter.

Calvert's model ignores the cost of running a campaign. Even if we suppose agency cost to be zero, we may still recognize the positive cost of informing and convincing potential voters. The cost of running a campaign should relate inversely to the number of potential labor and capital suppliers who can derive amenity potential from the policies and candidates a party selects. A party attuned to median

154

voter interests (if these can be defined in a multiple-issue election) has an advantage provided (1) that it need not share its potential suppliers with other parties similarly attuned and (2) that more potential voters have preferences similar to rather than different from the median voter's.

The relevance of the distribution of voter preferences can be examined in a context of two political parties. Assume that the median voter has unique political preferences and that all other voter preferences lie either to the right or to the left of the median voter's. Furthermore, suppose that preferences to the right are uniformly distributed between the median voter and the extreme right, while preferences to the left are densely located somewhere far to the left. A party representing preferences similar to those of this left-leaning group will have access to considerable firmly committed resources to campaign and turn out the vote with. A party with an output mix the median voter prefers, or to the right of that mix, will not have low-cost access to as many committed supporters. The left-leaning party will be more effective in convincing not only its supporters to vote for it but, in a world of ignorance and imperfect knowledge, will also find it easier to misguide voters on the right side of the political spectrum. The party of the median voter or of the right will turn out fewer supporters and misguide fewer left-leaning voters because it will not be as amply endowed with low-cost, politically committed resources. In this context, amenity potential must shift both parties to the left of the median voter, but by differing amounts, even if the only objective these parties have is to win the election.

In contrast to median voter models of the electoral process, the distribution of political preferences about the median voter matters. Asymmetry in this distribution, such as we have already hypothesized, can cause winning policies and programs to differ from those that the median voter would favor. This tendency will be stronger for some asymmetrical distributions than for others, depending on whether new parties face barriers to their formation.

Ease in forming new parties tends to equalize the support available to all parties. In the case already outlined, more new parties could form to the left of the median voter's preferences than to the right, tending to equalize the low-cost support available to all parties and thus to equalize the chances of winning for all parties. The number of parties with similar policies that can practically be accommodated depends on how limited the scale of efficient political organization is. Still, the existence of more parties to the left of center than to the right would seem to imply a higher probability that the winning *program* will reflect left-of-center preferences.

155

The further the left-of-center group's policies are from median voter policy preferences, the more costly in terms of election probabilities will catering to the left-of-center group be for it. To win the low-cost support of a sizable internal constituency, a party must win the left-leaning group by offering policies it prefers. The more left-leaning the group is, the more these policies will differ from those of the median voter. The adoption of these policies will make it more difficult for parties to convince right-leaning voters to support the party seeking low-cost support from left-leaning voters. Thus, amenity potential and the need to attract votes from outside the internal constituency combine to make the left-leaning party's election more likely if the left-leaning group the party draws support from is not too far left.

If this analysis is not too far off the mark, it implies that representative democracy can yield outcomes different from those suggested by assuming that competition between political parties results in voter sovereignty (if by voter we mean a member of the external constituency). However, the influence this analysis ascribes to internal constituencies should not be interpreted as a source of inefficiency. There is nothing necessarily inefficient in allowing full sway to the amenity potential and indivisibilities of political activity. My claim is much more modest. If we wish to understand political parties' internal organization and the output mix that competition between parties yields, we must take amenity potential and indivisibilities into account.

Suggested empirical tests

Treating political parties as if they are the same as business firms neglects, slights, or denies the greater importance of amenity potential and collective consumption for political parties. The comparison here implies that taking these differences into account will yield an improved understanding of politics. Which view is more useful depends largely on explanatory power. Some observations on empirical implications are therefore in order.

One test has already been offered. The internal constituencies of business firms will not favor their firms' outputs as much as the internal constituencies of political parties favor their parties' programs. A brief pause to consider this proposition obviates any need for extensive study. Most business firms employ workers to produce goods that they never knowingly consume and for which, therefore, they have no known consumption preferences. Employers of lumberjacks and oil drill riggers are not concerned about, and do not seek knowledge of, their workers' preferences for things made from wood or petroleum. Even automobile producers give employees discounts to entice them to

156

purchase their models. Even with such discounts, many Fords, Chryslers, and Toyotas stand on General Motors employee parking lots. More to the point, General Motors does not require its employees to prefer its products.

Political parties are much more concerned about the political affiliations of their internal constituencies, who are in turn also much more concerned about their parties' politics. A Republican administration surely seeks to identify the political affiliations of potential appointees and tries hard to find suitable Republicans to fill positions before turning to Democrats. Such favoritism rewards diligent effort, but, because it also applies to people who have not been active in the party, it also reflects the presumed importance of amenity potential. Indeed, civil service was created partly to protect career employees from the employment preferences of the party that happens to be in power.

A second test produces results that are not so easy to predict. If a political party's internal constituency exerts a significant influence on its selection of programs and candidates, that influence must on average be to create a divergence between the product mix the party offers and the one external constituencies prefer. This means that a political party typically holds more stubbornly to its product mix than does a business firm. This is because a change in its product mix alienates a political party's internal constituency more than a shift in a business firm's output mix alienates its management and employees. The cost of shifting output mixes is thus higher for political parties.

Business firms are not completely immune from control that is exercised in stubborn fashion, but owner interests usually restrain management's independence. Therefore, firms are especially exposed to stubborn management when owners are also managers. Henry Ford held stubbornly to a view of automobile production that gave his firm a dominant market share, but then undermined the firm's ability to maintain that dominance. The company's management simply could not shake the old man's view of the sources of success.

Extreme situations such as Ford's, however, are atypical. More usually, firm owners bring stubborn management to heel, although they sometimes require a corporate takeover to do so. No person or group in a political party has an owner's interest, even in the special sense of maximizing the probability of winning office; the gains and costs of winning office are dispersed widely, and the office, if won, cannot be sold for full value. Its internal constituency controls a party; the goal of winning office is tempered for that constituency by the "selling" of a favored viewpoint. The typical business firm, on the other hand, has a keen interest in altering its product mix to suit unexpected developments in consumer preferences. It cannot always move easily or

157

Harold Demsetz

economically to satisfy newly revealed tastes, but it has less reason to resist such a move than a political party does. Political parties that are out of favor should continue to be out of favor longer than business firms would. Assuming that voter preferences change with about the same frequency and intensity as consumer preferences do, the greater reluctance of parties to modify output mix should make their market shares less stable than those of business firms.

The difficulty political parties have in altering their product mix — or, more accurately, the preference of political parties not to alter their product mix — has profound consequences for their organization. Political parties are not owned in the sense that business firms are. We need not examine data to know that this is so. Owners of business firms have an equity stake that can be sold and that frequently is sold. Political parties do not. To a degree, of course, some stakeholding occurs within parties. Mayor Richard J. Daley held a considerable stake in Chicago's Democratic Party; in a limited sense, he owned the machine — but in a limited sense only. He could try to use his stake for personal gain, but he could not do so openly and completely. He could, and did, attempt to bequeath this stake to his son. Beyond such maneuvering even in a case as extreme as this, a political party is not owned. It has no capital value that belongs to an individual or group of individuals. It is controlled through party organization, but it is not owned outright. Why not?

Owners are residual claimants. They profit if gains exceed the value of the obligations they enter into; they lose otherwise. The pressure market forces exert on the personal fortunes of owners is therefore intense. It constrains their ability and willingness to market goods that consumers do not prefer. Even owners of missionary newspapers can ignore reader preferences only somewhat without draining their personal coffers in an attempt to market a losing social perspective. Such marketing may continue for a time, in the hope that consumers develop a taste for the goods offered to them, but it cannot continue for long periods.

Political parties often produce output mixes that deviate from voter preferences because they cater to the personal preferences of their internal constituencies. The more ideological the political party is, the more insistent it will be *not* to conform to the changing mood of the electorate. If parties were owned outright, their owners would be under intense pressure to give the public what it wants. Positions on slates of candidates would be marketed to the highest bidders, sold to people who could personally gain from holding office or who could win at the polls by giving voters what they want. Programs would be offered on the same basis. A party's politics would be for sale. One does not need

158

to be a political expert to know that this occurs, but, again, it occurs only to a limited extent and not openly.

Parties and political procedures are organized to reduce incentives to behave in this fashion. An important element in such organizations is denial of outright ownership. In its place is committee control and an internal constituency's cost sharing. No single person or group bears most of the implicit profit or loss that results from the party's actions. Hence, no person, however much control he or she may exercise in a party's affairs, has an owner's incentive to conform to the external constituency's demands. Only this incentive's absence can explain the Democratic Party's selection of presidential candidates in recent years and the Republican Party's selection of Barry Goldwater in 1964. It is difficult to understand why political parties avoid outright ownership and why they so often ignore voter preferences; the importance of amenity potential in a context of consumption indivisibilities helps explain why parties behave in these ways.

An empirical example

To examine how responsive political parties and business firms are to external constituencies, I have calculated the votes Democratic presidential candidates won over a specified period as a percentage of the combined votes cast for Democratic and Republican candidates; I have also calculated total General Motors automobile sales as a percentage of the combined sales of General Motors and Ford. I recorded automobile sales figures at four-year intervals to match the frequency of presidential elections. The standard deviation of each of these variables, divided by the variables' mean value, yields an index of variability of market share for each of these two competitive arenas (business and political). The time period used to calculate this index covers three decades (1932–1964 for the political arena, 1931–1964 for the business arena); this includes the years during which Ford dramatically lost market share to General Motors. For Democratic vote as a percentage of two-party vote, this index equals 13.13 percent; for General Motors sales as a percentage of two-company sales, it equals 9.13 percent. By this sample, political market share varies more than does business market share. This is as we would expect if internal constituencies matter more in politics than in business.

If the period of time used in the index is shortened to eliminate the years in which Ford suffered its most rapid losses, confining the study to 1948–1964, the index of variability in market share for the political and business arenas, respectively, equals 14.88 percent and 3.44 percent. Over this shorter period, General Motors consistently did better

159

than Ford. We can recalculate this index by using Ford sales as a percentage of two-company sales, and, correspondingly, by using Republican vote as a percentage of two-party vote. The standard deviation of market shares calculated this way, divided by mean value of market shares, yields an index of variability equal to 14.96 percent for the political arena and 6.40 percent for the business arena. Again, business market shares seem less volatile than political market shares.

These differences in the relative stabilities of business and political market shares may, of course, reflect the fact that political preferences change more frequently or dramatically than do economic preferences. I know no better reason for supposing this than for supposing the contrary. It is difficult to put forward a general theory of preference changes that would be convincing as well as practically applicable. I leave this task for the future.

PART III

Reflections on theoretical foundations

6

Political science and rational choice

WILLIAM H. RIKER

The impulse to study politics scientifically is both old and persistent. Aristotle collected 158 constitutions in order to generalize about events and institutions in the *Politics*. Early in the Renaissance, Machiavelli revived the Aristotelian program in the *Discourses* and *The Prince*, although he did not seem to have as clear a vision of the scientific method as did Aristotle. Late in the eighteenth century, when the term *political science* came into general use, John Adams studied republics in exactly the Aristotelian spirit and with, perhaps, an even bolder claim for political science:

The vegetable and animal kingdoms, and those heavenly bodies whose existence and movements we are, as yet only permitted faintly to perceive, do not appear to be governed by laws more uniform or certain than those that regulate the moral and political world. (Adams 1850–1856, vol. VI, p. 218)

By the twentieth century, however, hardly anyone shared Adams's faith in the relative certainty of social and physical science. Surely few people now believe that our laws of political life are as certain or as useful for making predictions as are the laws employed in sending a man to the moon or in eradicating smallpox. In 1778, however, when Adams started his book, electricity had been identified but hardly understood, chemistry consisted mainly of the story of phlogiston, and no one had ever thought that bacteria were connected with disease. Consequently, eighteenth-century social science, with its elementary interpretation of the competitive market and the law of demand, does not, at least in retrospect, seem significantly inferior to eighteenth-century biological or physical sciences. In the interim, however, the latter sciences have produced large numbers of well verified and practically useful generalizations, whereas social science, even economics, has developed very slowly.

In order to investigate this slow development, I will first consider the reasons for it (some invalid, some valid). Then, after interpreting the

163

nature of science, I will show why rational choice theory fits in with it and helps social science develop more swiftly.

SUBJECTIVITY IN SCIENCE

In the twentieth century, many writers have tried to explain the startling variations in the rates of development of various scientific fields. Initially, Max Weber and Karl Mannheim offered the most popular explanations. In their views social science developed slowly because its sentences about human affairs necessarily depended on and incorporated various authors' interests, motives, values, and prior histories. These subjective elements were said both to be necessary for understanding sentences in social science and to compromise the accuracy of their descriptions.

Mannheim (1949) carried this epistemological relativism to an extreme. He started from and accepted the Marxist view of classical economics as ideology. Its descriptions of nature, he said, were primarily rhetorical, in the sense that they justified and cajoled others into accepting property rights, the sale of labor, and other features of market exchange. This rhetoric had, in the Marxist view, only incidental and accidental validity as description. Of course, Marx used equally effective rhetoric in calling his opponents ideological in order to cast doubt on the truth of their utterances and, inferentially, to suggest the objective validity of his own self-proclaimed science. But Mannheim then turned Marx's rhetorical sword against him, showing that Marx's sentences were just as rhetorical as those of the classical economists and as much distorted by interest and taste. Mannheim pointed out that Marxist pronouncements justified revolution and cajoled others into accepting the utopia in which Marxists, not capitalists, ran things.

Mannheim's argument led to an inference that the truth value of every description of human affairs is dubious. If all such descriptions are distorted for the sake of rhetorical and political advantage, then one should not expect social science to accumulate more or less verified sentences the way the biological and physical sciences do.

This explanation for the lack of progress in social science is, in my opinion, neither correct nor convincing. Just because an author has a political purpose in uttering a sentence does not make the sentence untrue. Nor does an author's special affinity for a subject (Weber's *verstehen*) crucially affect the validity of that author's statements. The truth of a descriptive sentence is ascertained in ways that bypass the author's state of mind. That is, a statement can be shown to be false if one offers counterexamples or shows that it is inconsistent with other accepted statements. If it survives these tests, its next test is to see whether or not it predicts better than an established standard or alternative statements. If the tested sentence is not certainly falsified and predicts adequately, then one looks for a theoretical explanation that subsumes it. If the explanation is convincing, then the sentence is said to be as true as scientific sentences can be. Nothing in this conventional scientific procedure involves investigation of the author or the sociology of knowledge. Nothing in it precludes a politically motivated rhetorician from uttering a truthful sentence, although, of course, deliberate dissimulation can usually be exposed. Furthermore, because all descriptive sentences, whatever their subject, contain rhetoric, the rhetoric, by itself, cannot prevent the progress of science.

On the basis, then, of my interpretation of the scientific method, I can reject Weber's and Mannheim's concerns as simply irrelevant on theoretical grounds. Speaking practically, there is another reason for rejecting their explanation. Physical science, as described, for example, by Kuhn (1970), is also presented historically. Looking backward, one sees that Kuhn's scientific revolutions are disputes about value assumptions (mostly about whether or not naive human perception, as, for example, the naive perception of an earth-centered planetary system discarded in the Copernican revolution, is adequate for description). These value assumptions did not prevent the accumulation of knowledge nor the improvement of theory. The scientific "revolutions" came about because, following the scientific method, counterexamples and alternative theories were pitted only against existing laws and theories, with no examination whatever of the values contained in the contested sentences or of the motives of their original authors. Indeed, the moral assumptions that supported losing theories have typically been revealed by looking back over completed revolutions. So one can say, first, that the moral assumptions of physical science were not usually noticed before they were rejected, and second, that many laws and theories that are at least adequate for prediction developed while these moral elements were unrecognized.

Many, if not most, contemporary opponents of social science fail to recognize that Kuhn's book has a twofold message: It recognizes the subjectivity of scientific assumptions, but it also demonstrates that science can be effective despite this subjectivity. The valid inference from Kuhn is that, if subjectivity has not prevented the development of biological and physical science, then it need not prevent the development of social science. This means that to explain the slow development of social science, one must look at something other than the subjectivity of its assumptions.

GENERALIZATIONS IN SCIENTIFIC DISCOURSE

The first place I propose to look is in the classes used in the generalizations of scientific discourse.

The essence of science is, of course, the accumulation of more or less valid generalizations. Information about particular events or particular objects, while often humanly interesting, is not, by itself, useful for either prediction or explanation. These activities require generalizations asserting that a subject class is included in a predicate class: "All A is B," where A and B are well-defined classes. Consider, then, the use of generalizations to predict: A prediction is an assertion about some individual member of class A: "Since a_i belongs to A, a_i *belongs to B*" (because, by reason of the generalization *"A* is included in *B*," all members of A are also members of B.) Thus, one can attribute a specific property (namely, the defining property of class B) to an object known to be in class A. Using as an example Duverger's law, a typical prediction about a particular government belonging to the subject class (i.e., "Governments in which single member districts, plurality decision rules, and unique nominations are used to select legislative and executive officials") is, then, that this government will have a predicted property (say, exactly two political parties or a low index of fractionalization).

In the absence of the generalization (Duverger's law), it would be difficult, I think, to make a good prediction about the correlates of two-party systems. Indeed, before this law or something like it was widely discussed and understood, most political scientists wrongly attributed two-party systems entirely to some sort of bifurcating civil war, even though two-party systems occur fairly frequently, whereas truly bifurcating civil wars are rare (Riker 1982).

Suppose that one tries to predict from hermeneutical investigation. One asserts, in interpreting a particular event on the basis of what appear to be its significant features, that these features will appear in some subsequent similar event. In the absence of a generalization, however, one does not know whether or not the features chosen as significant and possibly persistent are in fact the ones that will show up in the future event. We have, indeed, an often-quoted, sarcastic observation about just this failure of hermeneutical prediction: Generals always prepare to fight the last war. The study of history, which is often said to be essentially hermeneutical, is often justified on the ground that "those who fail to learn from history are compelled to relive it." I

166

agree about the consequences of failure, but I insist that hermeneutical investigation is not the way to learn from experience. Instead, one must generalize – which is to say that the only way to learn from history is to do social science.[1]

EXPLANATION IN SCIENTIFIC DISCOURSE

What I have said about prediction applies also to explanation. To explain an event is to subsume it under a covering law that, in turn, is encased in a theory. We often say, however, that it is enough to know how an object or event was generated or how its parts fit together to explain it. One may indeed feel comfortable with objects or events by rendering them familiar in these ways, yet familiarity is not an explanation. Suppose one knows exactly how an event came about. A question remains, however, about which antecedents of the event are necessary or sufficient or both for the event to occur and which are merely coincidental and irrelevant. If one observes that there are a system of secret ballots and a system of two political parties, can one conclude that secret ballots are "essential" to the two-party system? Perhaps yes, perhaps no, and a detailed history of the party system is not likely to be of much help. This is why explanation, just like prediction, needs a covering law.

The difference between prediction and explanation is that explanation requires much more convincing support. The value of a generalization for prediction is measured by comparing it with alternatives. Law h is better than law j if the probability of accurate prediction with h is higher than with j. Furthermore, some law h is usable in many circumstances even if the probability of accurate prediction is less than one. A social scientist can use a probabilistic law, if its predictions are better than random, to design institutions or strategies in just the same way that an engineer uses similarly probabilistic laws about stress to design machines – by building in a large safety factor, which allows for the inaccuracy of the law.

Explanations, on the other hand, are not very convincing if they are only probabilistically accurate and only empirically justified. What one wants from an explanation is the assurance that the antecedent in a conditional clause describes an event (A) that is necessary and sufficient for the event (B) described in the consequent. If the antecedent is sufficient, then, if A occurs, B must occur. If the antecedent is necessary, then, if A does not occur, B does not occur. With such an explanation one knows that B both had to happen and could not have happened any other way. One knows especially that B is not accidental but is entirely dependent on the existence of A.

167

Since empirical laws are always probabilistic, they cannot, by themselves, have the necessary and sufficient character of an explanation. Consequently, for an explanation to be adequate, a covering law must be encased in a deductive theory. The idealized, nonprobabilistic form of the empirical law is, then, a theorem properly inferred from axioms and from other theorems. Once reinforced so that it is theoretically valid as well as empirically (mostly) accurate, the law is reasonably justified. One knows from empirical testing that the avowed relationship between classes exists, and one knows from deductive support that there is good reason for this relationship to be the way it is.

CLASSES IN SCIENTIFIC DISCOURSE

The main task of scientific investigation is, thus, to utter satisfactory generalizations. This boils down to constructing subject classes that truly are subsets of predicate classes. The main difference, in my opinion, in the rates of development of physical/biological science and social science is that constructing appropriate classes has turned out to be harder (i.e., less in accord with naive intuition) in social science.

One reason this is so is that the events studied in physical and biological science are in some ways neater, or less ambiguous, than the events studied in social science. An event is ambiguous when speakers are uncertain about its content. Suppose one asks this question, "Is this actor (or mover) in events in this class?" And suppose the answers are "sometimes" or "partly" or "in anticipation" or "in some events in the class but in not others." Then, if a generalization about the class of these events turns on the dubious presence of the actor (or mover), clearly the generalization cannot be very useful or accurate. To avoid this kind of ambiguity, events must have temporal and spatial boundaries that precisely indicate what's in and what's out (Riker 1957).

Events have two parts: the motion and action they contain and their boundaries. The motion and action are continuous in space and time – that is, events don't stop at a temporal or spatial edge of observation. They exist, I assume, whether or not people differentiate and observe them. In that sense they are objective.

Observation requires us, however, to slice up this real-world continuity into pieces that we can observe. We do so by inserting static boundaries into dynamic reality. I call these boundaries *situations* – that is, the arrangement and interconnection among movers and actors just when an event begins or ends. At those points static situations are not to be thought of as real because they are instantaneous (i.e., without elapsed time, and hence also eternal). They have no significance other than to demarcate the portion of the continuous and real event

Political science and rational choice

that we wish to discuss. To compare events and situations, think of reality as a continuous image on a screen (the phenomenal world, perhaps). Suppose we stop the projector at, say, frame 1207. The nonmoving image on this frame is then a situation – the starting point of an event. Starting the projector again, we observe, metaphorically, reality that is, the moving picture – until we stop it at, say frame 1295, – where the motionless image is the terminal situation of the event. The event is the motion between frames 1207 and 1295, while the situations are the images on those two frames when the projector stops.

This metaphor is somewhat misleading, however, because it requires that the events contain all the contiguous elements of the two situational frames. In actual social science, models omit many features of reality. In all sciences one wants to allow for the exclusion of, especially, those features of situations that might move in or out of the event. For example, one might wish to generalize about how wars begin with the assumption that in such events there is a unique decision maker on each side (Bueno de Mesquita 1981). This means that the numerous people who influence or constrain the decision maker are deliberately excluded from the initial situation and hence from the event. This exclusion permits the scientist to determine how much predictive power is lost by the simplification in the model. If little is lost, the assumption is usable; otherwise it is not. Similarly, one can excise people's (say, decision makers') concerns about others or about the future. It is a question, then, of empirical testing to determine the magnitude of the loss in predictive or explanatory power.

It is easy to see from this interpretation of events that they include both subjective and objective elements. The objective elements are the motion and action. The subjective elements are the situations. Nothing in this interpretation of events limits the subjectivity of discourse to social phenomena. Instead, all observation contains a subjective element – namely the demarcation undertaken for the purpose of uttering particular sentences. This is why it is erroneous to attribute the slow development of social science to the subjectivity of social observation. Were subjectivity a barrier to knowledge, we would have no science at all.

EVENTS IN SOCIAL SCIENTIFIC DISCOURSE

The inadequacies of social science lie rather in the way social scientists have constructed events. Physical and biological sciences have gradually come to concentrate on quite precisely delimited events – for example, in astronomy, the differences in the locations of light sources on photographs; in chemistry, the motion in a test tube during a chemical re-

169

action; in geology, the differences in measurements of core samples. Because of the increasing precision in definitions, it is less and less likely that the events studied will be ambiguous. This development has not gone as far in social science, where, by and large, scientists have not taken care to prevent ambiguity.

An event is unambiguous when the movers and actors of its initial and terminal situations are the same. Indeed, strictly speaking, only such events can be properly called events. (For a rigorous proof of this proposition, see Riker 1957.) To appreciate this, observe that, if all the movers and actors of the initial situation are not in the terminal situation, then the event ends more than once, so that there are really as many events as endings. This means that it is impossible to generalize about events with multiple endings because the scientist does not know which of the events to include in a generalization. Similarly, if movers and actors other than those in the initial situation are in the terminal situation, then the event must begin more than once, with similar consequences for generalization. Thus, to prevent ambiguity in an event, its terminal situation must contain all the movers and actors of its initial situation and only those movers and actors.

Consider how often this minimum requirement of clarity is violated. When I first thought about this subject, I used Marx's and Toynbee's theories of history as examples. Marx's three grand events, feudalism, capitalism, and communism, occur over most of human history and the future. No wonder these events are ambiguous and that any generalization about them is meaningless. Toynbee (1936) sought to generalize, so he used twenty-seven rather than three events. But the events (civilizations) themselves were so huge and lasted so long (usually several hundred years) and were such complex agglomerations of culture and institutions that they also were ambiguous and meaningless.

It seems to me that the reason many writers discuss ambiguous events is that they accept as classes for investigation those that are given by the common language ("capitalism," "civilization," etc.) rather than those that serve some scientific purpose. Of course, ambiguity is more likely if, like Marx, writers intend to persuade people to political action, because persuasion is easier if the categories used in the argument are well established in the common language. In that sense Mannheim was correct about Marx's rhetorical distortion in order to justify his utopia. But Toynbee had no apparent rhetorical purpose. Instead, he intended, I believe, to explain the rise and fall of civilizations not for the sake of promoting either movement but rather merely to satisfy his own curiosity and win literary fame. Thus, he accepted, probably without realizing their deficiency, a question and categories that, while of great human interest, were inherently ambiguous.

Political science and rational choice

EVENTS IN INDIVIDUAL DECISION

It might seem that the appropriate way to avoid ambiguity is to concentrate on small events. Indeed, the most successful social scientists have done exactly that. Although in the eighteenth and nineteenth centuries economics concerned itself with "the wealth of nations," a humanly interesting but ambiguous question, directed in good part by Adam Smith himself, it later concerned itself with the determination of prices. This investigation led to the law of demand and thence to price theory and general equilibrium theory, which are today the core of economic science. Price offerings and price takings are, of course, very small events, even when they are considered to include the preferences and calculations of the offenders and takers. They still do not include whole people, but only those parts involved in intelligent, willful, and goal-directed choosing. Hence, it is easy to avoid ambiguity in generalizing about prices.

But it is not just the size of events of price offering and taking that renders prices amenable to scientific investigation. Were size the only consideration, it would, by analogy, be fairly easy to develop other social sciences by analyzing only small events. We have made some progress by, for example, substituting voting acts for entire elections in our studies of citizens' political actions. Still it is possible to generalize usefully about relatively large events, provided they are properly constructed. We do not fully understand Duverger's law, which concerns a class of huge events (i.e., two-party systems), and it has yet to be embedded in a convincing theory. But it is strongly supported empirically by studies of strategic voting by individuals and of decisions on entry by parties and candidates – that is, by studies of small decisions related to the larger constitutions. These studies have permitted us to restate the law with appropriate qualifications, just as in the case of the law of demand (Riker 1982). The law of federal origins, which I set forth in *Federalism* (1964) and *The Development of American Federalism* (1987), also concerns huge events (i.e., federal constitutions) and is strongly supported empirically – perhaps even more strongly than Duverger's law. It, too, depends for its success on reshaping events to emphasize individual decisions at crucial points in the making of constitutions.

In each case, the feature that makes generalization possible is that the central propositions are about rational decisions by individuals: Duverger's law involves rational choices on voting and entry; the law of federal origins involves choices on constitutional concessions by rulers of central and provincial governments. One can even study matters involving, for example, overlapping generations by carefully restricting

171

events to decisions in one generation at a time. In short, events are amenable to generalization not just because they are reduced in size – although size itself is very important – but also because the contents of new events can be unambiguously defined.

THE RATIONAL CHOICE MODEL

What renders these events unambiguous is the concentration on rational decision. The main action in the event is the choice made by people who are only partially included – that is, who are included only with respect to their concentration on the precise institutional situation for choosing. Thus, the action categorized is quite similar to the action of price takers. The size of the event is thus controlled not so much by the grand attendant circumstances as by the restrictions on the choosers' concerns.

The rational choice model consists of the following elements:

1. Actors are able to order their alternative goals, values, tastes, and strategies. This means that the relation of preference and indifference among the alternatives is transitive so that, for a set of alternatives, A: $\{a_1, a_2, \ldots, a_m\}$, if a_i is preferred or indifferent to a_j and a_j is preferred or indifferent to a_k, then a_i is preferred or indifferent to a_k.

2. Actors choose from available alternatives so as to maximize their satisfaction.

Note that the chooser assumes the set of alternatives to be finite and fixed in content at the time of choice. This means that matters the chooser ignores or believes to be irrelevant are not possible choices. While this accords with commonsense perception, it generates uncertainties in both theory and investigation. One way out of the difficulty is to assume that the choice set contains all conceivable alternatives. Even though economists commonly make this assumption, it too entails difficulties of interpretation when the subject of investigation is itself more complicated than money. (For example, does the observer or theorist know what all the conceivable alternatives are, and whether or not some should be regarded as conceivable?) In this discussion I will assume that the choice set contains what choosers regard as relevant, noting that this assumption thus requires the observer and theorist to determine just what the choice set does contain. (It is important that this assumption eliminates the unnecessary distinction between strict rationality and bounded rationality.)

Note, secondly, that this definition requires only maximizing choices from among ordered tastes. It does not require that actors do not err in interpreting the meanings of alternatives or in choosing among them. It is quite possible for people to choose alternative actions that frustrate their primary goals. It is also quite possible that, lacking information about others' choices, people choose actions (even ones with undesired consequences) that would be different from those they would choose with full information. In short, this definition requires only that, within the limits of available information about circumstances and consequences, actors choose so as to maximize their satisfaction.

Many would argue that this formulation renders every choice rational – that is, quite foolish choices can be explained as a result of incomplete information. True, but this does not mean that the formulation is scientifically useless. It would be, perhaps, if social scientists were studying individual psychology; but political science, economics, and sociology are intended to interpret social outcomes, not psyches. For this purpose, the assumption is just right. It does not allow supposedly foolish actions to be consigned to the unfathomable world of the irrational; instead it suggests inquiry into the degree of the actors' ignorance or into the kinds of their misinformation. Even more important, it suggests that the observer reevaluate his or her preconceptions about how sets of alternatives might be ordered.

Note, thirdly, that this definition of rationality does not specify any particular goal. Everybody is presumed to be self-interested, choosing what provides the most satisfaction, but the content of the self-interest is not specified.[2] As in the case of possible error or incomplete information, it is often said that the assumption of abstract goals (i.e., ideal points in space) is tautological in the sense that every choice is rational. That is, if only the process is required to be consistent, then any outcome, even one that appears to be inconsistent, can be said to be consistent with some set of initial tastes. To take an extreme case, suicide is said to be a rational choice if we assume that the chooser wishes to die.

Rationality as so defined requires merely the best choice from the choice set. In many practical circumstances the choice set is so restricted by nature that neither the chooser nor the observer has any difficulty in specifying the order of its alternatives. In that case, then, a particular goal is indirectly specified. For example, in a legislature the minimum choice set on a motion is {yes, no, pair, abstain}, where orderings for each participant are often quite obvious. Of course, even this simple situation may be complicated by the existence of several related motions, by electoral considerations, and so on, in which case no ordering is easily inferable. (See Denzau, Riker, and Shepsle 1985.)

The dispute remains, therefore, about tautological rationality. To analyze the dispute, I distinguish between *procedural rationality,* or *revealed preference* (in which neither goals nor outcomes are specified in advance), and *substantive rationality,* or *posited preference* (in which

173

particular goals, like maximization of wealth, or a hierarchy of goals –
satisfying hunger first, sex second, wealth third, etc. – are stipulated in
advance). Procedural rationality assumes that the process is consistent.
Choice reveals preference because one can infer backwards from an
outcome and a consistent process to what the goals must have been to
get to that outcome. With substantive rationality, on the other hand,
the observer posits preferences for the chooser and then discovers
whether or not the process and outcome are consistent with this posited goal.

In general, the assumption of procedural rationality leads to interesting discoveries about tastes and institutions. Suppose it is known that
minimum wages contribute more to unemployment for marginally employable workers than to redistribution of income to the poor. Should
we then attribute irrationality (or stupidity) to the legislator who justifies voting for minimum wages on the ground of redistribution? Or
should we recognize that the legislator, while really seeking to reduce
competition for the fully employable, is pretending to help the poor.
That is, should we accept the legislator's own substantive specification,
which renders him or her inconsistent, or should we assume that the
legislator is consistent but is dissimulating about goals? According to
the model of procedural rationality, the legislator is dissimulating;
according to the model of substantive rationality, the legislator is
inconsistent.

Social scientists, unlike psychologists, are not usually interested in
investigating the degrees of human consistency, even though that is, of
course, an important subject in the philosophy of science. Hence, substantive rationality plays a lesser role in social science than procedural
rationality does. Nevertheless, in actual practice, social scientists move
back and forth between the two assumptions. Consider investigations
of potentially sophisticated voting in connection with Duverger's law.
Assuming substantively that people vote for the candidate they like best
reveals that electoral outcomes are inconsistent with the assumed
choice of strategy. Hence, changing to the procedural assumption that
choice is consistent reveals that many voters prefer a good chance for
their second-best candidate to a poor chance for their best candidate.

ADVANTAGES OF THE RATIONAL CHOICE MODEL

The primary advantage of the rational choice model is that it permits
scientists to generalize about events (choices, actually) that are as small
and precise as the events of price taking. But as the example just mentioned suggests, the model has numerous other advantages, the most
important being that it permits generalizations about intentions.

Many who denounce social science assert that it denies people's humanity, turning them into mechanical objects driven by mechanical forces, with no room for human intentions except as automatic responses to material forces. This charge is true with respect to some pseudosciences: Dialectical materialism, for example, reduces all history and behavior to simple accommodations to random (or possibly determined) technological change. But as the economic and political failures of contemporary Marxist-Leninist governments indicate, generalizations based on mechanistic social philosophy are not very useful either for prediction or for explanation.

Perhaps in reaction to these and other mechanistic, deterministic, and hence inhumane philosophies, many social critics have insisted that intentions are unique to individuals and hence not subject to generalization. For example, some have argued that the meanings of actions and decisions are to be found only in the specific culture within which they occur – (what meaning can a witch's curse have outside the community of believers?). As another example, others have argued that intentions are necessarily rooted in concrete circumstances. Hence, outcomes from actors' intentional actions are to be understood only in terms of the efforts of individuals to grapple with these circumstances.[3]

These arguments are indeed fundamental to hermeneutics, which confines social studies entirely to the interpretation of specific events. Writers in this tradition have not, unfortunately, understood that when reasonable people who have the same goals are placed in similar social situations they behave similarly. This then becomes the basis for generalization about intentions. An example is the previously mentioned law of federal origins, which relates the adoption of federal constitutions to governmental leaders' responses to military circumstances.

By far the most important feature of generalizations about intentions, however, is their use in equilibrium models of social interaction. Equilibria are valuable, indeed essential, in theory in social science because they are identified consequences of decisions that are necessary and sufficient to bring them about. An explanation is, as I have already argued, the assurance that an outcome must be the way it is because of antecedent conditions. This is precisely what an equilibrium provides.

The only equilibrium theories I know of in social science are those that deal with intentions through rational choice models. It seems to me impossible for alternative scientific methods (such as behaviorism) to generate theories of equilibrium. Behavioral laws, when properly constructed, exclude intentions. (Intentions are, of course, matters of thought and are identified and appreciated by observing people who, by introspective knowledge of their own thoughts, interpret others'

175

thoughts. Strict behaviorists, confined to observing the externally visible or audible behavior of other creatures, are thus precluded from discussing intentions.)

Behavioral laws specify simply that organisms, subjected to a particular treatment, behave in a particular way. For example, behaviorists assert that people who respond to questions on surveys that they belong to party A also say that they intend to vote for party A's candidate. (This is the famous or infamous law of party identification that has from time to time been the center of controversy between the behavioral and rational choice schools.) Such sentences, in my opinion, though I am willing to be instructed on this point, cannot be put into a form that allows for interaction among actors that leads to an equilibrium. The same holds true for so-called sociological laws that relate behavior on a mass scale to social outcomes, for example, the proposition that numerous political parties are associated with governmental or cabinet instability. Behavioral or sociological laws of the sort I have mentioned may be well supported, sufficiently well, indeed, to provide adequate predictions and justify social engineering; but they cannot, in the absence of an interpretation of a giant social mechanism far too complex for our present understanding, be placed inside a theory of equilibrium. This is why behavioral and sociological laws may be used to predict, but not to explain.

To see why this is true, note, for example, that an explanation of the behavioral assertion about party identification requires that the scientist give reasons why the following two sentences should both be true: (a) if i identifies with A, then i votes for A; and (b) if i votes for A, then i identifies with A. Entirely aside from doubts about the empirical validity of these sentences, what kind of argument might be offered to support necessity and sufficiency? Showing that these sentences have always been true — though, of course, they are not — is not enough, because such a showing involves only an empirical regularity and is no proof of validity. It does not reveal the reason for the regularity. Suppose, then, one creates a theory from which necessity and sufficiency are deduced. What kind of axioms can in each case relate the antecedent to the consequent? Perhaps one might offer a Skinnerian argument: To say i identifies with A means that i has been reinforced to approve of A. Hence, when choosing between A and another party (which by definition of reinforcement i has not been conditioned to approve), i chooses A. But how then can one explain reinforcement? In the end, I think it must involve some axioms about preferences and, hence, intentions.

In response to one of my readers who found this claim extreme, I point out that physical and social equilibria have different properties.

Physical equilibria occur when forces balance one another so that a process repeats itself (such as orbits) or comes to rest (as in completed reactions). The scientist explains such equilibria by showing that, in an equilibrium, the forces must in fact balance; or that, in a disequilibrium, the forces must fail to balance. Human actions do not, however, consist of mechanical properties that can be balanced. What must be balanced is choices of actions – that is, intentions, which are thus analogous to physical forces. Social equilibria occur when actors choose in the most advantageous way, given the choices of others, and reach an outcome they would not wish to depart from. That is, they would not wish to have chosen differently because the outcome reached is the best they can achieve under the circumstances. Defining equilibria in this way does not mean that actors are always happy with outcomes, which may be negative for all participants (as in prisoners' dilemmas, total wars, and so on); nor does it mean that actors always analyze or choose correctly. Indeed, error (which I equate with unintended consequences and disequilibria) is common enough in the world. Still, it is hard to see how one can explain equilibria that do occur without taking account of what actors seek to accomplish. This means that the explanation must involve choices and, since equilibria are defined by actors doing the best they can, that the choices must be rational. Since explanations are the identification of necessary and sufficient conditions, which are also equilibria, and since social equilibria in turn require rational choice models, it follows that such models are necessary for explanation.

WHY SOCIAL SCIENCE HAS DEVELOPED SLOWLY

I revert now to the puzzle I described at the beginning of this essay: How can one account for the great disparity in development between the physical and biological sciences, on the one hand, and the social sciences on the other? The main clue is that the major achievements in social science during the bicentennium since Adam Smith and John Adams have been in microeconomics. Within that field scientists have offered some genuine explanations of social outcomes. Explanations are, in my opinion, the whole point of science and microeconomists have explained phenomena by deduction in a rational choice model of theorems that parallel empirical laws. So my interpretation of the disparity in development is that social science generally   microeconomics excluded – has not been based on rational choice models. I believe and hope, however, that, as the appreciation and understanding and use of these models spread, we will see a considerable increase in achievements in political science and in other social sciences.

There is reason to hope this will happen. Political scientists have never completely rejected rational choice notions. Indeed, apart from the temporary ascendancy of behavioral models in the 1960s and 1970s, the rational choice model has been implicit, although not consciously recognized, throughout the history of the academic discipline, which can be conveniently dated from 1875 when Harvard awarded its first Ph.D. in the subject. At about the same time (actually 1869) Henry Droop stated an early form of Duverger's law in which, in equilibrium, rational action by voters is associated with the number of political parties (Riker 1982). This kind of institutionalism, which relates structure to participants' incentives, continued to characterize political analysis right up to the 1950s. At the same time, the development of pluralism in the writings of, for example, Arthur F. Bentley (1908), Pendleton Herring (1940), David Truman (1951), and Robert Dahl (1961) also unconsciously expressed the rational choice model because policy outcomes were said to be the products of vectors of interests. Unfortunately, like their institutionalist colleagues, the pluralist writers mostly interpreted rather than generalized, so they missed the advantage of the rational choice model. Yet so deeply ingrained was this model that V. O. Key, the leading representative of the older institutionalism as seen in *American State Politics* (1956), produced, at the very height of the behavioralist movement, a defense of rational choice: *The Responsible Electorate* (1966). So it is fair to say that, throughout much of the history of political science, the rational choice model has rather loosely guided it.

But that model has shaped political science only loosely because in contrast to economists, political scientists frequently have been methodologically unsophisticated. They have conducted empirical research without articulating a political theory. As a result their unconsciously accepted theories have not been critically analyzed and revised. Nevertheless, some developments in the last generation give me confidence that the rational choice model will succeed.

Consider the Median Voter Theorem, certainly the greatest step forward in political theory in this century. It was first articulated and proved by Black in 1948 (and republished and elaborated in 1958), and since then it has been gradually absorbed into some portions of the political science community. This theorem and the model in which it is embedded can, in my opinion, be expected to play about the same role in political theory as the law of demand does in economics. The theorem asserts that, for a committee or electoral decision made by majority rule, if voters' preferences over alternatives can be arranged on a scale so that every voter has a best alternative and so that the greater

178

the difference between the best and some other alternative the lower the voter's evaluation of this other alternative, then the social choice of the whole set of voters consists of the median voter's best alternative (i.e., when just under half of the several best alternatives lie to the right of the median and just under half to the left). When the antecedent condition is met (often called the condition of single peakedness), this theorem identifies an equilibrium on one dimension of judgment.

The significance of the Median Voter Theorem has been estimated in a variety of ways. Niemi and Weisberg (1968) have calculated the chance of single peakedness given a random distribution of preferences. Although this chance goes to zero with infinite voters, Niemi (1969) has also estimated the chance of equilibrium even if the antecedent is not fully satisfied. Even with random preferences, this chance turns out to be quite high, which justifies the use of this model in studying nature.

One obvious limitation of the Median Voter Theorem is that an equilibrium is identified only for one dimension. Plott (1967) has, however, extended the definition to two or more dimensions, and McKelvey (1976) has shown that, in this case, there may be complete disequilibrium, in the sense that all possible alternatives are in a preference cycle. While Ferejohn, McKelvey, and Packel (1984) have modified this result by showing that, practically, the cycles are limited to a relatively small set of similar points, Riker (1983) has shown that full disequilibrium can be revived by increasing the number of dimensions. All of this theoretical development leads to the conclusion that the model is applicable to nature when it can reasonably be interpreted as one-dimensional, though otherwise perhaps not, except for interpreting political manipulation and consciously achieved disequilibrium. Fortunately Poole and Rosenthal (1985) have shown with large empirical studies of congressional voting that, in the absence of grand manipulation, a considerable part of political life is one-dimensional.

Political scientists have begun to use the Median Voter Theorem to interpret political institutions. Consider, for example, legislative committees. Shepsle (1979) has shown that, in legislatures with committees, a committee's jurisdiction provides a quasi-unidimensional scale of judgment, resulting in – given single peakedness – equilibria that might not otherwise be expected. Gilligan and Krehbiel (1987) have shown, again unidimensionally, that the relation between committee bills and floor amendments should be sharply different according to whether rules are closed or open. Shepsle and Weingast (1987) then investigated why, even with open rules, something of the closed rule effect appeared – an empirical result that probably could not even have been thought of without the background of the Median Voter Theorem.

179

The most extensive and informative use of the median voter theorem is by far the study of agenda control, which is also a subject that was neither well understood nor frequently studied prior to the publication of this theorem. McKelvey's theorem (1976) showed that those who controlled the agenda could engage in all sorts of manipulation. Plott and Levine (1978) conducted a seminal experiment to show just how much control was possible. Riker (1983) surveyed the feature of agenda control and offered a variety of concrete examples in *The Art of Political Manipulation* (1986).

It is clear that the median voter theorem – and through it, the rational choice theory – has had a salutary impact on political science. Furthermore, a forecasting model based on the theorem has attracted repeat customers in the worlds of business and government (Bueno de Mesquita, Newman, and Rabushka 1985). While commercial success says nothing about scientific explanation, it does at least indicate that the model using the median voter theorem is better for prediction than alternatives (which are mostly nontheoretical and intuitive). Unplanned reality testing of this sort gives me, at least, some confidence that rational choice theory is on the right track.

But lest we be overconfident, I conclude with a remark about the history of Duverger's law, which is usually explained with a rational choice theory. The part of this explanation concerned with sophisticated voting was first enunciated in 1869, before political science was an academic study (Riker 1982). Duverger (1953) and Rae (1967) assembled much system-level evidence for the law, and during the 1970s many scholars assembled voter-level and system-level evidence about the appropriate sort of sophisticated voting. But when I studied the history of the law in 1982, I found that scientists had not explained the connection between sophisticated voting, underrepresentation of minor parties, and the decision of prospective candidates to enter the electoral race. Since that time Cox (1987), Ferejohn and Noll (1987), Greenberg and Shepsle (1987), Palfrey (1988), and, especially, Feddersen, Sened, and Wright (1989) have explained parts of that connection. Nevertheless it remains true that a rational choice explanation of an important political institution, an explanation first suggested before academic political science existed, has not yet been worked out. However, the fact that the rate of successful theorizing seems to have picked up in the last two decades – under, I believe, the influence of rational choice theory – gives one reason to hope that an acceptably explanatory theory is just over the horizon.

Perhaps, however, the main practical benefit of rational choice theory to political science is that it has opened the door to political economy as a part of political science. This means that political scientists now use the tools of microeconomics to study political institutions. The law of demand, the idea of public goods, the notion of transaction costs, principal-agent theory, noncooperative games – all these assume rational choice. Now that political science is accepting rational choice, it is also accepting these additional tools to study political problems.

7

Institutions and a transaction-cost theory of exchange

DOUGLASS C. NORTH

Institutions are the humanly devised constraints that shape human interaction. They reduce uncertainty by providing a structure to political, social, and economic exchange. In order to understand the role of institutions in making choices we must rethink our views about human behavior and then explore the costs of exchange. In this chapter I shall first briefly examine the behavioral assumptions used in economics in order to develop a transaction-cost theory of exchange. I then apply the framework to both economic and political exchange. I conclude with a brief discussion of the implications of the theory for analyzing institutions.

THE BEHAVIORAL ASSUMPTIONS OF ECONOMICS

The basic behavioral assumption of neoclassical economics makes a direct connection between expected utility and outcomes with no intervening dilemmas of uncertainty. There are no institutions in such a setting. They are unnecessary precisely because this behavioral assumption ignores the uncertainty that arises from the incomplete and imperfect processing of information, a pervasive feature of human interaction. Institutions reduce the costs of human interaction from those that would be found in an institution-free world (although there is no implication in that statement that they are "efficient" solutions).

The behavioral assumptions of economics have recently been the subject of a good deal of critical scrutiny (Hogarth and Reder 1986), which has focused on the anomalies of intransitivity, preference reversal, framing, and inconsistent processing of subjective probabilities. Less attention has been given the much more fundamental issue of which behavioral assumptions are consistent with the existence of institutions. Herbert Simon (1986) has come closest to stating the issues:

If we accept values as given and consistent, if we postulate an objective description of the world as it really is, and if we assume that the decisionmaker's computational powers are unlimited, then two important consequences follow. First, we do not need to distinguish between the real world and the decisionmaker's perception of it. He or she perceives the world as it really is. Second, we can predict the choices that will be made by a rational decisionmaker entirely from our knowledge of the real world and without a knowledge of the decisionmaker's perceptions or modes of calculation (we do, of course, have to know his or her utility function).

If on the other hand we accept the proposition that both the knowledge and the computational power of the decisionmaker are severely limited, then we must distinguish between the real world and the actor's perception of it and reasoning about it. That is to say, we must construct a theory (and test it empirically) of the processes of decision. Our theory must include not only the reasoning processes but also the processes that generate the actors' subjective representation of the decision problem he or she frames. (pp. S210–S211)

Simon's quote captures two elements of human behavior that are essential to modeling institutions: motivation and deciphering the environment. Human motivation involves more than simple wealth maximization. People do trade wealth or income for other values, and institutions frequently lower the price people pay for their convictions, making them important in choices. Deciphering the environment means being able to connect choices with outcomes. Institutions facilitate that connection. Simon's statement explains why institutions play a critical role: They allow ideology derived from subjective perceptions of reality to play a major part in making choices.[1] They reflect the incompleteness of our information, the complexity of the environment, and the fumbling efforts we make to decipher that environment. They focus on the need to develop regularized patterns of human interaction in the face of such complexities, and they suggest that this structure may be inadequate or far from optimal. What is it about the environment of the individual in economic or political exchange that is complex and costly to decipher?

MEASURING TRANSACTIONS COSTS

The costliness of economic exchange distinguishes the transaction-cost approach from traditional economic theory inherited from Adam Smith. For 200 years the gains from trade made possible by increasing specialization and division of labor have been the cornerstone of economic theory. In turn, specialization could be realized by the increasing size of markets, so that as the world's economy grew and division of labor became ever more specific, the number of exchanges occurring in economies expanded. But the many economists who built this approach

183

into an elegant body of economic theory did so without regard to the costliness of this exchange process. Today economists for the most part still do not appreciate that the costliness of transacting is going to force a basic reconstruction of economic theory. The reason for this reconstruction is that an exchange process involving transaction costs suggests significant modifications in economic theory and very different implications for economic performance.[2]

A recent study (Wallis and North 1986) measuring the size of the transaction sector in the U.S. economy indicated that more than 45 percent of national income was devoted to transacting. This number reflects the proportion of resources going through the market that are devoted to transacting. The total production costs consist of the land, labor, and capital involved in transforming the physical attributes of a good (i.e., its size, weight, color, location, chemical composition, etc.), plus the land, labor, and capital involved in defining and enforcing property rights over goods (the right to use, to derive income from the use of, to exclude others, to exchange), known as the transaction function. Once we recognize that the production costs are the sum of transformation and transaction costs, we must construct a new analytical framework of microeconomic theory.[3]

Our concern in this study is with a theory of institutions. Although that focus inevitably overlaps with some fundamental issues in microeconomic theory, it takes us in another direction. Our initial question, however – why is it costly to transact? – is common both to restructured microtheory and to a theory of institutions.

A TRANSACTION-COST THEORY OF EXCHANGE

In his celebrated essay "The Problem of Social Cost" (1960), Ronald Coase made clear that only in the absence of transaction costs did the neoclassical paradigm yield the implied allocative results: With positive transaction costs, resource allocations are altered by the structures of property rights. Neither Coase nor authors of many of the subsequent studies of transaction costs have attempted to define exactly what it is about transacting that is so costly, but those costs are central to this chapter. The costs that arise from defining goods and services and enforcing exchanges underlie transaction costs. Let me take each in turn, keeping in mind that the aggregate of the two determines transaction costs.

We owe to Lancaster (1966), Becker (1965), Cheung (1974), and Barzel (1982) the insight that utility comes from the diverse attributes of a good or service as well as from the diverse attributes that constitute the performance of agents. This means, in commonsense terms, that when I consume orange juice, I get utility from the quantity of juice I drink, the amount of vitamin C it contains, and its flavor, even though the exchange itself consisted simply of expending two dollars for fourteen oranges. Similarly, when I buy an automobile, I choose color, style, interior design, gasoline mileage, and so on – all valued attributes, even though an automobile is all I buy ultimately. When I buy the services of a doctor, that person's skill, bedside manner, and the inverse of time spent waiting in an office are of value. When as head of an economics department I hire an assistant professor, it is not only the quantity and quality however measured of teaching and re-search output (again, however measured) but a multitude of other as-pects of his or her performance that matter. Meeting classes on time, good class preparation, providing external benefits to colleagues, being cooperative in department affairs, not abusing his or her position vis-à-vis students nor calling a boyfriend (girlfriend) in Hong Kong at departmental expense are also factors. The value of the exchange to the parties then, is the value of the different attributes lumped into the good or service. It takes resources to measure these attributes, and still additional measurement to define and police rights that are transferred.

Because of the positive costs of measurement, the rights to all valued attributes are never completely specified and measured. Therefore, the transfers that occur in an exchange entail costs that result from both parties attempting to determine what the valued attributes of these as-sets are. Thus, as a buyer of oranges, I attempt to purchase an amount of juice, an amount of vitamin C, and the flavor of oranges, even though I simply purchased fourteen oranges for two dollars. Similarly, when I purchase an automobile, I attempt to ascertain the value of the attributes important to me in a car. The same holds for the purchase of doctor's services. I try to determine the doctor's skills, bedside manner, and the time I'll be kept waiting in the office.

Let me generalize from the particulars in the foregoing illustrations. Commodities, services, and the performance of agents have numerous attributes and their level *varies* from one specimen or agent to another. The measurement of these levels is too costly to be comprehensive or fully accurate. The information costs in ascertaining the level of indi-vidual attributes of each unit exchanged underlie the costliness of this aspect of transacting. But even if all individuals involved in exchanges had the same objective function (for example jointly maximizing the wealth of a firm that employed them), the transaction would still entail the costs of acquiring the necessary information about the levels of at-tributes of each exchange unit, the location of buyers (sellers), and so on. This search would consume substantial resources. Yet the analysis of transaction costs would be mundane, only a "friction" of some constant proportion. In fact, however, asymmetries of information amongst the players, and variations in the underlying behavioral function of individuals, in combination produce radical implications for economic theory and for the study of institutions.

Let me take up the issue of asymmetry first. In the foregoing illustrations, the seller of oranges knows much more about the valuable attributes of oranges than buyers do; the used car dealer knows more about the valued attributes of cars than buyers do (Akerlof 1970); and the doctor knows more about the quality of his or her services and skills than patients do. Likewise, the prospective assistant professor knows much more about his or her work habits than the department chairman, or, to take another example, the purchaser of life insurance from an insurance company knows much more about his or her health than the insurer does.

Not only does one party (sometimes the buyer and sometimes the seller) know more about some valued attribute than the other party, but that person may stand to gain by concealing that information, which takes us to the behavioral assumptions we use in economics. Following a strictly wealth-maximizing behavioral assumption, a party to an exchange will cheat, steal, and so on, when the payoff to such activity exceeds the value of the alternative opportunities available to that person. Indeed, this assumption has been the basis of Akerlof's famous article (1970) on "lemons" as well as of the dilemmas posed by adverse selection in the purchase of life insurance and of a multitude of other issues that have emerged in the literature over the last dozen years in what is called the New Industrial Organization. While sometimes exchanging parties have an interest in concealing certain kinds of information, at other times they have an interest in revealing information. We can develop some generalizations about a transaction-cost model of exchange with this background.

Let us begin with the standard neoclassical Walrasian model. In this general equilibrium model, commodities are identical, the market is concentrated at a single point in space, and exchange is instantaneous. Moreover, individuals are fully informed about the exchange commodity and about the terms of trade. As a result, exchange requires no more than dispensing an appropriate amount of cash. Prices, then, become a sufficient allocative device to achieve highest value uses.

Let us now retain in our model individuals' maximizing behavior, the gains that result from specialization, and the division of labor that produces exchange, but let us add to the model positive costs of information, which specify the costs of measuring the valued attributes of goods and services and the performance of agents. Now, gains from exchange are gross gains (the standard gains in neoclassical theory and in the international trade model), minus the costs of measuring and policing an agreement and the losses resulting from imperfect monitoring.

It is easy to see that we devote substantial resources and efforts to measurement and to enforcement, or the policing of agreements. Warranties, guarantees, trademarks, resources devoted to sorting and grading, time and motion studies, the bonding of agents, arbitration, mediation, and judicial processes all reflect the ubiquity of this problem. Because it is costly to measure the valued attributes fully, the opportunity for capturing wealth by devoting resources to acquiring more information is always present. For example, sellers of commodities such as fruits and vegetables may find it too costly to sort and grade those commodities precisely. On the other hand, buyers may find it worthwhile to pick and choose from among the fruits and vegetables available. In one case sellers put into the public domain the variability of attributes that buyers can in part capture by devoting time and effort to sorting them out. The same can be said for purchasers of used automobiles or of medical services. Because of the enormous variety in the characteristics and the costliness of measuring attributes of goods and services and the performance of agents, the "ideal" ownership rights, with respect to these assets and resources, frequently may take a variety of forms. In some cases, the ideal form is that the parties involved divide rights. The buyer of a durable good, for example, may own some rights to it, yet its manufacturer keeps others in the form of performance guarantees.

As a generalization, the more easily others can affect the income flow from someone's asset without bearing the full costs of their actions, the lower is that asset's value. As a result, the maximization of an asset's value involves an ownership structure in which parties who can influence the variability of particular attributes become residual claimants over those attributes. In effect the parties are then responsible for their actions and have incentives to maximize the potential gains from exchange. The rights to an asset generating a flow of services are usually easy to assure when the flow can be ascertained — that is, easily measured — since it is easy to impose a charge commensurate with a level of service. Therefore, when services are known and constant, rights are easy to assure. If they are variable but predictable, rights are still easy to assure. When the flow of income from an asset can be affected by the parties to an exchange, assigning ownership becomes more problematic. When income is variable and unpredictable, it is costly to determine whether or not the flow is what it should be. In that case, because of the costliness of accurate measurement, both parties will try to capture some part of the contestable income stream.

Douglass C. North

A useful way to think of measurement is to conceive of all valued attributes in an exchange as remaining in the public domain (i.e., no property rights exist over them). But the parties in an exchange have different costs of acquiring information about valued attributes and hence value an exchange differently. Given the costs of measurement (and ignoring enforcement costs), what would be ideal property rights – that is, what rights would maximize exchange in the traditional neo-classical model? Because conditions vary among exchanges, rights cannot be fully defined economically, and only one ownership structure does in fact maximize an asset's net income and its value to an original owner. The general principle of maximizing the allocation of owner-ship is that the more easily a party can affect the mean income an asset can generate, the greater is the share of the residual that party assumes. I shall draw out the implications of this public domain approach to property rights, but first I must turn to the other source of transaction costs – the costs of policing and of enforcing agreements.

ECONOMIC EXCHANGE

No problem exists at all in the Walrasian model, which assumes that no costs are associated with enforcing agreements. Indeed, as long as we maintain the fiction of a one-dimensional good transacted instanta-neously, the problems of policing and enforcement are trivial. However, when we add the costs of acquiring information, and specifically of measuring, the problems become major ones. The issues arise because we don't know the valued attributes of a good or service or all the characteristics of the performance of agents and because we have to devote costly resources to measuring and monitoring them.

Let us begin with policing agents. I start with the most extreme ex-ample, the relationship between a master and slave. An implicit con-tract exists between the two, because in order to get maximum effort from a slave, an owner must devote resources to monitoring and meter-ing the slave's output. Because of increasing marginal costs to measur-ing and policing performance, the master will stop short of perfect policing and will instead police until marginal costs equal the addi-tional marginal benefits from such activity. The result is that slaves ac-quire certain property rights from their own labor. That is, owners are able to enhance the value of their property by granting slaves some rights in exchange for services the owners value more. Hence slaves become owners too. Indeed it is only this that made possible a slave's ability to purchase his own freedom, as was frequently done in classical times and even occasionally in the American South.[4] The slave exam-ple, an extreme form of the agency problem, nevertheless highlights the

188

issues involved in agency. Monitoring and metering the various attributes that constitute performance of agents mean that, in contrast to the standard neoclassical frictionless model of workers being paid the value of their marginal product, workers are paid that amount minus the costs of monitoring and policing.[5] Moreover, in the illustration already presented I implicitly introduced property rights when I referred to a master owning a slave. Indeed, in all discussions of monitoring we assume that principals can discipline agents and can therefore enforce agreements.

One cannot take enforcement for granted. It is, and always has been, the critical obstacle to increasing specialization and division of labor. Enforcement poses no problem when it is in both parties' interests to live up to agreements. But without institutional constraints, self-interested behavior will prevent complex exchange, because one party will be uncertain that the other will live up to the agreement. The transaction's cost will reflect the uncertainty by a risk premium, the magnitude of which will turn on the likelihood of defection by one party and the consequent cost to the other. Throughout history this premium's size has largely prevented complex exchange and therefore limited economic growth. Enforcement can come from the first party's internally enforced codes of conduct, from the second party's effective retaliation, or from a third party's imposition of costs on the first party. In this last instance third-party retaliation can come from effective societal sanctions or from a coercive party, such as the state. Let me now apply the same framework to modeling political exchange in order both to develop a complementary analytical framework and to focus on the key dilemma of third-party enforcement.

POLITICAL EXCHANGE

I start with a simple model of a policy consisting of a ruler and diverse constituents (this model is elaborated in "A Neo-Classical Theory of the State" in North 1981). The ruler acts like a discriminating monopolist, offering to constituents, in exchange for tax revenue, "protection and justice" or at least reduced internal disorder and protection of property rights. Since different constituent groups have different opportunity costs and bargaining power with the ruler, different bargains result. There are economies of scale in providing the (semi-) public goods of law and enforcement; hence, total revenue is increased. The division of the incremental gains between ruler and constituents depends on their relative bargaining strength. Changes at the margin, either the violence potential of the ruler or constituents' opportunity cost, will result in redividing the incremental revenue. Moreover the ruler's gross and net revenue differ significantly because of the necessity of developing agents (a bureaucracy) to monitor, meter, and collect revenue. All the consequences inherent in agency theory apply at this point.

This model becomes more complicated when I introduce a representative body to reflect constituent group interests in bargaining with the ruler. This step parallels the origins of Parliaments, Estates General and Cortes in early modern Europe and reflects the ruler's need to obtain agreements to get more revenue in exchange for providing certain services to constituent groups. The representative body, by aggregating a group of wealth and income constituents, facilitates exchange between the parties. On the ruler's side, this aggregation leads to the development of a hierarchical structure of agents. The simple (if extensive) management of the king's household and estates is transformed into a bureaucracy that monitors constituents' wealth and income.

When we move from the polities of early modern Europe to modern representative democracy, our story is complicated by the development of multiple interest groups and by a much more complicated institutional structure, one still devised to facilitate (again given relative bargaining strength) the exchange between interest groups. This political transaction-cost approach is built on the recognition of the multiplicity of interest groups reflecting concentrations of voters in particular locations. Thus, there are elderly in Florida and Arizona, miners in Pennsylvania and West Virginia, artichoke growers in California, automobile manufacturers in Michigan, and so on. Each legislator's district has concentrations of only a few of the large number of interest groups. Therefore, acting alone, legislators cannot succeed; they must make agreements with other legislators, who have different interests. What kind of institutions will evolve from exchange relationships between legislators reflecting multiple interest groups? Previous work, beginning with Buchanan and Tullock, focused on vote trading, also known as logrolling. This work was certainly a step forward in recognizing how legislators can engage in activities that facilitate exchange. However, such an approach was far too simple to solve the fundamental problems of legislative exchange. It assumed that all bills and payoffs were known in advance, and it had a timeless dimension to it. But in a variety of exchanges, today's legislation can only be enacted by making future commitments. In order to lower costs of exchange, a set of institutional arrangements that would allow for exchange across space and time had to be devised. Note the parallels with economic exchange, as already described. How does credible commitment evolve to enable agreements to be reached when its payoffs are in the future and on completely different issues? Self-enforcement is important in such exchanges and a reputation is a valuable asset in repeated dealings. But as in economic exchange, the costs of measurement and enforcement – discovering who is cheating whom, when free riding will occur, and who should bear the cost of punishing "defectors" – make self-enforcement ineffective in many situations. Hence political institutions constitute *ex ante* agreements over cooperation among politicians. They reduce uncertainty by creating a stable exchange structure. The result is a complicated system of committees, with both formal rules and informal methods of devising structures. Its evolution in the U.S. Congress is described in a recent study by Weingast and Marshall (1988).

Even though political institutions facilitate exchange among bargaining parties, there is no implication of economic efficiency as an outcome. Given the interests of the parties involved, efficient political exchange can create or alter economic institutions that may raise or lower the costs of economic exchange. I earlier argued (North 1981) that there were two basic reasons why rulers typically produced inefficient property rights (defined here as rules that do not produce increases in output). The first is that the competitive constraint on the ruler simply means that that ruler will avoid offending powerful constituents who have close ties to alternative rulers. The ruler will agree to a structure of property rights favorable to those constituents regardless of its efficiency. The second reason is that even though efficient property rights would lead to higher societal income they might not lead to higher tax revenues because of the high costs of monitoring, metering, and collecting those revenues. Granting guilds monopolies in Colbert's France may not have been efficient, but it did improve tax collecting as compared to an unregulated decentralized economy.

The same constraints have existed throughout history. Inefficient economic institutions are the rule, not the exception. Political entrepreneurs would like economic growth, but constraints seldom make such choices feasible.

IMPLICATIONS FOR ANALYZING INSTITUTIONS

We are now ready to explore the relationships among behavioral assumptions, the characteristics of transacting previously developed in this chapter, and a society's institutional structure. Property rights consist of the rights individuals appropriate over their own labor, the goods and services they possess, and so on. Appropriation is a function of legal rules, organizational forms, enforcement, and norms of behavior. Because transaction costs are positive, rights are never perfectly specified and enforced. Some valued attributes are in the public domain, and it pays individuals to devote resources to their capture. Because the transaction costs have changed radically throughout history and vary equally radically in contemporary economies, the mix between the formal protection of rights and individuals' attempts to capture rights or to devote resources to protecting their own rights varies enormously. We have only to compare property rights in Beirut with those in a modern community in the United States to cover the spectrum. In Beirut, most valuable rights are in the public domain, to be seized by those violent enough to be successful. In the United States, communities have legal structures that define and enforce rights; valuable rights in the public domain tend to be allocated by conventions and traditional norms of behavior. The difference between these two is a function of the institutional structure in each. In each case formal and informal constraints and their enforcement – that is, the institutional framework – define the opportunity sets of the players and hence the way the system works.

Institutions provide the structure for exchange that, together with the technology employed, determines the cost of transacting and the cost of transformation. How well institutions solve coordination and production problems is a function of the motivation of the players involved (their utility function), the complexity of the environment, and the players' ability to decipher and order the environment (measurement and enforcement).

The institutions necessary to accomplish economic exchange, however, vary in their complexity, from those that solve simple exchange problems to those that extend across space and time and numerous individuals. Complexity in economic exchange is a function of the type of contracts necessary for exchange in economies of various degrees of specialization. The greater the specialization – that is, the greater the number and variability of valuable attributes – the more weight must be put on reliable institutions that allow individuals to engage in complex contracting with a minimum of uncertainty about whether the contract's terms can be realized. Exchange in modern economies with many variable attributes extending over long periods of time requires the kind of institutional reliability that has only gradually emerged in Western economies. There is nothing automatic about "the evolution of cooperation" from simple forms of contracting and exchange to the complex forms that have characterized modern "successful" economies. Nor is there any implication about the "efficiency" of the institutions we observe.[6]

Institutions to undertake economic exchange exist in an enormous variety of forms that do, however, fall into general types that are consistent with the transaction-cost model of exchange. In its simplest form, the kind of exchange that has occurred throughout most of economic history can be characterized as personalized exchange involving small-scale production and local trade. Repeat dealing, cultural homogeneity (that is, a common set of values), and a lack of third-party enforcement (and little need for it) have been typical conditions. Under them transaction costs are low, but because specialization and division of labor are rudimentary, production costs are high.

As the size and scope of exchange has increased, the parties involved have always attempted to "clientize," or personalize, exchange. Indeed, this is still true today. But the greater the variety and numbers of exchange, the more complex the kinds of agreements that have to be made, and the more difficult it is to make them. Therefore, a second pattern of exchange that evolved was impersonal exchange, in which the parties were constrained by kinship ties, bonding, exchanging hostages, or merchant codes of conduct. Frequently exchanges were made possible by the reinforcement that came from setting the exchange in a context of widely held beliefs in rituals and religious precepts in order to constrain the participants. Early long-distance and cross-cultural trade and the fairs of medieval Europe were built on such institutional constructs. They permitted a widening of the market and the realization of the gains from more complex production and exchange, extending beyond the bounds of a small geographic area. In early modern Europe these institutions led to the state increasing its role in protecting merchants and adopting merchant codes as the revenue potential of such fiscal activities increased. However, in this environment the state's role was at best ambiguous. The state was as often the source of increasing insecurity and higher transaction costs as it was the protector and enforcer of property rights. Throughout most of history rulers of states have found that acting like the modern Mafia (given the time horizons they possessed) was the optimal maximizing behavior rather than protecting and enforcing property rights and receiving the gains that resulted from the productive consequences of more efficient exchange.

The final form of exchange is impersonal exchange with third-party enforcement. It has been the critical underpinning of successful modern economies involved in the complex contracting necessary for modern economic growth. Third-party enforcement is never ideal, never perfect, and the parties to exchange still devote immense resources to attempting to clientize exchange relationships. But neither self-enforcement nor trust can be completely successful. It is not that ideology or norms do not matter, because they do, and immense resources are devoted to attempting to promulgate codes of conduct. Equally,

193

however, in such complex societies the returns on opportunism, cheating, and shirking rise in this context. A coercive third party is essential to constrain the parties to exchange when the contracts essential to realizing the productive potential of modern technology extend across time and space and involve impersonal exchange with others. One cannot have the productivity of a modern high-income society with political anarchy. Indeed, third-party enforcement is realized by creating an effective set of rules that then enhance a variety of effective informal constraints. Nevertheless, the problems of having third parties enforce agreements, the development of an effective judicial system that carries out, however imperfectly, such terms, are only very imperfectly understood and a major dilemma in the study of institutional evolution.

8

The costs of special privilege

GORDON TULLOCK

The first time I saw Milton Friedman was at a public debate on free enterprise versus socialism at the University of Chicago. He based his entire lecture on what a benevolent dictator would do. Admittedly, he intended this simply as a rhetorical device to argue for a free economy. Of course, Friedman himself was not in favor of a dictatorship. He was, however, using a benevolent dictator as a means of avoiding all discussion of politics.

In this, he was typical of the economists of that time. They investigated optimal policies and considered what well-intentioned people would do if they had control of the government. Insofar as they had an argument for this approach, it was based on the division of labor. They would have said that politics was best left to political scientists. As a matter of fact, political scientists were not doing very well with politics, essentially because they lacked the tools that economists had. Public choice is, in the real sense, the use of economic and economiclike tools developed for special application in a field that political scientists traditionally taught.[1]

Let us turn to the more scientific aspect of public choice. I am going to give an example of the kind of work we do. This example is particularly interesting because it is a case in which for some two hundred years economists were simply wrong. Furthermore, they erred not solely in their analyses of government activity but also in their analyses of the private market.[2]

Economists were wrong in a very simple and straightforward way. In dealing with the social costs of monopolies, they considered the monopolists themselves members of society so that those people's gains to some extent counterbalanced the losses of others. Economists thus counted total monopoly profit as a mere transfer from some members of society to others. Socially, it was neither a gain nor a loss. Even

195

though economists noticed and proved that monopolies were generally harmful to society, they considered the actual costs of them were small.

Economists erred in failing to notice that the creation of monopolies would require resources. They had no reason to believe that resources invested in the creation of monopolies would be more profitable than those invested in anything else. After all, if greater profits were to be earned by creating monopolies, we would expect people to shift their resources out of building factories until such time as the returns from building factories and creating monopolies were about equal. This rather simple insight – that resources would be consumed in creating monopolies – increased the estimated cost of monopolies by a factor of at least ten. Monopolies were a much more important problem than had been previously realized.

This chapter explores several consequences of that insight in shaping the politics of organizing for special privileges. We compare the social cost of monopolies to the costs those seeking to create monopolies incur. This gives a better idea of the returns available from this sort of activity. We also explain why the resources actually consumed in seeking monopoly appear small compared to the potential benefits monopolists might gain. The explanation lies in a requirement to use inefficient technology, and we discuss the roles of voter ideology and ignorance in that requirement.

RENTS AND RENT SEEKING

In order to understand economists' mistake about monopolies and its correction, together with a later correction of the correction, consider Figure 8.1, adapted from Tullock (1988). On the horizontal axis we show some commodity, we will call it wheat, that can be produced at a price of CC. There is a demand for wheat, shown by DD, and tracts of land of varying fertility. A competitive market would produce Q units because the demand curve, DD, crosses the cost line at that point. (We assume the situation involves perfect information and no transaction costs.) In equilibrium, the price is thus P, and land of poorer quality to the right of Q is not farmed. The Ricardian land rent is the area above CC and below P, and the owners of the land wheat is produced on collect it.

Now, the wheat producers could invest to lower the cost of production, as described in Tullock (1988). Or they might organize a cartel, or monopoly, to drive up prices by restricting production. This second behavior is what we call rent seeking. Today most monopolies are organized by getting the government to put some kind of restraint on competition, but this has not always been so. In the nineteenth

The costs of special privilege

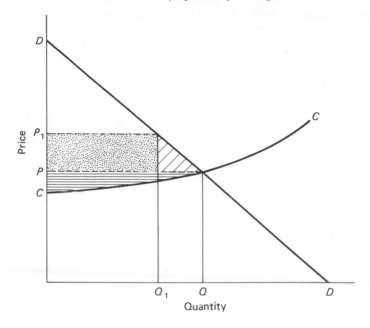

Figure 8.1. Costs of monopoly

century, monopolies were far more likely to be organized privately. Even today some monopolies do not depend on government support, although they are rare. The result of this rent seeking, of organizing this monopoly, is that production is restricted to Q_1, with a consequent increase in price to P_1.

The traditional argument, one that I taught for so many years before I saw the error of my ways, was that the reduction of production to Q_1 and the rise in the price to P_1 had two consequences. First, an amount corresponding to the dotted rectangle in Figure 8.1 was transferred from consumers to monopolists; second, society lost an amount represented by the slant-lined triangle. This triangle represented the benefit consumers would have obtained from buying the units between Q_1 and Q if the price had not been raised. Economists normally said that monopolists and consumers were both members of the same society and hence that the dotted rectangle was merely a transfer between them and not a cost when looked at from the standpoint of society as a whole. My students always objected to this view, and my eventual discovery that they were right was a little embarrassing.

Since my first article (Tullock 1967) in this area, a hidden assumption has been realized: that monopolists get their monopolies through

197

divine favor. In the real world, they have to work for them. Whether this work involves complicated, devious market manipulating by J. P. Morgan, or complicated, devious manipulating in the halls of Congress, so as, for example, to get quotas on car imports, it clearly has a cost. Further, this cost should be about the same as that of any other investment bringing in an equivalent return. If an automobile company can make a better return on its money by investing in manipulation in Washington than it can by building a new and improved factory, then it will not build the new plant but will instead put resources into congressional manipulation. Over time, the two rates of return will be brought into equality.[3]

I have not here exhausted the topic of total cost. The bulk of the literature stops here, but recently I have realized that there is a further cost, shown in Figure 8.1 by the horizontally lined region. This cost is the gain that society would have made had the resources being used to create these rents (the lobbyists in Washington, etc.) instead been used constructively.[4] For instance, as I discuss elsewhere (Tullock 1988), the same costs could have been applied to investment to reduce the costs of production *CC*.

I have been accused here of double counting, so let me go through the reasoning carefully. Suppose that a contractor uses a bulldozer to repair roads. If the contractor just stopped using the bulldozer one day, society would incur a cost equivalent to the full amount the bulldozer would normally produce. If on the other hand, the contractor begins digging large holes in a road with the bulldozer, then the cost to society is both the holes in the road *and* the work that the bulldozer would otherwise have produced. The dotted rectangle in Figure 8.1 represents the holes in the road, and the horizontally lined area below it represents the work the bulldozer would otherwise have produced.

In general, the slant-lined triangle in Figure 8.1 is a deadweight social loss, the dotted rectangle is a transfer that results from rent seeking (for example, what might have been consumer surplus becomes producer surplus), and the trapezoid is an additional social cost from resources directed not to socially productive activity but rather to achieving the transfer. It should be pointed out that there is no necessary reason for the latter two areas to be exactly the same size. Indeed, in my construction they are not. Which is bigger cannot be deduced from pure theory, but the difference should not be great.

Let me turn to a real-life example, although I am going to be drawing on an account in William Faulkner's *The Reivers*. In the early part of this century, roads in the United States were in a horrible state, and cars, newly introduced machines, tended to get stuck in mud holes. Farmers would then turn up with their teams and, in return for a fee, pull them out. It occurred to some farmers that this was a business opportunity and that they could either artificially create mud holes or improve existing mudholes. They therefore would plow up pieces of road. Note that this is a completely private creation of a negative externality, although it was illegal and farmers had to have enough political pull to be sure that they would be kept out of jail.

The first cost of this activity was, of course, the inconvenience to car owners. But a second cost was the loss to society of the wheat that farmers would otherwise have produced had they not been plowing up roads. If the farmers had simply stopped work, their output would have been reduced. When they not only stopped work but also used their equipment to cause positive ill to society, then the cost was even greater.

Economists frequently have difficulty with this point. I think the basic reason is that if contractors or farmers simply stopped work the cost of that stopping would fall entirely on them. Presumably, if they stopped voluntarily, they had some reason, so that in the real sense society was no worse off. If instead of stopping farmers shifted to some other activity, let us say growing corn, then society loses the wheat that they would have produced but gains the corn. If they stopped producing wheat to produce mud holes, however, society loses on both sides.

Rent seeking as we defined it is the collusive pursuit by producers of restrictions on competition that transfer consumer surplus into producer surplus. Returning to Figure 8.1, rent seeking would cause the horizontally lined trapezoid and the slant-lined triangle simply to disappear. They are things that might have, but as a matter of fact have not, come into existence. The dotted rectangle, however, should come into existence. We would expect that the rectangle would represent actual work, possibly by lobbyists in Washington or by other things. In any event, it in fact involves the use of resources to generate something, and the resources should be detectable.

THE SCALE OF INVESTMENT IN RENT SEEKING

The problem which immediately concerns me is that the resources we can detect seem to be too small for their apparent value. To take but one example:

Overall, the allegedly altruistic tax-writing politicians accepted striking amounts of money during the Ninety-ninth Congress. The fifty-six members of the House Ways and Means and Senate Finance Committees raised $6.7 million from PACs and $19.8 million overall in 1985 as the tax season got underway. This compares with $2.7 million received from PACs and $9.9 million received by these members overall in 1983, the most recent nonelection year. Though the members of the tax committees comprise only ten percent of the

Congress, they garnered almost a quarter of the PAC money given in the first half of 1985. Moreover, these figures do not include the contributions received during 1986, when tax reform became an even bigger issue.

(Doernberg and McChesney 1987, p. 901)

An interesting feature of this particular quotation is that the Tax Reform Bill involved literally billions of dollars – even tens of billions – compared to which the contributed amounts are, indeed, very small.[5] Indeed, if we multiply these numbers by ten on the grounds that the publicly disclosed expenditures are only 10 percent of total expenditures, they still look trivial. This is nevertheless true of many contemporary political situations.

New York Congressman Mario Biaggi, for example, intervened with the federal government to save, temporarily, a gigantic Brooklyn dockyard from bankruptcy. He was tried and convicted for having accepted from the management of the dockyard three Florida vacations valuing a total of three thousand dollars.[6] This appears to be a minute sum compared to the amount of money potentially involved in the bankruptcy.

As another example, Chrysler paid the lobbyists it hired to promote its federal bailout a total of $390,000 (Reich and Donahue 1986, pp. 204–205). Once again, this seems a trivial amount. In both cases, there were probably some additional payments that were not publicized. Even if those payments were ten times as much as the payments made public, however, they would still be insignificant compared to the size of the government actions.

By the same token, campaign contributions also seem too small. If we assume that in the average election contributions total $500 million (that is probably an overestimate), that amount is still small compared to the various restrictions imposed on the economy to benefit particular groups. For example, the direct budgetary costs of our agricultural program, not counting increases in prices, run between $15 billion and $30 billion a year. Total campaign contributions from farmers equal only a small part of that.

Further evidence of this lack of proportion can be found in the life-styles of U.S. politicians. Unlike some Third World leaders, U.S. politicians do not retire with vast wealth. They are no doubt well-off, but their life-styles indicate that they are far, far from extremely wealthy. Considering the value of the benefits they have conferred on special interest groups, let alone the total social cost of the resulting distortions that they have imposed on the economy, this seems odd.[7]

To take a specific example, the members of the Texas Railroad Commission conferred benefits worth many billions of dollars on the oil industry. The commissioners were elected officials, and their life-styles,

200

both when on the commission and when retired (one served for thirty-three years), indicate that they lived mainly on their modest salaries. These were, of course, frequently supplemented by elaborate dinners and visits to expensive resorts, but their returns were small compared to the effects of their decisions (Libecap 1987).

INEFFICIENCY AND RENT DISSIPATION

The disparity between the benefits politicians confer and the payments they receive is the first observation that seems to contradict existing rent-seeking theory. The second is simply that the rents are normally transferred extremely inefficiently. Giving someone a monopoly is generally a socially inefficient way of transferring profit to that person. Furthermore, in most cases where valuable production controls are politically provided, they are not awarded to one single person or organization but to a considerable group of producers. These producers enjoy a higher price than they would get from an unhampered market, but because of the difficulties of coordinating their activities, each increases production competitively in order to take advantage of that price. Libecap (1987) demonstrates that the Texas Railroad Commission did not even come close to maximizing the profits of the Texas oil producers.

At the same time, in the case of airline regulation,

the CAB [Civil Aeronautics Board] controlled price competition, but allowed airlines to compete for customers by offering non-price frills like free drinks, movies and half empty planes. The airlines competed away, through additional costs, the rents granted them by the prices the CAB set.

(Mueller 1989, Ch. 15)[8]

In the later days of regulation one transcontinental airline actually had a piano bar on its flights. Such attempts at attracting passengers at the CAB price simply reflected the fact that most planes were half empty. The airlines were, in fact, not making markedly higher profits than they do today, when seats are closer together, more fully occupied, and cheaper.

Why, then, do we observe both inefficient rent seeking and the dissipation of rents through competition? (Note that I have given no extended citations to other cases because I presume readers can simply look around.) My answer to this question will be given later, but I should warn readers that it is not uncontroversial. In Figure 8.2, I show a situation in which rent seekers confront technical difficulties. Specifically, they can only get their rents by choosing an inappropriate technology of production. In order to simplify the diagram, the horizontally lined and slant-lined areas of Figure 8.1 have been omitted.

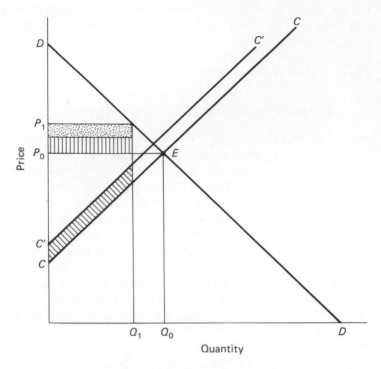

Figure 8.2. Hampered rent seeking

These are still costs, but they do not affect the argument here. I defer discussing why rent seekers would be forced to choose an inappropriate technology until I have explained the basic theory.

Figure 8.2 contains the usual demand and supply curves. The supply curve *(CC)* in this case is variable cost. The triangle CEP_0 is the rent owners of fixed resources in this industry derive. If we consider the resources to be land for growing wheat, this is a Ricardian rent. Suppose that the producers now organize and obtain a government-mandated price rise to P_1. The specific details of the restriction would be determined by political considerations that are outside the scope of this article.

Assume here, however, that the trade restriction producers obtain carries with it adoption of a less efficient production method shown by the increase of cost to $C'C'$. With the price rise to P_1 quantity falls to Q_1. The standard rent-seeking rectangle is shown to the left of Q_1 between P_0 and P_1. I have broken the rectangle into two categories in the figure for reasons that will become obvious later.[9]

202

The costs of special privilege

If the rent-seeking activity has carried with it not only a restriction but also a requirement to use inefficient technology, the cost line goes up to $C'C'$, and a net loss from the inefficient technology is shown by the area within the slanting lines. Because the people still remaining in the industry – that is, those not eliminated by the restriction – have to use this technology and it raises their costs, I have transferred this area up to the rent-seeking rectangle, where it is shown by the vertically lined lower part. The actual return on rent seeking for those who organized it, then, is the dotted upper part, a return much smaller than the total increase in price. This, of course, is a consequence of the need to net out the cost of having to use an inefficient method.

In farming, for example, the present program results in wheat production using less land and more fertilizer per bushel. Assume that the additional cost of production from this nonoptimal farming method is shown by the vertically lined area. The direct return to rent seeking would be the smaller dotted area above it. "Lobbying" expenses would not exceed the amount this rectangle represents, hence they would be much smaller than the $15 billion to $30 billion direct cost of the agricultural program. Part of the social cost would be eaten up by the necessity of using more expensive production technology, shown by the slant-lined area. Presumably the amount spent in hiring lobbyists and so on would not exceed the amount this rectangle represents.

While we are examining this construction, let me point out that empirically it immediately explains one of the two problems I mentioned earlier. The reason that the apparent payoffs to people who arrange the rents are so low in our society is that the actual "profit" to the beneficiaries of the rents is much, much lower than the traditional measure of the value of rent seeking. Thus, Congressman Biaggi may, in fact, have obtained the full value of his intervention.

But consider agriculture. The government program, in general, has taken the form of restricting the amount of real estate used in producing crops. This led farmers to change their production technology to an inefficient one using less land and more fertilizer and other resources. This change resulted in a higher production cost. (Were it not higher, farmers could have used this new production technology before.) Furthermore, the present system prevents certain technological changes that might improve efficiency. The long-run gain to farmers is much less than the price increase.

Most government restriction programs will have this effect. They are cartels without any binding restriction of the quantity of resources invested. Farmers, for example, for many years faced a restriction on the amount of land they could use but not on other resources. People can and do invest resources and change technology because of restrictive arrangements, and hence profits to the producers are considerably less than costs to purchasers. This occurs in addition to the deadweight loss the Harberger triangle shows. The situation should be described as handicapped competition rather than monopoly or oligopoly.

But for true rent seeking, the total cost in Figure 8.2 is not measured only by the dotted rectangle or even by the dotted rectangle plus the vertically lined area, which is the traditional rent-seeking cost. There is also the loss of what would have been produced if the same resources had been used productively (see Tullock 1988). The resources used for creating rents – for example, lobbying the government for some restriction – are not only wasted but are positively detrimental, as in the case of the Luddites, who devoted their energies to destroying machines. Their cost is the sum of the positive damage and the simple waste of those resources.

But what about the use of the inefficient technology in this case? The arguments so far appear to apply only to the dotted rectangle, or possibly the dotted rectangle minus the loss of standard Ricardian rents shown by the lower small triangle. Resources used in producing inefficiently would appear to be simply wasted. We have here what amounts to a metaphysical problem, one that has to do with the meanings of waste and of injury. Since we are assuming that the government requires this particular wasteful method of technology as a payoff for the restriction, the resources involved in producing the technology are also part of the resources used to reduce production.

The professional lobbyist the farm lobby hires tells farmers that if they really want to get a government subsidy, they must take the subsidy in a form that lowers the agricultural sector's technological efficiency. They must use less land and more fertilizer. The change in technology is as much an effort to reduce total product and gross national product as was the money directly spent on (or by) the lobbyist.

The total costs of inefficient production methods as part of rent-earning activity may be quite hard to measure. This is because such inefficient technologies may generate external effects on people who are not even in the industry in question. The arrangement under which airlines flew half-empty planes across the continent was supposed, among other things, to increase the demand for planes; it quite possibly did, although this is a subject of dispute. What we can say is that the industry itself will only fight for a system under which the costs of the inefficient technology are less than the benefits it obtains from the restriction. Further, it will use resources in the usual rent-seeking way (for example, in lobbying) up to the point where the rent-seeking activity fully absorbs the surplus above production costs under the inefficient technology and the price that can be derived under the restriction.

As readers who have seen my "Efficient Rent-Seeking" (Tullock 1980) and the various articles that have come out of it (see Rowley, Tollison, and Tullock 1988, pp. 91–146) will know, I am not sure that this is true. But, the standard approach to the cost of rent seeking from the time of "The Welfare Costs of Monopolies, Tariffs, and Theft" to the present has been to assume that there is no reason for the return on lobbying and other rent-seeking activity to differ from the return on investment in, let us say, building a steel mill. If that is so, then the rent-seeking cost would always fully absorb the present discounted value of the restriction in equilibrium.

Manufacturers planning on making money would be indifferent to the choice between improving their steel mills and trying to get a quota on Japanese steel imports from Congress. In spite of the doubts raised in "Efficient Rent-Seeking," I am going to use that assumption throughout this chapter. I sincerely hope that the present state of the "Efficient Rent-Seeking" debate, which is mired in paradox, is simply a transitional stage. With luck, someone will solve the problem in the near future.

IDEOLOGY, IGNORANCE, AND INEFFICIENT TECHNOLOGY

So far, readers may be a little unhappy with this chapter. I have discussed rent-seeking costs under the assumption that rent seeking normally requires not only that prices be increased but that inefficient technologies be adopted. I have so far offered no explanation as to why the latter should be so, although, as I have pointed out, it quite commonly is so if we look at how government actually functions. Let us then turn to why it is so. Briefly, it is because of voter ideology and lack of knowledge. As we shall see, these are not entirely bad things.

Consider an efficient transfer scheme. For the purpose of illustration, let us use what we will call the Tullock Economic Development Program. This involves placing a dollar of additional tax on each U.S. income tax form and paying the resulting funds to Tullock, whose economy would develop rapidly. All of my readers will agree that were I to propose this measure, politically, regardless of its desirability, it would have not the slightest chance of being adopted.

Let us compare the Tullock Economic Development Program with the Tucson Air Quality Improvement Program. Tucson, like many cities, has an air pollution problem; it is not very serious, but it is real. It has a lot of people excited about it. No one, however, really wants to incur the expenses and suffer the inconveniences that would be necessary to reduce the pollution. This is normal. A number of gestures that have a minor effect on pollution but make people feel good and do not cost much are the most that we can expect.

In order to understand the Tucson Air Quality Improvement Program, we must realize that Tucson has a heavily subsidized bus line. Part of the subsidy comes from the federal government, part from the city of Tucson. Since the buses are much underused,[10] transportation cost in terms of passenger miles must be extremely high. The buses also probably increase total pollution. They run all the time, whether empty or with only a few passengers, and generate more pollution than I believe cars would generate carrying the same number of passengers. The subsidized buses are, however, supported by three pressure groups: their drivers, the people who actually do depend on them, and environmentalists.

The Tucson Air Quality Improvement Program itself consists of doubling the size of the bus line while at the same time starting a research project. This project will naturally be allocated to the University of Arizona's Economics Department, and two friends of mine, one an engineer and the other a locational geographer, will share in it. The grant for Tullock in this program is $30,000. A research grant, of course, is not the same as $30,000 in cash, but it is not too different. Each of my friends would also get $30,000, and there would be additional funds for such things as hiring research assistants, because we would actually do some research. Basically, however, the bulk of the money would simply go to buying and subsidizing more buses.

Given my choice between the Tullock Economic Development Program and the Tucson Air Quality Improvement Program, I obviously would favor the first. But, if I had to choose one to put $10,000 of my own resources (in the form of lobbying effort or building a supporting coalition) into, I would choose the Tucson Air Quality Improvement Program. I estimate that I might have about a 50–50 chance of getting my $30,000 as a return on the $10,000 in this program. My chances of getting many millions of dollars for putting $10,000 into lobbying for the other are so small that its present discounted value is far below the $5,000 (net of lobbying cost) of the Tucson Air Quality Improvement Program.

Economically, if one ignores rent-seeking costs, the Tullock Economic Development Program is an efficient transfer. Economically, the Tucson Air Quality Improvement Program, which we will assume has exactly the same cost, is a ghastly mistake. Nevertheless, I would predict that any democratic legislature would pass more programs like the Tucson Air Quality Improvement Program than like the Tullock Economic Development Program.

The costs of special privilege

We see the same thing in the farm program. From the very beginning and right up to the present, the farm lobby has fought vigorously against any proposal to pay farmers directly in cash.[11] But at much less cost to the rest of us, we clearly could give farmers the same benefits they now receive in their present program by instead giving them direct cash payments equal to the discounted value of that program, but with no crop restrictions. Superficially, this is a little puzzling.

However, the explanation is simple and straightforward. Farmers are aware that such a program would be too raw – voters would not buy it. In another paper, I referred to public image (see Rowley et al. 1988, pp. 51–63) as a problem for rent seekers. To please its citizens, the government has to cover over any transfers to the well-to-do that it undertakes. Changing the technology with which something is produced can frequently disguise the government's real objective – say, improving total production or helping people without directly paying them. Direct payments would not work.

To take one example, from the Civil Aeronautics Board's organization until very nearly its end, it permitted no trunk line carrier to enter the industry. Suppose instead of preventing entry to the industry the government had simply put a tax on all trunk line airplane tickets and paid the resulting cash to the companies operating trunk lines at the time the legislation creating the CAB was enacted. For the airlines and air travelers, this procedure would obviously have been superior to the system that was in fact adopted. Like the Tullock Economic Development Program, however, it would obviously have failed to pass Congress. The risk-prone entrepreneurs who had entered the airline business in the 1930s had to adapt to the inefficient method if they were to be offered any aid at all.

Moreover, something a bit like this also applies to private monopolies. When we look at the history of such monopolies, and it is, of course, a long one, we note that almost never do monopoly organizers openly avow raising prices and increasing profits as their motive. They claim instead to be concerned with stabilizing prices, improving quality, guaranteeing a production reserve for possible use in war, and so on. These slogans are less effective when private monopolies use them than when government-sponsored monopolies do, but even private monopolies rarely admit to purely exploitative motives.

The cover of public interest the government uses to hide its motivations for its restrictions is thicker and much, much more expensive both to rent seekers and to society as a whole. Thus, if Figure 8.2 represented a private monopoly the rent-seeking rectangle to the left would have very little motivation to adopt inefficient technologies. The vertically lined area would be very small, and the dotted area showing the resources invested in obtaining the monopoly would be very large. When we deal with the government, the reverse situation is likely to be true.

Public misunderstanding of the actual situation is more or less necessary for the average rent-seeking activity. There, total losses are greater than total gains, and hence a superior strategy is obviously available to people if they are fully informed and can coordinate their activities. Furthermore, as a normal rule, the number of people who gain is much smaller than the number who lose.

Logrolling in legislatures, of course, can frequently pass laws that benefit a minority at a dispersed cost to the majority. This is easier to do, however, if you can deceive the majority so as to minimize their opposition. Hence, in a democratic system, a straightforward transfer from the poor to the wealthy wheat producers would certainly not occur. There are then two ways such a transfer can be accomplished. People can be deceived about or simply not informed about the action. Minor revisions in proposals to benefit small groups are frequently implemented by the latter strategy.

Obviously the average citizen cannot possibly be familiar with all the clauses in even one major bill, so proposals can always slip through legislatures. This procedure is, however, decidedly risky. Scandals attract newspaper attention, and the public is likely to be indignant about them. For example, at the time I drafted this chapter (May 1987), Colorado's Democratic Senator Gary Hart had just withdrawn from the 1988 U.S. presidential race after being accused of committing adultery. Simultaneously, the U.S. Congress was investigating the possible illegal diversion of $10 million to $12 million to aid the Nicaraguan contras. Both of these defaults, from the standpoint of the normal functioning of the U.S. government, were trivial, but they both attracted attention and developed into major scandals. In trying to sneak something past the public, a special interest must always realize that such a public reaction is possible.

More commonly, programs are designed so that at least superficially plausible explanations account for them. Designing programs to have such superficial plausibility makes it necessary to use inefficient means. Direct cash payments are usually the most efficient way of helping interest groups, but they will not do. The costs of inefficient methods may be very great, particularly because, in general, a good deal of complication and indirection is desirable.

Political scientists have realized since Downs (1957) that if voters do not pursue politics as a hobby, they are usually very badly informed about it. Indeed, if they rationally choose subjects to read in newspapers, they will be "rationally ignorant" (Tullock 1976). Recently, another problem has been realized. In voting people may be motivated not by the actual outcome of the matter up for vote but by a desire to express their own emotion, feeling of virtue, and so on.[12] They may, in fact, vote directly against their interests because they realize that their votes have very little, if any, effect on the actual outcome of the election. Hence, they can get a feeling of moral satisfaction out of casting a virtuous vote without bearing a significant cost. Expressive votes may well lead to more waste than corrupt votes.

Ideology is also of great importance in voting. Whether this ideology is devotion to the nineteenth-century economic encyclicals of the pope of socialism, it is, in any event, not likely to lead to highly efficient policies. When it comes to rent seeking, we almost by definition are dealing with inefficient policies.[13]

CONCLUSION

I can think of no formal test of this hypothesis. I believe, however, that if readers consider the matter a little and think about how members of Congress act, how newspapers report political activities, and so on, they will accept it. Consider automobile quotas. The squabble is not just between U.S. auto manufacturers and unionists and potential purchasers of new cars. Other Americans not directly involved are apt to vote ideologically, if the matter is brought to their attention. Therefore, measures must be packaged so that they appear to voters to be somehow in accord with their ideology. Quotas are far better ways of doing that than are direct taxes and subsidy combinations.

Moreover, people not directly involved in an issue are overwhelmingly more numerous than special interests on either side. They must, therefore, be kept from intervening. Inefficient technology is the answer, and once again, it is what we observe. Politicians balance the interests of direct gainers and losers against each other. However, overwhelmingly important additional players – outsiders to a particular squabble – must be convinced that something other than a simple fight for pork is involved.[14]

My position that an inefficient technique is necessary to deceive voters is empirically fairly easily, but somewhat subjectively, testable. I have mentioned various efforts to have minor special interest provisions inserted in bills in the hopes they would not attract attention and the dangers of such efforts. An empirical study of cases in which secrecy has failed and matters have been brought to public attention would do. Additionally, the dissolution of the Civil Aeronautics Board and the current sharp restriction on the Interstate Commerce Commission both seem to have come about, at least in part, because the monopolylike managements of these two organizations became well-known. Derthick and Quirk's (1985) careful study agrees.

I would like to end by pointing out that, although I have been arguing that the required use of inefficient techniques is very expensive to society, it may be cheaper than direct cash payments. If obtaining special privileges requires the use of highly inefficient production techniques, then the resources that will be put into rent seeking for them are much lower than they would otherwise be. It is likely, therefore, that less of this restrictive special interest legislation will be passed than would be passed if direct payments were permitted.

Consider, for example, two proposals, one to make a direct cash payment to some group of people, the other to hire them at a price somewhat above their opportunity costs to build a dam somewhere. Assume that $1 million is available. In the first case, it would be paid directly to them, but in the second they would make a net profit of $100,000 after spending $900,000 building a dam (which we will assume is totally useless). The net social waste in each case is the same.

Nevertheless, the amount of rent seeking that we would expect is quite different in each case. Where direct payments to special interests are permitted, the resources invested in rent seeking are much larger: in the above case, $1 million as opposed to $100,000. Clearly, more special interest legislation would be passed under those circumstances. Thus, common citizens, in requiring that those government acts that do come to their attention fit into their ideas of what government should do, are probably doing good.

There is another advantage to this type of inefficiency. Almost all economists, whatever they say, are actually reformers who would like to improve the world. Their particular tool in this campaign is their ability to analyze various economic projects. A project that gives special benefits to some interest group by employing an inefficient production technique is the kind of thing economists are in a good position to attack. Pointing out that direct cash payments to farmers could give them the same amount of money that they get from the current program at less expense to consumers is fairly easy. It is also politically devastating to the farm program. Indeed, that is probably the reason the farmers have always been so violently opposed to talking about it in these terms.

Average voters, as we said above, are apt to be badly informed but interested in scandals. The inefficiencies we have described allow economists to convert special interest programs into scandals with the tools of their profession. A direct cash payment does not have this disciplinary connection, although economists, like political scientists or even philosophers, could complain about it. Hence, even though the main objective of this chapter has been to make the rent-seeking literature accord more with what we observe in everyday governmental activity, we end with the suggestion that what appears to be an extremely inefficient characteristic of democracy may actually improve the total efficiency of the system.

9

Toward a unified view of economics and the other social sciences

MANCUR OLSON

In the 1950s and 1960s, the main line of conceptual development in most of the social sciences was contradictory to that in economics. In most social sciences other than economics, the single most influential framework was probably the one the late Talcott Parsons presented. Economics, on the other hand, was not influenced by this framework and even proceeded along an opposing line. Diversity and debate are, of course, desirable, so these differences had their uses. Still, in another respect they were (or should have been) troubling. The substantive domains of the social sciences overlap a great deal, so the mutually contradictory frameworks sometimes led to opposing results that could not all be true. Scientific progress normally leads to scientific consensus, presumably because results become so compelling that all competent investigators are persuaded and professional disagreements focus on new and not-yet-settled issues that are, in turn, eventually often also resolved.[1]

In more recent years, the theoretical evolutions of the different social sciences have perhaps been more encouraging. The habits of thought in these sciences are probably not so different now as they were a couple of decades ago. Significant numbers of leading people in each of the social sciences are working along quite resonant lines. Work is also going on in different disciplines that is cumulative across disciplines. This is clearly true, for example, in the work on the Arrow paradox, on the theory of deterrence and strategy, on collective action and public goods, and on spatial models of political interaction.

I shall argue here that this tendency toward convergence is highly desirable and ought to be accelerated. In part, this is because of the old idea that reality is not divided into departments the way universities are. The same individuals are active in the marketplace, in the political system, and in social institutions such as friendships and families, and most of them act most of the time out of a single life plan or general purpose. The line of inquiry outlined in this chapter is accordingly inspired by the conviction that any effort to compartmentalize the substantive domains of disciplines is inevitably artificial and arbitrary.[2]

To be sure, everyday observation and common sense tell us that most individuals treat loved ones – and enemies – differently than they treat strangers or anonymous individuals. Thus the role that self-sacrifice and enmity play in social interaction obviously varies from circumstance to circumstance. But there are probably as many close relationships and as many enmities in, say, business as in government, so these differences in circumstances do not justify traditional disciplinary divisions. As it happens, a broader conception of human interaction can help to explain whether or not interactions are likely to be with anonymous individuals. Thus, I will argue here that no natural divisions separate economics and the other social sciences; all of them deal with one seamless reality.

On the other hand, some indivisibilities limit the supply of information available to researchers and policy makers in some areas of social science. These indivisibilities mainly explain the differences between economics (or rather, certain parts of economics) and the disciplines that have traditionally focused on the study of the political system and the social system.

I will attempt to make the foregoing claims meaningful by setting out five eccentric but practically important questions. It will be obvious, I think, that none of these questions could be answered within the *traditional* confines of the familiar disciplines; none could, for example, be answered within the discipline of economics as it was defined in Alfred Marshall's time. My contention is that I can make some limited progress toward answering these questions with an approach that treats the whole domain of economics and the other social sciences as one undivided field.

THE QUESTIONS

The first of my questions is about the puzzling relationship between economic growth and some other social phenomena. If there is a true increase in real income there is, of course, an expansion of the opportunity set. Individuals can obtain more of whatever goods they choose to consume. Thus, if other things are equal, it seems reasonable as well as customary to conclude that contentment or satisfaction has also increased.

Nonetheless, measured economic growth definitely does not have the clear positive correlations with independent measures of contentment or the clear negative correlations with some obvious signs of discontent that would naively be expected. As Easterlin (1973) first pointed out and as several subsequent studies have confirmed, economic growth does not by any means have the clear correlation with social psychologists' measurements of contentment that might be expected. It would be much too hasty to conclude that this means psychologists' measures are wrong, for vast numbers of surveys by many different investigators reveal a consistent and plausible pattern. In any society individuals with relatively high incomes give themselves higher contentment ratings (on arbitrary quantitative scales from 0 to 10, for example) than do people with low incomes. Yet average contentment ratings across societies show no (or virtually no) correlation with measured real per capita income and no increase over time when average real income increases.

This finding could perhaps still be dismissed as an artifact if other indications did not apparently reinforce it. Suicide must indicate a desperately low level of satisfaction. Yet preliminary research suggests that suicide rates tend to be markedly higher in rich societies and groups than in poor ones. The suicide rate across countries appears to be a fair measure of differences in levels of economic development. Similarly, increasing real incomes also appear to do little if anything to abate rates of mental illness, although any categorical conclusion on this point must await further research.

In addition, I claim to have shown elsewhere (Olson 1963) that rapid economic growth is by no means correlated with political manifestations of contentment and stability and has in an astonishing number of cases been followed directly by political protest and upheaval. The subsequent literature on this subject, mainly by political scientists and historians, has more often than not tended to support the claim in that article. Since 1963 the upheaval in newly rich Iran and the political protests in the United States during the prosperous 1960s have underlined the paradox.

The second question to which this research is addressed unfortunately does not initially appear to be at all precise, but it should become more meaningful when the concepts and tentative answers set out in the rest of this chapter have been presented. The question grows out of the everyday observation that when people greatly increase the proportion of their incomes they spend on some good, they usually speak favorably of that good. Thus, if the demand for personal computers or Japanese automobiles increases, there are usually also some other comments or signs of enthusiasm besides the increase in demand. There are exceptions, as when a cold winter brings an increased demand for fuel, but the idea that a shift in demand in the direction of a good would generally be associated with some other favorable assessments of the good is surely plausible.

Among the goods people in the United States and in other developed democracies have apparently decided to spend much larger proportions of their incomes on are those produced by governments. Over the last half century, and especially in the last two decades, the proportions of the national incomes of developed democracies that have been devoted to goods or services produced by governments (and also to transfers of income through governments) have increased dramatically (see Borcherding 1977, Peltzman 1980, or Meltzer and Richard 1981). As any student of the theory of social choice knows, one cannot blithely assume that elections in a democracy closely reflect an electorate's changing patterns of demands or preferences. Yet such a huge, long-lasting, and pervasive increase in the role of governments could not have occurred if there had not been a public demand for it.

But do we hear the same favorable comments and see the same signs of enthusiasm about governments, public bureaucracies, and politicians that are evident for most other goods to which increasing proportions of incomes are devoted? Surely people show nothing like the same enthusiasm about expanding public bureaucracies that they show for, say, more personal computers. Some of the complaints about big government come, of course, from those who have regularly espoused anti-government ideologies. Such complaints involve no paradox and so will be left aside here. But the impression that government bureaucracies are not especially efficient or responsive and that politics often leads to poor choices is also widespread on the left and in the center. Many people are enthusiastic about this or that candidate and sometimes also about a political party, but they appear to have little enthusiasm for government bureaucracy and politics per se. The paradox was perhaps illustrated best in the 1976 campaigns for the presidential nominations, where the four candidates who received the most votes in the primaries, including the ultimate winner of the office, all ran against Washington and big government, as did the winner of the next two presidential races. But the share of the net national product that the federal government consumes or transfers has not fallen significantly. Some similar phenomena occur in at least parts of Europe, with shorter tenures for incumbent governments, increasing dissatisfaction with governments, and even separatist movements occurring at the same time as governmental outputs and transfers take larger proportions of national incomes. Admittedly, the paradoxical question being posed here may not be altogether clear until the rest of the argument in this chapter has been stated, and readers are asked to suspend judgment until then. Still, there is surely already some intuitive meaning in the question, Why are the developed democracies consuming more government without appearing to enjoy it more (and maybe even enjoying it less) than before?

The third question grows out of the observation that public administration is not the same as business or private administration. Public administration is characterized by merit systems and other civil service or military regulations, by competitive bidding rules, and by reputedly greater quantities of red tape (the phrase *red tape* itself is derived from the color of the ribbon once used to tie bundles of papers in the British government). The differences between public and private administration are great enough that university courses in public administration are far removed from those in business administration.

So the question is, Why is public administration necessarily different from private administration? The merit systems and other peculiarities of public administration are often explained simply by the need to keep governing parties from using the entire governmental work force for patronage and thus corrupting the democratic process.[3] It turns out that, although this explanation contains an important element of truth, it is far from sufficient, as might be guessed from the fact that some dictatorships also use much the same civil service systems as democracies do and from the fact that the nationalized industries in many viable democracies do not follow civil service procedures.

The fourth question is, Why are some research fields or disciplines less tractable or less amenable to the rapid advance of knowledge – or simply less advanced – than others? The perception that some disciplines, like physics, are highly advanced whereas others, like sociology, are not, is well-nigh universal. The danger is, nonetheless, that the question just posed may be unoperational or metaphysical unless some objective or independent standard tells us how advanced different fields of research are. Although it has some shortcomings, scientific consensus will do as a standard here. A consensus among researchers, at least for a considerable period of time, suggests that there is a good probability of some compelling findings. A lack of consensus suggests that none of the contending schools of thought has come up with anything compelling. Every field of research will, of course, always contain some open or unsettled questions, but some will reach consensus on many findings and on basic theory. There is, for example, more consensus in physics than in sociology, in microeconomics than in macroeconomics (see Mankiw 1989; Plosser 1989), and in inorganic chemistry than in ecology or environmental science.

People sometimes say that some disciplines are more advanced than others because they attract more talented people. This explanation is, at best, insufficient, among other reasons because it neglects the requirements for equilibrium in the labor market. If an average physicist could become the Copernicus of sociology, he or she need only shift fields in order to obtain immortal distinction, and it is beyond belief that all able physicists would resist such a reward. The lesser consensus in macroeconomics than in microeconomics could also not possibly be explained by any differences in talent in the two fields, since leaders in the one field of economics are often also leaders in the other. It is much more reasonable to hypothesize that some aspects of reality are more tractable, or easier to get a handle on, than others. The ideas that are set out later in this chapter provide an explanation of why some aspects of reality are more amenable to research than others.

The final question is one I am defensive about. This defensiveness arises because of the long and honorable role of specialization in science and scholarship. We have known since the time of Adam Smith that the division of labor can often increase productivity in an economy, and modern economic growth has undoubtedly been associated with increased specialization. In science and scholarship specialization has surely brought similar benefits, and almost anyone who has directed student research knows how important it is to pass on a feel for narrow and manageable research projects. Scientists are perhaps most of all specialists who know their places.

Yet colossal as the gains from specialization are, they do not alter the fact that specialization also has some costs and that occasionally the findings and models in different specializations need to be integrated. Within disciplines this is done from time to time in survey articles, interpretive books, and even in textbooks. But it is rarely done across disciplines, at least in the social sciences. Yet, as was argued earlier in this chapter, integration is occasionally needed here, too; words such as "economic," "political," and "social" do not refer to well-defined and independent spheres of reality.

Thus the final question is, How can we theoretically unify all of social science? The subsequent portions of this chapter explain how I believe this question should be answered.

INDIVISIBILITIES AND UTILITY FUNCTIONS

Let us now examine the idea that will be used here to begin to answer the first of the foregoing questions, about why economic growth often is associated with increased discontent. This idea also is expected to provide a part of the answer to the fourth question, about why some fields of research are more tractable than others.

These questions are, it is argued, intimately bound up with the question of what goods do and do not fall under what A.C. Pigou, following Alfred Marshall, called "the measuring rod of money." One essential feature of these matters can be stated rather easily. Marshall almost hit on the essence of the matter when he tried to explain why he believed economics had made more progress than the other social sciences.

The advantage which economics has over other branches of social science appears then to arise from the fact that its special field of work gives rather larger opportunities for exact methods than any other branch. It concerns itself chiefly with those desires, aspirations and other affections of human nature, the outward manifestations of which appear as incentives to action in such a form that the force or quantity of the incentives can be estimated and measured with some approach to accuracy; and which therefore are in some degree amenable to treatment by scientific machinery. An opening is made for methods and the tests of science as soon as the force of a person's motives – *not* the motives themselves – can be approximately measured by the sum of money, which he will just give up in order to secure a desired satisfaction; or again by the sum which is just required to induce him to undergo a certain fatigue.

Thus though it is true that "money" or "general purchasing power" or "command over wealth," is the centre around which economic science clusters; this is so, not because money or material wealth is regarded as the main aim of human effort, nor even as affording the main subject-matter for the study of the economist, but because in this world of ours it is the one convenient means of measuring human motive on a large scale.

(*Principles of Economics*, 8th ed., 1920)

In the modern economist's language what Marshall said was that whenever individuals can take more or less of each of any pair of goods they consume, they will so adjust their consumption that the marginal rate of substitution between the two goods equals the ratio of their prices. This also means, as we know, that individuals can have greatly different tastes and incomes, yet if they face the same price ratios they have the same marginal rates of substitution between every pair of goods they consume, as is the case of the two consumers depicted in Figure 9.1. This surely helps explain why national income statistics and cost-benefit studies of public projects attract so much interest.

Marshall somehow did not ask what distinguished those phenomena, generally studied by other branches of social science, that cannot so readily be measured monetarily. Yet the answer is obvious. Consumers reveal their marginal valuations of the goods economists traditionally have studied by taking a little more or less until the marginal evaluation equals the price; *the goods that do not readily come under the measuring rod of money are those which, because of one type of indivisibility or another, the individual cannot take a little more or less of,* at least over some pertinent range.

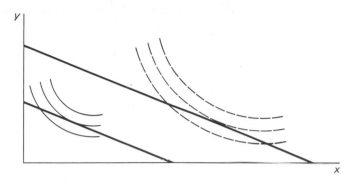

Figure 9.1. Equal marginal rates of substitution for two consumers.

This idea has long been understood for the special case of classical public goods, where it has long been understood that the indivisibility that entails collective consumption tends to prevent different individuals from consuming or receiving different amounts of the public good. But the problem of the nonrevelation of preferences for public goods is only a special case of a vastly more general set of problems. All of the social and political problems that have proved more difficult than ordinary market phenomena to understand are more difficult principally because they contain certain indivisibilities. One of the ways these indivisibilities make the problems more difficult to analyze is by limiting the revelation of preferences – by obscuring what Marshall called "the force of a person's motive."

Indivisibilities in utility functions complicate social and political problems in several different ways, but it may be sufficient to discuss just one of them. Suppose we ask what differentiates an acquaintanceship from a friendship. It would surely be agreed that "*n* acquaintances" are not always a perfect substitute for "one true friend." But why not? Whatever else it involves, a friendship lasts a certain time and implies some mutual commitment. But if so, friendship entails at least some degree of indivisibility; at least a certain minimum interaction, commitment, or other expenditure is required to get any friendship at all. A lesser outlay buys something qualitatively different.

Similarly, one of the things that distinguishes a marriage from, say, transactions with a prostitute is not that prostitution involves exchange. Marriage also involves the exchange of valuable goods and services, and this is even recognized in everyday language, such as when people speak of an "unequal marriage." But a relationship cannot be a marriage unless it involves at least some minimal duration, interaction, or commitment – unless it involves an indivisibility; a smaller involvement gives something qualitatively different. I expect eventually to be able to show convincingly that other distinctively social groups, such as social clubs and cohesive communities (and all groups in which the concept of status can be meaningful), also entail indivisibilities. These indivisibilities also obscure preferences to some extent. A relationship subject to indivisibilities may be intact only because it provides minuscule net benefits, or it may be intact because it provides colossal benefits. Preferences will only be clearly revealed if it is dissolved.[4]

To see the practical significance of this, return to the paradoxical relationship of measures of economic growth and other signs or measures of contentment and discontent. Rapid economic growth cannot occur unless rapid changes of one kind or another causes it. New technologies must be exploited or new resources discovered or new capital goods employed. Whatever the source of the growth, it will often be optimal for labor to work in new combinations or work groups, often in new locations. The incentive to innovate and to take risks, which is usually tied up with rapid growth, will also imply that many rise in the social order whereas others fall – there will be nouveaux riches and nouveaux pauvres.

So rapid economic growth with its recombinations of workers and geographical and social mobility entails the disruption of a wide array of valued social links and relationships (Olson 1982). Some valuable new social relationships will emerge in any new situation, but because of the indivisibilities, they take time to develop; their development may also be disrupted by continued rapid growth.

Long-standing social relationships that are broken up during periods of rapid change and growth presumably produced some valuable outputs to those involved in them or else they would not have been maintained in the first place. These valuable outputs are not usually measured in income statistics because they fall beyond the measuring rod of money. The gains from the increased output of marketed goods that rapid growth brings about are measured in national income statistics, but the losses from the severance of valued social relationships are not measured. So, if we leave other important aspects of the matter aside, we can see that income statistics in a period of rapid growth and change tend to overstate welfare gains: They measure extra output but leave out what falls beyond the measuring rod of money.

The social costs of rapid economic growth must not be exaggerated. Presumably no social relationship would be abandoned, even in a period of rapid growth, unless the individual who abandoned it thought the gains from moving to a new work group, location, or social situation were greater than the losses entailed in abandoning the relationship. Therefore, there is no suggestion here that rapid growth on balance reduces welfare; the point is rather that in cases of rapid growth income statistics will, if other things are equal, overstate gains.

But some individuals may be worse off – even some individuals whose real money income appears to rise. Although individuals will not leave valued social groups unless they expect net gains by doing so, they may neglect the losses to *other* group members that result from their departure. To take a poignant example from modern life, consider a person who leaves an immobile employed spouse in order to obtain a good job in a distant city, thereby dissolving a marriage. The person who moved presumably anticipated net benefits, but both partners do not necessarily gain. To relate the argument to traditional society, consider the example of a traditional village, which in a period of rapid growth loses many of its residents to high-paying opportunities far away. Those who are left behind may lose a great deal, especially if the village also loses economies of scale. This helps to explain why traditional groups can bitterly rebel against all that is modern even as their measured incomes rise, a situation that has occurred recently in Iran.

To be sure, many other factors are involved in anything so complex and profound as a social upheaval, and I do not imply that such changes occur from one cause. It may nonetheless be useful to think about such upheavals from the perspective that has just been described here.

Though an important part of the explanation for why some fields of research are less tractable or advanced than others will not be evident even in an intuitive fashion until we get to the next section, the way one aspect of the matter could be studied should already be evident. As Marshall pointed out in the quotation set out earlier, the preferences for some goods – notably those readily traded in the market – easily fall under the measuring rod of money. The strength of the preferences for these goods is accordingly easily revealed, and behavior is more easily understood. By contrast, when indivisibilities are present, as they are when economists study public goods or when political scientists study politics (almost all of which involves public goods or other indivisibilities), relevant preferences are not readily revealed. Indivisibilities similarly obscure the relevant preferences or values when sociologists study social groups and social problems.

INDIVISIBILITIES AND PRODUCTION FUNCTIONS

We also need to examine the idea that I believe helps answer the second question (about why we are using government more and enjoying it less than before) and the third question (about what necessarily distinguishes public from private administration). This idea also helps provide the remainder of the answer to the fourth question (about why some fields of study are more difficult than others). This is the idea that there are also indivisibilities that obscure social production functions, or relationships between inputs and outputs in areas of public concern, and conceal the cause-and-effect relationships in intractable fields of research.

The idea that some indivisibilities prevent certain production function and cause-and-effect relationships from being revealed can best be examined by starting with areas where such indivisibilities are absent or insignificant. Such areas would include much of chemistry and physics. The study of atoms and molecules must have been handicapped by the invisibility of such minute phenomena (the diameter of a water molecule is about one hundred-millionth of an inch, or about one three-thousandth of the wavelength of green light), yet we know that physicists and chemists have learned a great deal indeed about them. One reason so much has been learned is that the number of atoms of any element or of the molecules of any compound is unimaginably large (by Avogadro's constant, there are 6.0225×10^{23}, or somewhat less than a trillion trillion, molecules in a mole of a substance). Information about a small number of the atoms or molecules in any given class will, because they are relatively homogeneous, provide knowledge about the rest.

It might seem at first that this is just another way of explaining that controlled experiments are possible in physics and chemistry and that such experiments have helped these disciplines become relatively advanced and exact. Not so. Consider stars, which could hardly be the object of controlled experiments but which are nonetheless surprisingly well understood. A likely explanation is that there are so many stars for astronomers to observe, even at each stage of stellar evolution (because the light from more distant galaxies takes longer to reach the earth), that they have come to understand the life cycles of stars relatively well. Stars, like molecules, constitute what will here be called *multitudinous sets*.

The immediate economic significance of multitudinous sets is evident from some practical problems this investigator has considered in previous publications, such as determining the dose-response relationship between nitrogen or some other plant nutrient and the yields of an agricultural commodity. About all that anyone needs to know about the extent to which varying levels of fertilization will change crop yields in different soil and moisture conditions can be determined from a few hundred experimental plots, each the size of a small room. Wheat plants are incomparably larger than molecules, and the conditions un-

222

der which they are grown are normally less homogeneous than the molecules and the conditions that might be of interest to the chemist. This can somewhat increase the cost of getting the dose-response relationships for fertilizers. Nonetheless, the cost of this information is minuscule in relation to the wheat crop's value; the cost of the experiments over the value of output approaches zero. It will, of course, pay to continue experiments into the dose-response relationship until the marginal cost of an additional experiment is equal to its expected marginal value. But even when this point is reached, the total cost of the experiments is likely to be very small in relation to their total value. The research of Zvi Griliches (1958) and others supports this conclusion by showing that the total cost of developing new plant varieties and other agronomic information has tended to be small in relation to total benefits.

If we now switch our attention to ecological systems we have an entirely different problem. An ecological system is by definition a mutually interdependent set of relationships – an indivisible system – so it is not possible to obtain the information that is needed about the whole system by experimenting with a limited number of plots or test tubes and assuming the results apply to all of phenomena involved. Something can be learned by comparing one ecological system with another, but because of the major indivisibilities involved there are far fewer ecological systems than molecules. These systems are, moreover, more heterogeneous than any particular class of molecules or variety of wheat plants. So it is no accident that ecologists more often fail to reach consensus than do researchers in most other physical and natural sciences.

By virtue of indivisibilities, ecologists are confronted not with a multitudinous set but with a *scant set*. At the extreme the set may contain only one member. Consider the hypothesis that continued burning of fossil fuels will create a greenhouse effect that will dangerously increase the temperature of our planet or the hypothesis that the release of chlorofluorocarbons from refrigeration equipment and aerosol sprays will destroy the ozone layer that protects us from deadly radiation. Here the fact that winds blow all around the earth and give the planet a single stratosphere and meteorological system introduces a worldwide indivisibility. Although the chemistry of carbon dioxide and of ozone molecules is well-known, years of expensive studies have so far failed to resolve scientific disputes about either the greenhouse effect or the ozone layer. In large part the problem is that no experiment could be decisive except for one on the whole planet and that decisive observations about experimental outcomes may be made only on one system in any one period. Here the distinction between experiment and

223

policy disappears, and the ratio of the cost of experiment to the value of the output becomes one.

What relevance do indivisibilities that obscure cause-and-effect relationships have for economic, political, and social life? Although some indivisibilities in nature have no special consequence for the social sciences, some of the most fundamental problems in economic and political life *never* occur unless there are indivisibilities. Specifically, an indivisibility always exists whenever either of the following exists:

1. A nonexclusive public good (that is, a good that nonpurchasers cannot be excluded from and so must be collectively consumed). In all such cases it is not possible for the good to be divided up into units that are provided to some consumers and denied to others, but all must share the same indivisible level of provision – there is what will here be called shared indivisibility.

2. Economies of scale in production. If all inputs are completely divisible, the combination of productive factors that at given factor price ratios produces the lowest production cost per unit can be replicated at lower levels of output to produce the same unit cost. The indivisibilities in productive inputs that generate economies of scale will here be called lumpy indivisibilities.

Though economies of scale are tied into interesting issues of market structure (if average costs did not rise no matter how small the firm, there could, of course, easily be so many producers of every product that there was always pure competition), the focus here is not on issues of industrial organization. It is rather on the extreme cases where economies of scale are so great in relation to demand that, at a Pareto-efficient level of provision of the good, the marginal cost of providing a unit to an additional consumer is negligible (or at least much less than the average cost). Under those conditions, any firm that provided anything approaching a Pareto-efficient supply without price discrimination could not cover its costs; if the good is to be provided, it will have to be provided publicly. Public goods that exhibit nonrivalness (more consumption by some does not mean less for others) but not nonexclusion (e.g., goods such as bridges and roads in areas where congestion is not an issue, so that the marginal social cost of an additional user is zero) can then be defined as the result of an economy of scale and thus to lumpy indivisibilities.

Consider first cases of shared indivisibility – that is, a public good from which nonpurchasers cannot be excluded. In all such cases there must be three important types of information loss or difficulty.

1. Because of the indivisibility, any experiment must involve the whole group that receives the good and is therefore more costly. More-

over, only one empirical observation of natural variation (unintended experiments) can occur per period. Public goods, and particularly those of concern to national governments and other large jurisdictions, thus constitute a scant rather than a multitudinous set. There are many interesting illustrations of this point, but this investigator's favorite is the difference in the existing knowledge of the relationship between smoking and health (which in general involves no significant indivisibility and has been estimated rather precisely) and the relationship between air pollution and health (which involves an indivisibility at the level of the metropolitan area or community and is still utterly unsettled despite many skilled studies). The persistent disagreements about what foreign and defense policies would best safeguard a nation's security or what public policies would best reduce crime arise mainly because indivisibilities obscure relevant production functions. How could France in the 1930s get empirical information about whether to defend itself with a Maginot line or with planes and tanks without actually fighting a war to find out? (Even now the answer isn't certain: France might have lost even with a different military strategy.) Ideologies are, of course, involved in most disagreements about public policies, but ideologies about what works or doesn't work can survive indefinitely only where empirical information about cause and effect is poor.

2. Because of a good's shared indivisibility, it is not divisible into units that can be counted or straightforwardly measured, which usually denies the government a direct measure of the quantity produced. Even if such a measure is available, the nonrevelation of preferences for public goods means the value of this output is not known. The government therefore cannot usually obtain the information about changes in its output's value that is normally available to a firm selling goods or services.

3. Because shared indivisibility entails that the supplier (government) must have a monopoly, at least over some area or group, society is denied the knowledge of how well or cheaply some alternative supplier could have provided the output (except in certain cases where Tiebout-like voting with the feet costs very little). This means that even if the existing government's production function and citizens' valuation of its output could be known there would still be ignorance about the production function and the value of the output of some other government or administration system.

Although it would take too long to go into nonrival public goods here, I claim that the first and third of the foregoing problems also necessarily apply to these goods, with the first problem being slightly less severe than with shared indivisibility.

The consequence of all this is that a government, when it is fulfilling functions that only governments can fulfill, faces a variety of exceptional information problems that are different from those the private sector confronts. These information difficulties have never been adequately analyzed or researched. They do not have a huge bearing on what a government's role ought to be, because they are inherent in the functions that involve such a degree of market failure that the private sector will normally not perform them at all (and if it did, it would have some of the same information problems). Although the familiar arguments against public provision of goods that would be efficiently provided by the market still apply, the *information* problems a government faces when it provides such goods (which are, of course, private goods that can be produced without any overwhelming indivisibility) are relatively minor in comparison with those it faces when undertaking activities only a government can perform.

SOME IMPLICATIONS

It is now clear how the foregoing argument relates to the second question, about why modern democratic societies are using government more but not enjoying or admiring it more, as people allocating more of their income to a good might be expected to do. If what has been said is correct, government activity or production must take place in the dark, or at best in dim light, because of its inherent paucity of information. There will accordingly always be wasted motion, stumbling, and ineffectiveness. The larger the proportion of a society's resources its government consumes, the greater the absolute value of the losses and the more serious the concern about them. By the foregoing argument, the inherent lack of information is bound to cause a lot of waste and ineffectiveness, but sometimes also needless (even inexcusable) mistakes and unnecessary losses will, of course, also occur.

My hunch is that average citizens acquire from experience the notion that government bureaucracies do not (in an intuitively meaningful sense) operate with acceptable efficiency but that this experience naturally does not explain the information problems that cause this inefficiency. Thus, average citizens may attribute too much quantitative significance to the needless mistakes and to the human shortcomings of leading managers and politicians. Accordingly, the public is greatly susceptible to political campaigns that promise to cut out "waste, fraud, and abuse" (Reagan), to reorganize the government on a "businesslike basis" (Carter), and so on. But waste, fraud, and abuse are unfortunately not line items in the federal budget, and the public soon realizes they have not been eliminated. Reorganization and the creation of new departments similarly cannot solve information problems, and the public soon realizes it has been beguiled by false promises. Meanwhile, perceptions, sometimes valid and sometimes invalid, of social problems or market failures require additional government action, and perceptions of political pressures (described in my *Rise and Decline of Nations*) make the government grow at the same time that incumbent presidents and bureaucrats are attacked for what is wrongly supposed to be entirely unnecessary waste and ineffectiveness. Of course, other factors are also relevant.

The implications of the argument in the foregoing section for the third question, about what necessarily distinguishes public from private administration, are absolutely fundamental. The foregoing section demonstrated that, when a nonexclusive public good is at issue, the production function is unknown, the quantity and value of the output of the public good is unknown, and the value an alternative government or administration could offer is also unknown. In these circumstances, citizens cannot know either what output they are actually getting from a government agency or what output they ought to get with the resources allocated to that agency. They have even less knowledge of how much output or value any civil servant adds, any particular expenditure adds, or any particular way of organizing public production adds. Thus, in the absence of special constraints, nothing stops public officials from diverting public moneys to their own pockets, from hiring additional officials because of their party affiliations or personal allegiances, from loafing on the job, from making purchases from favorite rather than low-cost suppliers, and so on. The impact of such neglect on the public trust will presumably be a less efficient government, but the extent of this diminution of efficiency cannot be measured or even documented for the reasons explained in the previous section. Government agencies producing public goods and the particular people and other resources that they employ accordingly cannot be assessed or paid in terms of their productivity. Piece-rate or commission payment is inherently impossible for activities that only governments can perform.

Skeptics should be persuaded of this argument's force the moment they think of the implications that would follow if it were *not* true. If the public knew of every sparrow's fall, there would be no need for special constraints on government personnel and procedures. If public officials hired family members for their staffs and bought government supplies from their relatives, there would be no more reason for concern than if the local grocer hired his son to work in the store; all citizens need to do is judge whether they are getting maximum value for the tax moneys devoted to the government. There would be no need to worry about the administration buying votes in the next election by giving government jobs to those who promised to vote for it, for this inefficient method of obtaining inputs would show up in a reduction of public outputs that would lead to the defeat of the incumbent government.

The manifest unrealism of the assumption made in the preceding paragraph should not only support the argument of the prior section but also remind us that the familiar explanation of government merit systems, competitive bidding rules, and so on, as rules required to maintain the integrity of the democratic process, is insufficient. Without the paucity of information described in the preceding section, the typical constraints on public bureaucracy would not be needed to protect the integrity of the democratic process.

I would also answer the third question, about what necessarily distinguishes public from private administration, by invoking the information problems inherent in indivisibilities. The special constraints in the form of merit systems, competitive bidding rules, and the like that characterize typical public bureaucracies should be regarded mainly as necessary substitutes for the lack of good information on whether each government agency or official has provided good value and as constraints against the special opportunities for misconduct that the lack of such information on value produced makes available. These special constraints, though usually necessary, also make public bureaucracies less flexible and innovative, thereby aggravating the difficulty of efficiently providing public goods.

This conception of the necessary peculiarities of public administration can be tested by examining government enterprises that do *not* provide public goods but rather produce private goods that markets normally supply. Can such public enterprises sometimes get along without special civil service constraints, as the argument in the foregoing section implies should be possible? Preliminary evidence suggests that nationalized firms operating in somewhat competitive markets, such as Renault in France or Volkswagen some years ago in Germany, have in fact not been subject to the usual civil service constraints and, as the theory predicts, appear to have been able to avoid gross abuses of public trust without them.

Consider also bureaucracies in business firms. Preliminary research again suggests that the rules constraining such bureaucracies are less confining than those applied to bureaucracies providing public goods, and that the strongest constraints applied to bureaucracies in the private sector are also explained by indivisibilities – indivisibilities due to economies of scale.

The argument in the preceding section also provides a fresh perspective on various efforts to reform and improve public bureaucracy and decision making, such as the Planning-Programming-Budgeting System of the Kennedy and Johnson administrations and the civil service reforms in the Carter administration. Preliminary and journalistic, but nonetheless interesting, evidence about these reform attempts is readily available. The *Washington Post,* for example, ran a series of articles in January 1983 on how the Carter administration reform of paying bonuses to civil servants who were exceptionally productive was working out. Their main finding was summarized in a headline on January 18 that read, "Without a bottom line, the merit system is earning demerits"; the most common view among the many interviewees close to the situation was that the allocation of the bonuses was arbitrary and divisive because the government did not know who was really productive. It does not follow from the argument in the preceding section that cash bonuses for cherished civil servants is necessarily a bad idea, given the federal government's rigid personnel system. Even so, the reactions to the bonus pay system are what the argument here would have led one to expect.

The implications of the arguments on indivisibilities in preceding sections for the fourth question, of why some research fields are less tractable than others, are no doubt already obvious, so very little needs to be said about them here. The field of macroeconomics, for example, is less tractable than microeconomics, because macroeconomics deals with a whole national economy as an indivisible unit and there are fewer national economies (and especially national economies that approximate closed systems) than there are individual markets, which are the concern of microeconomics. It should therefore be no surprise that there is consensus about most matters in microeconomics but conflicting schools of thought of macroeconomics. The study of social problems and sociology is made more difficult by the nonrevelation of preferences or values described early in this chapter. The empirical study of public goods and of political science is made more difficult not only by the nonrevelation of utility functions but also by the obscurity of production functions and cause-and-effect relationships in the presence of indivisibilities.

TOWARD A UNIFIED THEORY OF SOCIAL SCIENCE

The answer that will be given here to the fifth question, about how to unify the theory of social science, will long have been obvious to readers who have read very many of my prior writings. The method for unifying the social sciences that I use is not original with me but is evident even in the work of Adam Smith. It is essentially the same method used by economists such as Kenneth Arrow, James Buchanan, Anthony Downs, Thomas Schelling, and Gordon Tullock in their work on public or social choice and problems of strategy; the same method that an increasing number of deductively oriented students of politics (such as William Riker and his students) have used in developing a genuinely theoretical approach to political science; and the same method that has been used in the study of law and economics since at least Guido Calebresi's initial work on this topic.

Sometimes those with only a passing acquaintance with the foregoing writers suppose that they assume only materialistic or monetary motivations for individuals and are incapable of incorporating altruistic elements in human behavior. Although some writers have chosen to belittle altruistic and nonfinancial objectives, this is by no means inherent in the method. Roughly speaking, the method can be easily used so long as behavior is broadly purposive and generally consistent. Altruistic behavior need create no problems for a unified approach to social science, at least so long as the objectives, altruistic or selfish, are characterized by diminishing marginal rates of substitution. This is hardly a very restrictive condition.

Distant observers sometimes also suppose that any methodology with economic theory as one of its parents must inevitably be biased ideologically and perhaps also biased toward one or the other ideological extremes; it must support a classical liberal or a conservative viewpoint or alternatively be a type of Marxian economic determinism. This supposition is not, so far as I know, taken seriously by anyone who understands economic theory. Therefore, refuting it is a task for remedial education rather than for any work that strives toward scientific originality. It is nonetheless my hope that the foregoing questions are so obviously removed from the ideological conflicts of the time that any system of thinking, like economic theory, that helps answer them is unlikely to be a mere ideology.

As I see it, the only gulf that has stood in the way of a unified theory of social science has been a lack of awareness of the indivisibilities evident in every area of social science other than classical microeconomics – in every area that falls beyond the measuring rod of money. Once we recognize these indivisibilities and realize we must work in their shadow, many heretofore insoluble problems (like the often paradoxical association between economic growth and discontent) are readily clarified.

Unified view of economics and social sciences

Once these indivisibilities are understood, I claim the way is clear for a correct and unified approach to such once-distinct subjects as law and economics, for a theoretically unified core curriculum for schools of public affairs, and for a unified approach to social science in general.

Notes

2. MACROPOLITICAL ECONOMY IN THE FIELD OF DEVELOPMENT

1 The favorite political topic was racial tension in the United States; the favorite cultural topic, miniskirts.

2 Many of us in the development field began fully to comprehend what we had been told by Barrington Moore half a decade before: that rural dwellers provided the revolutionary class of our time (see Moore 1966).

3 Examples are provided in Peter Fishburn (1974); see especially the dominated winner paradox, in which a commonly employed voting procedure can lead to the choice of alternative y even though *every* voter would prefer alternative x.

4 Historically, the potential for external effects led to the endorsement of "big push" efforts at industrialization. As guardians of the collective welfare, governments were held to be more sensitive to the external benefits a productive investment creates than private firms would be (see Rosenstein-Rodan 1943; Nurske 1953; Scitovsky 1954). As Lal (1983) and other critics (Little 1982) presciently point out, there is no particular reason to expect governments to make the correct choice either. The failure of private decisions may imply the necessity for public ones, but not their correctness.

5 In this section I have not discussed a strand in the literature that has recently grown in prominence: the concept of the political market. For an example, see Hayami (1988).

The fact is that there is no political market. There are institutions other than markets through which preferences aggregate into outcomes. Some of these are political institutions. The challenge is to analyze the equilibria that are achieved within them and thus how political outcomes occur. The results of these analyses will not look like conventional economic results. They will not be the kinds of equilibria found in price theory or the results achieved by employing a social welfare function to assign weights to the preferences of different interest. Rather, they will look like equilibria achieved through the strategic choices of actors involved in games in which the rules of the political institutions influence their choices and thus final outcomes. A major point of this chapter is that it is time to apply such reasoning to the study of the politics of the developing areas.

6 How, then, do peasant rebellions occur? Popkin's contribution was to address this problem and to analyze how political revolutionaries overcome incentives to free ride (Popkin 1979).

7 Two closely related approaches vividly exhibit this tendency: the theory of rent seeking and capture theory. For the former, see Krueger (1974); Colander (1984); Lal (1984); and Srinivasan (1985). For an introduction to the latter, see Stigler (1971). An example is provided by the literature on campaign contributions (Jacobson 1980).

8 An illustration of the significance of these dynamics is offered by agricultural programs in the United States, where the creation of the Department of Agriculture led to the subsequent formation of new groups, some promoted by bureaucrats hoping to create active support in Congress for agricultural programs (see McConnell 1953).

9 A major implication of this analysis is that the proper role of large, organized interests in such instrumentalist theories is to account for the perpetuation of policies rather than their creation.

10 According to Black's Theorem, a sufficient condition for a majority rule winner to exist is that there be a unidimensional issue space and that preferences be single peaked (Black 1958; see also Rabushka and Shepsle 1972).

11 This insight motivated the early work of Guillermo O'Donnell (1973), whose formulation proved too broad and imprecise to withstand close scrutiny (Collier 1979). At more of a microlevel, I have employed this line of reasoning to account for the development and structure of agrarian institutions in Kenya (Bates 1989). Critical to the analysis of this problem is the work of Williamson (1985).

12 The relevant critiques and some significant steps at refounding the analysis on appropriate microfoundations are to be found in Cohen (1978), Roemer (1982), and Elster (1985).

For many reasons, the program will be difficult to complete. One main difficulty is that if this line of analysis requires institutions to be conceived of as investments made by optimizing agents, then innovations cannot be studied singly, as they are now. What would represent an optimum innovation would depend on the portfolio of other investments already held. To illustrate: An investor in an agricultural project in Florida would possess a different repertoire of instruments for handling risks than would an investor in Kenya; for that reason alone the Florida investor could be expected to create a different institutional form for that investment.

Williamson's analysis (1985), where given institutional designs are analyzed apart from the other means of dealing with risks, is thus not strictly valid. The problem becomes particularly significant when the origins of institutions are examined internationally and across systems with different kinds of capital markets.

3. BARGAINING COSTS, INFLUENCE COSTS, AND THE ORGANIZATION OF ECONOMIC ACTIVITY

1 Identifying efficiency with expected total wealth maximization requires assumptions that are maintained throughout most of this literature, including risk neutrality (preferences being linear in a freely transferable good, usually money, in terms of which values are expressed), access to a smoothly func-

tioning capital market, and common beliefs about the likelihoods of uncertain events. All of these are clearly restrictive. An important implication of the hypothesis of wealth maximization is that the actions that should (and will) be taken and the way in which benefits of joint action will be shared are determined separately. In particular, such factors as relative bargaining power are irrelevant in determining economic organization. This prediction contrasts sharply with those of Marxian theories, in which power and class interests are prime determinants.

2 Yoram Barzel (1982) credits Steven Cheung (1974) with introducing the idea that "markets are organized to minimize dissipation." Certainly, earlier authors were often less than careful, arguing that arrangements were made to minimize transaction costs rather than to maximize wealth, and one still sees such statements.

3 For example, the phenomenon of second-sourcing in the semiconductor industry involves accepting increased production costs through lost economies of scale and learning curve effects to reduce the transaction costs that would arise in a monopolized market. Firms developing new integrated circuits regularly assist competing firms to become second sources of supply for the product, even when this involves significant production cost inefficiencies because potential customers would otherwise be reluctant to design their products to use the new input for fear that, once committed, they would be exploited by the monopoly supplier. See Shepard (1987) and Farrell and Gallini (1986).

4 These core economic models are sometimes argued to be inconsistent with the ideas that (1) firms are managed by individuals with limited abilities to process information and to calculate and make consistent decisions; and (2) firms respond to changing circumstances in the short run simply by following established procedures or routines. To evaluate this argument, notice that the formal theory, as presented, for example, by Debreu (1959), incorporates the possibility that a production plan can be uncertain or contingent, using inputs and producing outputs in a way that depends on emergent events and past decisions. Such production plans can include uncertain research and development, organizational routines, the use of boundedly rational supervisory and managerial personnel as inputs to production, the development of skilled managers as outputs, and so on. Consequently, the propositions established by Debreu and others in the context of abstract, general economic models necessarily apply also to more specific and detailed models in which firms may be actively managed by boundedly rational managers or in which a firm's behavior is determined by standard procedures, provided that the firm, recognizing its production possibilities, including the constraints imposed by its managers' bounded rationality, chooses its plan optimally.

5 *The American Heritage Dictionary of the English Language* (Boston: Houghton Mifflin, 1980).

6 Chandler's impressive account (1962) of how management at Du Pont, General Motors, Sears, and Standard Oil of New Jersey discovered the multidivisional structure indicates the extent to which some managers can innovate to rationalize the organization of production.

7 The remainder of this section will focus on what may be called the asset specificity branch of transaction-cost economics. The second, measurement costs branch is discussed very briefly in the section on bargaining costs.

8 In economic terminology, a rent is an excess return: The rent a supplier receives consists of any portion of the receipts on a good or service in excess of the minimum amount needed to get the supplier to provide the good in the first place, before any commitments are made or investments sunk. (This minimum amount is called the *normal return*.) Quasi-rents, by contrast, are part of a normal return. They consist of the smaller of two amounts – the amount being received and the amount necessary to induce the original supply decision (the normal return) – minus the amount required to prevent a supplier from ceasing to produce. Thus, positive quasi-rents exist when the current price is sufficient to keep an existing supplier active, even if it is not high enough to have attracted the supplier into the industry *de novo*.

Normally, quasi-rents arise as a return on a sunk investment. For example, an employee whose high pay is attributable partly to long hours invested in learning the ins and outs of a company is said to earn quasi-rents.

As we use the terms here, buyers can also earn rents or quasi-rents. These can be measured as the difference between what buyers actually pay for their purchases and the highest amounts they would be willing to pay.

9 An asset is an owned factor of production, something that contributes to the production of goods or services. To say that it is specialized means that its value is greatest in one particular relationship. Another way to describe the same situation is to say that the relationship itself is an asset, a factor that increases production. It is a specialized asset because its value – the appropriable quasi-rents – evaporates when the relationship is dissolved. Note, however, a subtle but important difference in these formulations: A physical asset can presumably be sold, a relationship cannot.

10 Variations of this argument are given by Klein, Crawford, and Alchian (1978); Grout (1984); Williamson (1986); Tirole (1986); and Grossman and Hart (1986). We examine this argument critically in a later section, but first we recap the argument as it has been made before.

11 Levi Strauss's television advertising contract for the 1980 Olympic games, signed in 1977, gives some idea of how detailed (and prescient) some contracts can be. It specified that in the event the U.S. team did not compete, no payments would be due.

12 As General Motors and Fisher Body did in the example cited.

13 Notice that increases in the frequency of interactions among the parties in a mutually profitable relationship *reduces* the problem of rent appropriation because the parties will be reluctant to endanger their future relations. The frequency of opportunities for appropriation of rents, not the frequency of transactions per se, gives rise to the scale economies of specialized governance.

14 Of course, this leaves open the question of what the costs of common ownership might be.

15 Or wages paid to those who prepare bids and those who solicit and evaluate them in case competitive bidding is used to set the price.

16 This assumption includes the possibilities that the bargainers maximize the expected present value of profits at some fixed discount rates or at discount rates that properly reflect the correlation of project returns with other aggregate risks. These objectives for the firm are widely used in the theory of financial economics.

Interestingly, the assumption that the parties are risk-neutral maximizers of expected wealth without financial constraints plays an important role in our analysis. The assumed absence of financial constraints severely limits the applicability of the analysis contained in this section to the problem of investments in human capital, because laws against slavery prohibit the use of human capital as loan collateral. The assumption is also likely to fail in applications to public projects involving health, safety, or environmental quality – projects for which the public's preferences are not easily expressed in terms of risk neutrality and expected pecuniary gains.

When the assumption fails, the efficiency of actions can no longer generally be considered separately from distributional considerations.

17 This proposition was inspired by the related results of Crawford (1988) and Fudenberg, Holmstrom, and Milgrom (1990).

18 Of course, the parties do not know what conditions will later prevail, so the design decision they reach cannot be based on that information. By the *efficient decision*, we mean the decision that would be agreed to on the basis of the available information if perfect long-term contracting were possible.

19 Arrow (1974) gives primacy to the role of markets when he holds that "organizations are a means of achieving the benefits of collective action in situations in which the price system fails." Here, he interprets organizations broadly. "Formal organizations, firms, labor unions, universities, or government, are not the only kind. Ethical codes and the market system itself are to be interpreted as organizations."

20 See Williamson (1985, Ch. 6.1) for a discussion of earlier treatments of this issue.

21 In a related vein, Hall and Lazear (1984) have argued that simple labor market contracts that sometimes vest the residual power to decide on separations with labor and sometimes vest it with management are efficient responses to informational asymmetries that prevent complete contracts.

22 A further criticism is that the very notion of ownership of the firm becomes problematic when, as is the case in real companies, the firm has many assets and residual decision rights over them differ. See Milgrom and Roberts (1988b) for a further discussion.

23 See Roth (1986), for example, on the general issue of the efficiency of bargaining, and Hoffman and Spitzer (1982) and Harrison and McKee (1985) on the specific issue of the experimental testing of the Coase hypothesis.

24 Mixed strategy equilibria are best interpreted as follows. The probabilities a player adopts at equilibrium represent the other player's subjective uncertainty about the demand the first player will make. Mixed strategy equilibria allow each player to be consistently uncertain about the demands the other player will actually make without attributing irrationality or mistaken views to that player.

25 Actually there are many such equilibria, but to verify the claim it is sufficient to exhibit one. Let x and y be positive numbers whose sum is one or less. Suppose that player 1 demands x with probability $y/(1-x)$ and demands $1-y$ with the complementary probability, and that player 2 demands y with probability $x/(1-y)$ and $1-x$ with the complementary probability. This describes a Nash equilibrium in which player 1's expected payoff is x and player 2's is y.

26 Despite the widely held belief that the outcome of bilateral monopoly is indeterminate, whether it is in fact so depends on the rules under which the bargaining occurs and on how the bargainers behave. For example, if the bargainers alternate in making demands, if there is no a priori limit on the number of rounds of bargaining, if the bargainers both discount the future, and if in every eventuality the bargainers act selfishly and farsightedly (subgame-perfect equilibrium), then the outcome is unique and efficient (Rubinstein 1982).

27 We have in mind a refinement of the Nash equilibrium based on the idea of iterated dominance, applied to this game with an infinity of strategies for each player. To compute our equilibrium, we first limit the parties to naming integer multiples of some discrete unit, such as pennies. Next, we eliminate weakly dominated strategies to create a new game with a smaller strategy set and iterate, applying the dominance criterion recursively until the strategy set is reduced no further. We then compute the Nash equilibria of the reduced game. At every such equilibrium, each supplier demands approximately zero dollars and the buyer demands approximately one dollar. Passing to the limit as the unit of account grows small isolates this equilibrium of the original game.

28 Banri Asanuma (1988) has posited that, in Japanese subcontracting relationships, the supplier's technological prowess and the importance of the part supplied affect the distribution of bargaining power among parties just as asset specificity does. If these factors are also similar to asset specificity in creating indeterminacy in bargaining, then they threaten to cause coordination problems and may lead to the creation of specialized governance structures to alleviate the situation. In Japan, subcontractor associations (such as the Association of Toyota Suppliers) may fill this governance role.

29 This example was first noted by Barzel (1977).

30 The particular institution described presumably also assigns most of the gains to De Beers, reflecting its monopoly position.

31 Prepackaging, of course, brings with it other costs. Stores may be inclined to reduce quality, which customers can no longer observe. Warranties may provide a partial remedy for that, but they may be costly to exercise and may encourage customers to abuse goods.

32 Royalties also result in higher compensation, on average, for the author, even holding the publishers' information fixed. See Milgrom (1987).

33 See Sutton (1986) for a recent survey of noncooperative bargaining theory.

34 Coase (1937), p. 395.

35 Williamson (1986), p. 131.

36 This contrasts with Coase's view (1937, p. 389) that "the distinguishing mark of the firm is the supersession of the price mechanism" and with the view of Alchian and Demsetz (1972) that a firm is principally a "nexus of contracts."

37 Of course, this may not be easy. In particular, to the extent that the only way to provide incentives is to limit somehow the set of allowed interventions, worthwhile interventions may also be deterred. See the discussion that follows on limiting influence activities.

38 Arrow (1974, p. 33) holds that the "purpose of organizations is to exploit the fact that many (virtually all) decisions require the participation of many individuals for their effectiveness."

39 Lazear (1986) makes the related argument that wage "equality is desirable on efficiency grounds. The compression of wages suppresses unwanted uncooperative behavior" when employees compete for good jobs on the basis of comparative performance.

40 Abegglen and Stalk (1985, pp. 24–25) describe how three major Japanese companies, Mitsubishi Chemical, Sumitomo Chemical, and Showa Denko, responded to the crisis in bauxite smelting caused by the oil price increases of 1973. "The aluminum producing units have been separated from their parent companies to isolate the problem and the losses, and their production facilities are being steadily reduced."

41 "The Nikkeiren report [asserts] that the pre-tax annual compensation level at the top of the Japanese company is low – about $100,000. This generally low level of pay for Japanese top management is borne out by other reports; for example *Fortune* of 19 March 1984 reported on 'salaries of Japanese chairmen and presidents, which range from $50,000 to $250,000 depending on company size.' *Fortune* also commented on U.S. executive salaries. 'In 1982 at least 85 American chief executives earned more than $1 million.'" Abegglen and Stalk (1985, p. 192).

42 Abegglen and Stalk (1985, p. 204) report that "promotion is also a function of age in the Japanese firm, being provided within a predictable and narrow age range. Not everyone gets promoted – the escalator cannot carry everyone to the top floor – but promotion will rarely if ever take place until adequate seniority has been attained."

43 In this regard, the ability of Japanese firms to make differential use of such policies relative to their counterparts elsewhere around the world is in large part a function of the limited interfirm mobility of labor in Japan (Milgrom and Roberts, 1988a).

44 The account given here is based on that given by Williamson (1985, p. 158), who cites a *Wall Street Journal* article (February 9, 1982, p. 17) as his original source.

45 Of course, the former chief executive may have spent some time with bankers or in attempts to impress his stockholders and directors. Our presumption is that he or she had greater autonomy from these authorities and hence spent less time trying to influence them.

46 Some influence activities do occur across firm boundaries. The prime example of this is selling. A good salesperson is one who is successful at influencing the buyer's decision.

47 Mintzberg (1973) summarizes the results of the many diary studies of how managers spend their time with the remark (p. 36) that "gossip, speculation and hearsay form a most important part of the manager's information diet." Also (p. 38), "Virtually every empirical study of managerial time allocation draws attention to the great proportion of time spent in verbal communications, with estimates ranging from 57 percent of time spent in face-to-face communication by foremen to 89 percent of episodes in verbal interaction by middle managers in a manufacturing company."

48 As we have already indicated, centralization may reduce or eliminate bargaining costs for firms. Also, as Milgrom (1988) and Milgrom and Roberts (1988a) have argued, the influence activities may themselves play a role in improving decision making, since the influencing parties may have valuable information and suggestions. In similar fashion, lobbyists and other advocates may contribute to better government decision making, and that possi-

bility must be weighed in any fair evaluation of the economics of government intervention.

49 George Shultz, U.S. Secretary of State, testifying to the House Foreign Affairs Committee, December 8, 1986, as reported in the *Oakland Tribune,* December 9, 1986.

50 A traditional economic analysis of damage awards might hold that, because courts sometimes fail to find fault where they should and because damage awards must provide the economic incentive to protect against losses, the award should be larger than the actual damage suffered when a party is found guilty. This logic supports the treble damage rule in antitrust law.

4. CORPORATE CULTURE AND ECONOMIC THEORY

1 In writing this chapter, I had tremendous difficulties coming up with a term for what it is that textbook economics and the Porter approach to strategy does not analyze. I will use organizational efficiency and effectiveness and words of that ilk, but I confess much unhappiness with them.

2 The notion of a hierarchical transaction and its particular relevance to employment relationships is quite old – going back at least to Simon (1951).

3 The role of reputation in hierarchical transactions also appears in Simon (1951).

4 It might run thus: Concentrated ownership of capital can be, as they show, efficient. Capital ownership by an individual might subject the individual to too much risk. Hence, for purposes of risk sharing we invent the limited stock corporation.

5 The argument's flavor is easiest to suggest if we assume that the game will run precisely one hundred million rounds. In this case, roughly, the argument runs as follows: A, with many rounds to go, will want to test B to see if B will honor trust. At worst A loses $5 by doing so, and there is a one-in-one-thousand chance that A will make at least $10 in each of the many rounds left to go. But then what will B do when A tries him or her out? Even if B is not a moral person, B will honor that trust: To abuse it would reveal B's true character to A and would mean obtaining nothing in all subsequent rounds; honoring trust will cause A to take another chance for a long time to come, worth $10 each time.

6 The reader desiring a more exact analysis of the issues discussed here may wish to refer at this point to the Appendix near the end of the chapter, where a simple example is presented.

7 Well, that is a bit of an overstatement. One must trade off unambiguity and the overall efficiency of the arrangement. In our earlier example of easy and hard problems and problems that do or do not require calculus, applying the calculus rule might be completely unambiguous, but as we make the necessity of calculus less and less predicative of the difficulty of the job, we lower the surplus derived from basing payment on the necessity of calculus. We could lower the predicative power of calculus to just the point where the arrangement still lives (test [ii] is just passed with enough surplus left for B so that the maintained reputation is worthwhile), and then we would not wish to apply the unambiguous and not very productive calculus-based scheme. Some measure of ambiguity is worth tolerating if there is a corre-

sponding gain in the arrangement's efficiency. The Appendix near the end of the chapter contains an explicit illustration of this point.

8 Seemingly outside the scope of economic theory are notions such as the following: A strong corporate culture increases the degree to which individuals internalize the common good of the organization. But one can approach this notion within an economic framework on the supposition that control in the organization will be based on adherence to the culture. An easy approach is to view this form of control as a simple screen. Somewhat less direct would be a story in which individuals are happier in situations in which they will be evaluated by criteria that leave little to chance – where they have relatively greater control of their own destinies. This could be a primitive taste, or one induced from risk aversion to capricious evaluation. In either case, if adherence to the culture provides an evaluation criterion that is predictable in application, it can provide an economic bond to the organization.

5. AMENITY POTENTIAL, INDIVISIBILITIES, AND POLITICAL COMPETITION

1 A recent examination of the multiple constituencies involved in business transactions such as takeovers occurs in Schleifer and Summers (in press). On how voting rules affect the principal-agent relationship in corporations, see Easterbrook and Fischel (1983).

2 For an application of the firm analogy to another aspect of politics – the structure of legislatures – see Weingast and Marshall (1988).

3 For evidence bearing on the amenity potential of newspapers, see Demsetz (1988).

4 For one model of the effects of monopoly on product quality, see Spence (1975).

6. POLITICAL SCIENCE AND RATIONAL CHOICE

1 I do not mean to suggest that there is no room in the curriculum or in life for case studies or hermeneutical criticism. Not every subject of economic, political, or social interest has inspired the scientifically appropriate kind of study and generalization. Instead, many subjects of great human concern are so complicated or so rare that generalization about them is probably impossible. By default, then, hermeneutical criticism and case studies are the best we can do. But still we ought not to take the results very seriously as a guide to behavior.

2 Moon (1975) asserts that this model is often supplemented with an assumption of choosers' indifference to the preferences of others. As a procedural assumption, this is necessarily redundant because of the way choice is defined. Choosers select from an ordering that they have made. So, when maximizing, choosers are satisfying only themselves, and no assumption to this effect is necessary. As a substantive assumption about the content of tastes, on the other hand, this assumption is unreasonable because we have good evidence of tastes for self-sacrifice (which, procedurally, is also self-interested). There are circumstances (such as auction markets) in which it is appropriate to assume that no one has altruistic tastes; but deviation from

the general principle of allowing them (as a result of my first assumption) is a matter for empirical investigation, not a priori judgment.

3 Moon (1975) offers a fine summary of these hermeneutical arguments. Unfortunately, he accepts some of them, not appreciating that rational choice models are the best way to deal with intentions and to distinguish between relevant and irrelevant features of events.

7. INSTITUTIONS AND A TRANSACTION-COST THEORY OF EXCHANGE

1 By ideology I mean the subjective perceptions people possess about how the world around them is organized, which can be at the microlevel of individual relationships or at the macrolevel of organized ideologies like communism; in either case the theories individuals construct are also intimately connected with a perception of how the world should be organized.

2 The transaction-cost approach is consistent only in its agreement on the importance of transaction costs; it is far from unified in other respects. The approach developed here might most appropriately be characterized as the University of Washington approach, originated by Steven Cheung and elaborated, modified, and developed at the University of Washington, most notably by Yoram Barzel (1982) but also by Masanori Hashimoto (1979), Keith Leffler (see Klein and Leffler 1981), and Douglass North (1981 and 1984).

The best-known approach is Oliver Williamson's. His approach differs from the one developed in this chapter in a number of respects. He takes the political and property rights framework as a given and examines organizations as efficient solutions to problems of organizing economic activity in a competitive environment. I am focusing on the underlying institutional framework. A second difference is that he takes imperfect enforcement as a given (otherwise opportunism would not pay) whereas in my framework I attempt to analyze the degree of imperfection, which turns out to be a critical factor in the way contracts are written. Indeed, the effectiveness of enforcement is a key issue in this framework.

3 For the beginning of such a theory, see Barzel (1989), whose approach is a part of the foundation of the third and fourth sections of this chapter.

4 See Barzel (1977) for a detailed elaboration of this argument.

5 Jensen and Meckling, in a well-known essay (1976), have elaborated on the agency costs involved in monitoring, policing, and the shirking of agents.

6 The rest of this chapter is a drastic condensation of the section dealing with the relationship of institutions to economic performance in a forthcoming book by the author entitled *Institutions, Institutional Change and Economic Performance*.

8. THE COSTS OF SPECIAL PRIVILEGE

1 As a matter of intellectual history, political scientists were not the leaders of this movement, but at least one political scientist, William Riker, certainly was a very early proponent of it.

2 I can claim to have been the first person to detect the error and begin its repair. I say this, however, without any degree of pride because, as a matter

of fact, for a number of years before I detected it I joined my fellow economists in teaching the error in economics classes. Heaven knows how many students I misled!

3 Krueger (1974) measured the size of this rectangle for India and Turkey. In both cases, she considered not the total cost to society of all the various government impediments on free markets but simply the cost of one impediment – the use of foreign exchange certificates. She found that the actual cost for India of that one impediment was 7 percent of gross national product; for Turkey it was 15 percent of gross national product. These are not small figures, and they represent only a small part of the total amount of rent seeking that keeps those two countries mired in poverty.

4 There are, of course, good as well as bad lobbyists. They can, in general, be regarded as creating benefit for society, but they are unfortunately mainly simply trying to defend society from other lobbyists. Incidentally, I should say here that my own acquaintance with Washington lobbyists is small, but I was very much impressed with the ones I met. I think they are outstanding human resources. If they applied their talents to something constructive we would be very much better off.

5 The whole point of Doernberg and McChesney's essay is, in essence, to argue that in passing the Tax Reform Bill of 1986 members of Congress were selfishly motivated. Under the circumstances, it does not seem likely that the authors have left out any significant expenses.

6 Congressman Biaggi was also convicted in another, much larger scam. In this case, he was allegedly paid several million dollars, but the cost to the federal government was many times that large.

7 For an amusing example of the triviality of these things see Miller (1984, p. 395). Incidentally, Dr. Miller kindly read an early draft of this chapter and strongly approved of its theme. Given his combination of economic and governmental experience, I regard this as a strong endorsement.

8 Mueller cites Douglas and Miller, but this is a draft, and the citation is incomplete. See also Derthick and Quirk (1985, pp. 152–153).

9 The standard Harberger triangle and the larger area just below it are not specially shaded. This is to improve the diagram's clarity. I presume readers can recognize them on their own.

10 I have never seen a full bus.

11 Recently, disguises have become harder and harder to devise. As a result, some present programs impress most economists as direct payments. Fortunately for farmers, most voters are not economists.

12 I first suggested this idea in Tullock (1971), but Brennan and Buchanan (1984) have greatly elaborated and improved it. Recent unpublished empirical work by Gary Anderson and Robert D. Tollison casts a good deal of doubt on the whole concept.

13 A problem with direct monetary payments is in seeing that they go to the right people. A simple subsidy on wheat would attract people who had nothing to do with the lobbying effort. Paying owners of land for growing wheat would be a better targeting method, although a capitation payment for existing farmers would be even better.

14 In some cases, average citizens regard a straightforward fight for pork as excusable, if not virtuous. The argument that every other district has a dam and I should have one too seems to be regarded as morally unobjectionable.

Currently, moral fairness can take the form of everybody getting some of the loot.

9. TOWARD A UNIFIED VIEW OF ECONOMICS AND THE OTHER SOCIAL SCIENCES

1 On the methodology of economics, see, among others, Friedman (1953, especially pp. 3–43), Blaug (1980), and McCloskey (1985).
2 For applications of economic reasoning in research areas more often thought to belong to other disciplines, see Becker (1976).
3 However, there is evidence on the influence of interest groups on civil service pay. See Borjas (1980).
4 In the abstract, it is possible that what is (in some sense) a small amount of an indivisible good can be "purchased" if a lottery is organized in which the indivisible good is the prize. Then a person could for a small price buy a tiny chance of obtaining a good that, because of its indivisibility, could otherwise be bought only in a prohibitively costly amount. A king could, say, sell lottery tickets for the hand of his daughter in marriage, with each ticket so inexpensive that even the poorest men could afford one. Such lotteries are rare for several reasons. Even when they occur they do not provide accurate information about preferences because risk aversion and the taste for adventurous gambles vary among individuals.

References

Abegglen, J. C., and G. Stalk, Jr. 1985. *Kaisha: The Japanese Corporation.* New York: Basic.

Abreu, D., D. Pearce, and E. Stachetti. 1987. Towards a Theory of Discounted Repeated Games with Imperfect Monitoring. Mimeo, Harvard University.

Adams, J. [1778, 1788] 1850–1856. Defense of the Constitutions of the United States. *Works of John Adams.* Boston: Little, Brown.

Akerlof, G. 1970. The Market for "Lemons": Quality, Uncertainty, and Market Mechanisms. *Quarterly Journal of Economics* 84: 488–500.

Alavi, H. 1972. The State in Postcolonial Societies: Pakistan and Bangladesh. *New Left Review* 74: 59–81.

Alchian, A., and H. Demsetz. 1972. Production, Information Costs, and Economic Organization. *American Economic Review* 62: 777–795.

Ames, B. 1987. *Political Survival.* Berkeley and Los Angeles: University of California Press.

Arrow, K. 1951. *Social Choice and Individual Values.* New Haven, Conn.: Yale University Press.

——— 1974. *The Limits of Organization.* New York: Norton.

Arrow, K., and F. Hahn. 1971. *General Competitive Analysis.* San Francisco: Holden-Day.

Asanuma, B. 1988. Manufacturer–Supplier Relationships in Japan and the Concept of Relation-Specific Skill. Kyoto University Faculty of Economics Working Paper No. 2. *Journal of the Japanese and International Economies,* in press.

Balassa, B. 1981. The Newly Industrializing Developing Countries After the Oil Crisis. *Weltwirtschaftliches Archiv* 117: 1027–1038.

——— 1982. Structural Adjustment Policies in Developing Countries, 1978–1990. *World Development* 10: 23–38.

Barzel, Y. 1977. An Economic Analysis of Slavery. *Journal of Law and Economics* 20: 87–110.

——— 1977. Some Fallacies in the Interpretation of Information Costs. *Journal of Law and Economics* 20: 291–307.

——— 1982. Measurement Cost and the Organization of Markets. *Journal of Law and Economics* 25: 27–48.

——— 1989. *Economic Analysis of Property Rights.* Cambridge: Cambridge University Press.

245

References

Bates, R. H. 1976. *Rural Responses to Industrialization.* New Haven, Conn.: Yale University Press.

1981. *Markets and States in Tropical Africa.* Berkeley and Los Angeles: University of California Press.

1983. *Essays on the Political Economy of Rural Africa.* Berkeley and Los Angeles: University of California Press.

ed. 1988. *Toward a Political Economy of Development: A Rational Choice Perspective.* Berkeley and Los Angeles: University of California Press.

1989. *Beyond the Miracle of the Market: The Political Economy of Agrarian Development in Kenya.* Cambridge: Cambridge University Press.

Becker, F. 1965. A Theory of the Allocation of Time. *Economic Journal* 75: 493–517.

Becker, G. 1976. *The Economic Approach to Human Behavior.* Chicago: University of Chicago Press.

1983. A Theory of Competition Among Pressure Groups for Political Influence. *Quarterly Journal of Economics* August: 371–400.

Bentley, A. 1908. *The Process of Government: A Study of Social Pressures.* Chicago: University of Chicago Press.

Black, D. 1948. On the Rationale of Group Decision Making. *Journal of Political Economy* 56: 23–34.

1958. *The Theory of Committees and Elections.* Cambridge: Cambridge University Press.

Black, D., and R. A. Newing. 1951. *Committee Decisions with Complementary Valuation.* London: Hodge Publications.

Blaug, M. 1980. *The Methodology of Economics; or How Economists Explain.* Cambridge: Cambridge University Press.

Borcherding, T. 1977. *Budgets and Bureaucrats: The Sources of Government Growth.* Durham, N.C.: Duke University Press.

Borjas, G. 1980. Wage Determination in the Federal Government: The Role of Constituents and Bureaucrats. *Journal of Political Economy* December: 1110–1147.

Brennan, G., and J. Buchanan. 1984. Voter Choice: Evaluating Political Alternatives. *American Behavioral Scientist* 29: 185–201.

Brown, C., and J. Medoff. 1978. Trade Unions in the Production Process. *Journal of Political Economy* 86: 355–378.

Buchanan, J., R. Tollison, and G. Tullock. 1980. *Toward a Theory of the Rent Seeking Society.* College Station: Texas A&M University Press.

Buchanan, J., and G. Tullock. 1962. *The Calculus of Consent.* Ann Arbor: The University of Michigan Press.

Bueno de Mesquita, B. 1981. *The War Trap.* New Haven, Conn.: Yale University Press.

Bueno de Mesquita, B., D. Newman, and A. Rabushka. 1985. *Forecasting Political Events: The Future of Hong Kong.* New Haven, Conn.: Yale University Press.

Calvert, R. L. 1985. Robustness of the Multidimensional Voting Model: Candidate Motivation, Uncertainty, and Convergence. *American Journal of Political Science* 29: 71–95.

Chandler, A. D., Jr. 1962. *Strategy and Structure.* Cambridge, Mass.: MIT Press.

1977. *The Visible Hand: The Managerial Revolution in American Business.* Cambridge, Mass.: Harvard University Press.

Cheung, S. 1974. A Theory of Price Control. *Journal of Law and Economics* 17: 23–45.

246

References

Coase, R. 1937. The Nature of the Firm. *Economica* 4: 386–405.

———. 1960. The Problem of Social Cost. *Journal of Law and Economics* 3: 1–44.

Cohen, G. A. 1978. *Karl Marx's Theory of History: A Defense.* Princeton, N.J.: Princeton University Press.

Colander, D. C., ed. 1984. *Neoclassical Political Economy: The Analysis of Rent-Seeking and DUP Activities.* Cambridge, Mass.: Ballinger.

Collier, D. 1979. *The New Authoritarianism in Latin America.* Princeton, N.J.: Princeton University Press.

Congleton, R. 1989. Campaign Finances and Political Platforms: The Economics of Political Controversy. *Public Choice* August: 101–118.

Cox, G. 1987. Electoral Equilibrium Under Alternative Voting Institutions. *American Journal of Political Science* 31: 82–108.

Crawford, V. 1988. Long-Term Relationships Governed by Short-Term Contracts. *American Economic Review* 78: 485–499.

Crawford, V., and H. Haller. 1987. Learning How to Cooperate: Optimal Play in Repeated Coordination Games. Mimeo, University of California, San Diego.

Dahl, R. 1961. *Who Governs: Democracy and Power in an American City.* New Haven, Conn.: Yale University Press.

Debreu, G. 1959. *The Theory of Value.* New Haven, Conn.: Yale University Press.

de Janvry, A. 1981. *The Agrarian Question and Reformism in Latin America.* Baltimore: Johns Hopkins University Press.

Demsetz, H. 1988. *Organization of Economic Activity.* Vol. 2. Oxford: Blackwell.

Demsetz, H., and K. Lehn. 1985. The Structure of Corporate Ownership: Causes and Consequences. *The Journal of Political Economy* 96(2): 1155–1177.

Denzau, A., W. Riker, and K. Shepsle. 1985. Farguharson and Fenno: Sophisticated Voting and Home Style. *American Political Science Review* 79: 1117–1134.

Derthick, M., and P. J. Quirk. 1985. *The Politics of Deregulation.* Washington, D.C.: Brookings Institute.

Deutsch, K. 1953. *Nationalism and Social Communications.* Cambridge, Mass.: MIT Press.

Doernberg, R., and F. S. McChesney. 1987. Doing Good or Doing Well: Congress and the Tax Reform Act of 1986. *New York University Law Review* 62(4): 891–926.

Downs, A. 1957. *An Economic Theory of Democracy.* New York: Harper & Row.

Duverger, M. [1951] 1963. *Political Parties: Their Organization and Activity in the Modern State.* New York: Wiley.

Easterbrook, F., and D. Fischel. 1983. Voting in Corporate Law. *Journal of Law and Economics* 26: 395–427.

Easterlin, R. 1973. Does Money Buy Happiness? *The Public Interest* 30: 3–10.

Elster, J. 1985. *Making Sense of Marx.* Cambridge: Cambridge University Press.

Farquharson, R. 1969. *The Theory of Voting.* New Haven, Conn.: Yale University Press.

Farrell, J., and N. Gallini. 1986. Second-Sourcing as a Commitment: Monopoly Incentives to Attract Competition. University of California Department of Economics Working Paper No. 8618.

247

References

Feddersen, T., I. Sened, and S. Wright. 1989. *Sophisticated Voting and Candidate Entry Under Plurality Rule*. University of Rochester Public Policy Series.

Ferejohn, J., R. McKelvey, and E. Packel. 1984. Limited Distributions for Continuous State Markov Model. *Social Choice and Welfare* 1: 45–67.

Ferejohn, J., and R. Noll. 1987. Three's a Crowd: Duverger's Law Reconsidered. Mimeo, American Political Science Association.

Fiedler, R. 1972. The Role of Cattle in the Ila Economy. *African Social Research* 15: 327–361.

Fishburn, P. 1974. Paradoxes of Voting. *American Political Science Review* 68: 537–547.

Friedman, M. 1953. *The Methodology of Positive Economics*. Chicago: University of Chicago Press.

Fudenberg, D., B. Holmstrom, and P. Milgrom. Short-Term Contracts and Long-Term Agency Relationships. *Journal of Economic Theory*, in press.

Fudenberg, D., and D. Kreps. 1988. *A Theory of Learning, Experimentation and Equilibrium in Games*. Mimeo, Stanford University.

Fudenberg, D., D. Kreps, and E. Maskin. 1987. Repeated Games with Long- and Short-Lived Players. Mimeo, MIT.

Fudenberg, D., and E. Maskin. 1986. The Folk Theorem with Discounting and with Incomplete Information. *Econometrica* 54: 533–554.

1986a. Discounted Repeated Games with One-Sided Moral Hazard. Mimeo, Harvard University.

Geertz, C. 1983. *Local Knowledge*. New York: Basic.

Gibbard, A. 1971. Manipulation of Voting Schemes: A General Result. *Econometrica* 41: 587–601.

Gilligan, T., and K. Krehbiel. 1987. Collective Decision Making and Standing Committees: An Informational Rationale for Restrictive Amendment Procedures. *Journal of Law, Economics and Organization* 3: 287–337.

Goffman, I. 1959. *The Presentation of the Self in Everyday Life*. New York: Doubleday.

Green, E., and R. Porter. 1984. Noncooperative Collusion Under Imperfect Price Information. *Econometrica* 52: 87–100.

Greenberg, J., and K. Shepsle. 1987. The Effect of Electoral Rewards in Multiparty Competition with Entry. *American Political Science Review* 81: 525–538.

Griliches, Z. 1958. Research Cost and Social Returns: Hybrid Corn and Related Innovations. *Journal of Political Economy* 66(5): 419–432.

Grossman, S., and O. Hart. 1986. The Costs and Benefits of Ownership: A Theory of Vertical and Lateral Integration. *Journal of Political Economy* 94: 691–719.

Grout, P. 1984. Investment and Wages in the Absence of Binding Contracts: A Nash Bargaining Approach. *Econometrica* 52: 449–460.

Hall, R., and E. Lazear. 1984. The Excess Sensitivity of Layoffs and Quits to Demand. *Journal of Labor Economics* 2: 233–257.

Hardin, R., 1982. *Collective Action*. Baltimore: Resources for the Future by Johns Hopkins University Press.

Hardin, R., and B. Barry, eds. 1982. *Rational Man and Irrational Society?* Beverly Hills, Calif.: Sage.

Harrison, G. W., and M. McKee. 1985. Experimental Evaluation of the Coase Theorem. *Journal of Law and Economics* 28: 653–670.

References

Hart, O., and J. Moore. 1988. Property Rights and the Nature of the Firm. Mimeo, Department of Economics, MIT.

Hashimoto, M. 1979. Bonus Payments, On-the-Job Training, and Lifetime Employment in Japan. *Journal of Political Economy* 87: 1086–1104.

Hayami, Y. 1988. *Community, Market and State.* Elmhurst Memorial Lecture, 20th International Conference of Economists. Buenos Aires, Argentina.

Herring, P. 1940. *The Politics of Democracy: American Parties in Action.* New York: Norton.

Herskovitz, M. J. 1926. The Cattle Complex in East Africa. *American Anthropology* New Series 28:230–272, 361–380, and 633–669.

Hill, P. 1960. *The Gold Coast Cocoa Farmer.* London: Oxford University Press.

　　　1963. *The Migrant Cocoa Farmers of Southern Ghana: A Study in Rural Capitalism.* Cambridge: Cambridge University Press.

Hirschleifer, J. 1971. The Private and Social Value of Information and the Reward to Inventive Activity. *American Economic Review* 61: 561–574.

Hoffman, E., and M. L. Spitzer. 1982. The Coase Theorem: Some Experimental Tests. *Journal of Law and Economics* 25: 73–98.

Hogarth, R. M., and M. W. Reder, eds. 1986. The Behavioral Foundations of Economic Theory. *The Journal of Business* 59(4): S181–S501.

Holmstrom, B. 1979. Moral Hazard and Observability. *Bell Journal of Economics* 10: 74–91.

　　　1982. Managerial Incentives – A Dynamic Perspective. In *Essays in Economics and Management in Honor of Lars Wahlbeck.* Helsinki: Swedish School of Economics.

Holmstrom, B., and P. Milgrom. 1987. Aggregation and Linearity in the Provision of Intertemporal Incentives. *Econometrica* 55: 303–328.

Holmstrom, B., and J. Ricart. 1986. Managerial Incentives and Capital Management. *Quarterly Journal of Economics* 101: 835–860.

Holmstrom, B., and J. Tirole. The Theory of the Firm. In R. Schmalensee and R. Willig, eds. *Handbook of Industrial Organization.* In press.

Horowitz, D. L. 1985. *Ethnic Groups in Conflict.* Berkeley and Los Angeles: University of California Press.

Ilchman, W. F., and N. T. Uphoff. 1971. *The Political Economy of Change.* Berkeley and Los Angeles: University of California Press.

Jacobs, A. 1980. Pastoral Masai and Tropical Rural Development. In R. H. Bates and M. F. Lofchie, eds. *Agricultural Development in Africa.* New York: Praeger.

Jacobson, G. 1980. *Money in Congressional Elections.* New Haven, Conn.: Yale University Press.

Jensen, M., and W. Meckling. 1976. Theory of the Firm: Managerial Behavior, Agency Costs, and Capital Structure. *Journal of Financial Economics* 3: 305–360.

　　　1981. The Role of Market Forces in Assuring Contractual Performance. *Journal of Political Economy* 89: 615–641.

Kalt, J., and M. Zupan. 1984. Capture and Ideology In The Economic Theory Of Politics. *American Economic Review* 74(3): 279–300.

　　　The Apparent Ideological Behavior of Legislators: Testing for Principal-agent Slack in Political Institutions. *Journal of Law and Economics,* in press.

References

Kenney, R., and B. Klein. 1983. The Economics of Block Booking. *Journal of Law and Economics* 26: 497–540.

Key, V. O., Jr. 1956. *American State Politics*. New York: Knopf.
1966. *The Responsible Electorate: Rationality in Presidential Voting*. Cambridge, Mass.: Harvard University Press.

Klein, B., R. Crawford, and A. Alchian. 1978. Vertical Integration, Appropriable Rents, and the Competitive Contracting Process. *Journal of Law and Economics* 21: 297–326.

Klein, B., and K. Leffler. 1981. The Role of Market Forces in Assuring Contractual Performance. *Journal of Political Economy* 89: 615–641.

Kramer, G. H. 1977. A Dynamical Model of Political Equilibrium. *Journal of Economic Theory* 16: 310–334.

Kreps, D. 1988. On Modelling Unforeseen Contingencies. Mimeo, Stanford University.

Kreps, D., P. Milgrom, J. Roberts, and R. Wilson. 1982. Rational Cooperation in the Finitely Repeated Prisoners' Dilemma. *Journal of Economic Theory* 27: 245–252.

Kreps, D., and R. Wilson. 1982. Reputation and Imperfect Information. *Journal of Economic Theory* 27: 253–279.

Krueger, A. 1974. The Political Economy of the Rent-Seeking Society. *American Economic Review* 64: 291–303.

Kuhn, T. 1970. *The Structure of Scientific Revolutions*. Chicago: University of Chicago Press.

Lal, D. 1983. *The Poverty of Development Economics*. Hobart Paperback 16. London: The Institute of Economic Affairs.
1984. The Political Economy of the Predatory State. Development Research Department, World Bank.

Lancaster, K. 1966. A New Approach to Consumer Theory. *Journal of Political Economy* 74: 132–157.

Lazear, E. Pay Inequality and Industrial Politics. Hoover Institution Working Paper No. E-86-12.

Lerner, D. 1958. *The Passing of Traditional Society*. New York: Free Press.

Levi, M. 1988. *Of Rule and Revenue*. Berkeley and Los Angeles: University of California Press.

Levine, M., and C. Plott. 1977. Agenda Influence and Its Implications. *Virginia Law Review* 63: 561–604.

Libecap, G. D. 1987. Political Economy of Fuel Oil Cartelization by the Texas Railroad Commission 1933–1972.

Lindblom, C. E. 1959. The Science of "Muddling Through." *Public Administration Review* 19: 79–88.

Little, I. 1982. *Economic Development: Theory, Practice and International Relations*. New York: Basic.

Mankiw, N. G. 1989. Real Business Cycles: A New Keynesian Perspective. *Journal of Economic Perspectives*. Spring: 79–90.

Mannheim, K. 1949. *Ideology and Utopia*. New York: Harcourt Brace & World.

McCloskey, D. 1985. *The Rhetoric of Economics*. Madison: University of Wisconsin Press.

McConnell, G. 1953. *The Decline of Agrarian Democracy*. Berkeley and Los Angeles: University of California Press.

McCubbins, M. D., and T. Sullivan. 1987. *Congress: Structure and Policy*. Cambridge: Cambridge University Press.

References

McKelvey, R. D. 1976. Intransitivities in Multidimensional Voting Models and Some Implications for Agenda Control. *Journal of Economic Theory* 12: 472–482.

    1979. General Conditions for Global Intransitivities in Formal Voting Models. *Econometrica* 47: 1085–1112.

    1986. Covering, Dominance, and the Institution-Free Properties of Social Choice. *American Journal of Political Science* 30: 283–314.

McKelvey, R. D., and P. C. Ordeshook. 1976. Symmetric Spatial Games without Majority Rule Equilibria. *American Political Science Review* 70: 1172–1184.

    1986. Information, Electoral Equilibria, and the Democratic Ideal. *Journal of Politics:* 909–937.

Meltzer, A., and S. Richard. 1981. A Rational Theory of the Size of Government. *Journal of Political Economy* October: 914–927.

Milgrom, P. 1986. Quasi-Rents, Influence and Organizational Form. Mimeo, Yale University.

    1987. Auction Theory. In Truman Bewley, ed. *Advances in Economic Theory, Fifth World Congress.* Cambridge: Cambridge University Press.

    1988. Employment Contracts, Influence Activities, and Efficient Organization Design. *Journal of Political Economy* 96: 42–60.

Milgrom, P., and J. Roberts. 1986. Relying on the Information of Interested Parties. *Rand Journal of Economics* 17: 18–32.

    1987. An Economic Approach to Influence Activities and Organizational Responses. Mimeo, Stanford University.

    1988a. An Economic Approach to Influence Activities in Organizations. *American Journal of Sociology* 94 (Supplement): S154–S179.

    1988b. Theories of the Firm: Past, Present and Future. *Canadian Journal of Economics* 21: 444–458.

Miller, J. 1984. Is Organized Labor Rational in Supporting OSHA? *Southern Economic Journal* 50(3): 881–885.

Miller, N. 1980. A New Solution Set for Tournaments and Majority Voting. *American Journal of Political Science* 24: 68–96.

Miller, N., and R. Aya, eds. 1971. *National Liberation.* New York: Free Press.

Mintzberg, H. 1973. *The Nature of Managerial Work.* New York: Harper & Row.

Moon, J. D. 1975. The Logic of Political Inquiry. *Handbook of Political Science.* F. Greenstein and N. Polsby, eds. *Political Science: Scope and Theory.* Vol. I: 131–228.

Moore, B. 1966. *The Social Origins of Dictatorship and Democracy.* Boston: Beacon.

Morgenstern, O., and G. Schwodiauer. 1976. Competition and Collusion in Bilateral Markets. *Zeitschrift für Nationalökonomie* 36: 217–247.

Mueller, D. 1979. *Public Choice.* Cambridge: Cambridge University Press.

    1989. *Public Choice II.* Cambridge: Cambridge University Press.

Munro, J. Forbes. 1975. *Colonial Rule and the Kamba.* New York: Oxford University Press.

Myerson, R., and M. Satterthwaite. 1983. Efficient Mechanisms for Bilateral Trading. *Journal of Economic Theory* 28: 265–281.

Nash, J. 1950. The Bargaining Problem. *Econometrica* 18: 155–162.

    1953. Two-Person Cooperative Games. *Econometrica* 21: 128–140.

References

Nelson, J., A. McGill, and D. McCloskey, eds. 1987. *The Rhetoric of the Human Science: Language and Argument in Scholarship and Public Affairs.* Madison: University of Wisconsin Press.

Nelson, R., and S. Winter. 1982. *An Evolutionary Theory of Economic Change.* Cambridge, Mass: Harvard University Press.

Niemi, R. 1969. Majority Decision-Making with Partial Unidimensionality. *American Political Science Review* 63: 489–497.

Niemi, R., and H. Weisberg. 1968. A Mathematical Solution for the Probability of the Paradox of Voting. *Behavioral Science* 13: 317–323.

Niskanen, W. 1971. *Bureaucracy and Representative Government.* Hawthorne, N.Y.: Aldine.

North, D. C. 1981. *Structure and Change in Economic History.* New York: Norton.

1984. Government and the Cost of Exchange in History. *Journal of Economic History* 44: 255–264.

North, D. C., and R. Thomas. 1973. *The Rise of the Western World: A New Economic History.* Cambridge: Cambridge University Press.

North, D. C., and B. Weingast. 1987. Constitutions and Commitment: The Evolution of Institutions Governing Public Choice in 17th Century England. Mimeo, Hoover Institution.

Nurske, R. 1953. *Problems of Capital Formation in Underdeveloped Countries.* Oxford: Blackwell.

O'Donnell, G. 1973. *Modernization and Bureaucratic Authoritarianism: Studies in South American Politics.* Berkeley, Calif.: Institute of International Studies.

Olson, M. 1963. Rapid Growth as a Destabilizing Force. *Journal of Economic History* December: 529–552.

1965. *The Logic of Collective Action.* Cambridge, Mass.: Harvard University Press.

1982. *The Rise and Decline of Nations: Economic Growth, Stagflation, and Social Rigidities.* New Haven, Conn.: Yale University Press.

Palfrey, T. 1988. A Mathematical Proof of Duverger's Law in a Large Electoral System. Mimeo, California Institute of Technology.

Palma, G. 1978. Dependency: A Formal Theory of Underdevelopment or a Methodology for the Analysis of Concrete Situations of Underdevelopment. *World Development* 6: 881–924.

Peltzman, S. 1980. The Growth of Government. *Journal of Law and Economics* October: 209–287.

1984. Constituent Interest and Congressional Voting. *Journal of Law and Economics* April: 181–200.

1985. An Economic Interpretation of the History of Congressional Voting in the Twentieth Century. *American Economic Review* September: 656–675.

Plosser, C. 1989. Understanding Real Business Cycles. *Journal of Economic Perspectives* Spring: 51–77.

Plott, C. 1967. A Notion of Equilibrium and Its Possibility Under Majority Rule. *American Economic Review* 57: 787–806.

Plott, C., and M. Levine. 1978. A Model Agenda Influence on Committee Decisions. *American Economic Review* 68: 146–160.

Poole, K., and H. Rosenthal. 1985. A Spatial Model for Legislative Roll Call Analysis. *American Journal of Political Science* 29: 357–384.

References

Popkin, S. P. 1979. *The Rational Peasant*. Los Angeles and Berkeley: University of California Press.

Porter, M. E. 1987. From Competitive Advantage to Corporate Strategy. *Harvard Business Review* 65: 43–59.

Posner, R. 1975. The Social Costs of Monopoly and Regulation. *Journal of Political Economy* 83: 807–827.

1980. A Theory of Primitive Society, with Special Relevance to Law. *The Journal of Law and Economics* 23: 1–53.

Quine, W. 1960. *Word and Object*. New York: Wiley.

Rabushka, A., and K. A. Shepsle. 1972. *Politics in Plural Societies*. Westerville, Ohio: Merrill.

Rae, D. 1967. *The Political Consequences of Electoral Laws*. New Haven, Conn.: Yale University Press.

Reich, R., and J. Donahue. 1986. *New Deals, the Chrysler Revival and the American System*. New York: Penguin.

Riker, W. 1957. Events and Situations. *The Journal of Philosophy* 54: 57–70.

1958. Causes of Events. *The Journal of Philosophy* 55: 281–291.

1962. *The Theory of Political Coalitions*. New Haven, Conn.: Yale University Press.

1964. *Federalism: Orgin, Operation, Significance*. Boston: Little, Brown.

1977. The Future of the Science of Politics. *American Behavioral Scientist* 21: 22–38.

1982. The Two-Party System and Duverger's Law: An Essay on the History of Political Science. *American Political Science Review* 76: 753–766.

1986. *The Art of Political Manipulation*. New Haven, Conn.: Yale University Press.

1987. *The Development of American Federalism*. Boston: Kluwer.

[1983] 1988. *Liberalism Against Populism: A Confrontation Between the Theory of Social Choice and the Theory of Democracy*. New York: Freeman.

Roberts, J. 1987. An Equilibrium Model with Involuntary Unemployment at Flexible, Competitive Prices and Wages. *American Economic Review* 77: 856–874.

Roemer, J. E. 1982. *A General Theory of Class and Exploitation*. Cambridge, Mass.: Harvard University Press.

Rogers, E. M. 1962. *Diffusion of Innovations*. New York: Free Press.

Rosenberg, N., and L. E. Birdzell. 1986. *How the West Grew Rich*. New York: Basic.

Rosenstein-Rodan, P. 1943. Problems of Industrialization of Eastern and South Eastern Europe. *Economic Journal* 53: 202–211.

Roth, A. 1988. Bargaining Phenomena and Bargaining Theory. In A. Roth, ed. *Laboratory Experimentation in Economics: Six Points of View*. Cambridge: Cambridge University Press.

Roth, A., and F. Schoumaker. 1983. Expectations and Reputations in Bargaining: An Experimental Study. *American Economic Review* 73: 362–372.

Rothchild, D., and Olorunsula, V., eds. 1983. *State Versus Ethnic Claims: African Policy Dilemmas*. Boulder, Colo.: Westview.

Rowley, C. K., R. Tollison, and G. Tullock, eds. 1988. *The Political Economy of Rent-Seeking*. Boston: Kluwer Academic.

Rubinstein, A. 1982. Perfect Equilibrium in a Bargaining Model. *Econometrica* 50: 97–110.

References

Satterthwaite, M. 1975. Strategy-Proofness and Arrow's Conditions: Existence and Correspondence Theorems for Voting Procedures and Social Welfare Functions. *Journal of Economic Theory* 11: 187–217.

Savage, L. 1954. *The Foundations of Statistics*. New York: Wiley.

Schelling, T. 1960. *The Strategy of Conflict*. Cambridge, Mass.: Harvard University Press.

Scherer, F. M. 1971. *Industrial Market Structure and Economic Performance*. Skokie, Ill.: Rand McNally.

Schneider, H. 1979. *Livestock and Equality in East Africa: The Economic Basis for Social Structure*. Bloomington: Indiana University Press.

Schultz, T. W., ed. 1978. *Distortions of Agricultural Incentives*. Bloomington: Indiana University Press.

Schwartz, T. 1970. On the Possibility of Rational Policy Evaluation. *Theory and Decision* 1: 89–106.

Scitovsky, T. 1954. Two Concepts of External Economies. *Journal of Political Economy* 52(2): 143–151.

Scott, J. C. 1976. *The Moral Economy of the Peasant*. New Haven, Conn.: Yale University Press.

Scudder, T. 1966. Man-made Lakes and Social Change. *Engineering and Science* 29 (6): 18–22.

Selten, R. 1978. The Chain-Store Paradox. *Theory and Decision* 9: 127–159.

Shepard, A. 1987. Licensing to Enhance Demand for New Technologies. *Rand Journal of Economics* 18: 360–368.

Shepsle, K. A. 1979. Institutional Arrangements and Equilibrium in Multidimensional Voting Models. *American Journal of Political Science* 23: 27–59.

Shepsle, K. A., and B. Weingast. 1981. Structure-Induced Equilibrium and Legislative Choice. *Public Choice* 37: 503–519.

    1987. The Institutional Foundations of Committee Power. *American Political Science Review* 81(1): 85–104.

Shleifer, A., and L. Summers. Breach of Trust in Hostile Takeovers. In A. Auerbach, ed. *Corporate Takeovers: Causes and Consequence*. Chicago: University of Chicago Press, in press.

Simon, H. 1951. A Formal Theory of the Employment Relationship. *Econometrica* 19: 293–305.

    1965. *Administrative Behavior*. New York: Free Press.

    1978. Rationality as Process and as Product of Thought. *Paper and Proceedings of the American Economic Association* 68: 1–16.

    1986. Rationality in Psychology and Economics. In R. M. Hogarth and M. W. Reder, eds. *The Behavioral Foundations of Economic Theory*, supplement to the *Journal of Business* 59: S209–S224.

Skinner, W. 1974. The Focused Factory. *Harvard Business Review* 52: 113–121.

Spence, A. M. 1975. Monopoly, Quality, and Regulation. *Bell Journal of Economics* Autumn: 417–429.

Srinivasan, T. N. 1985. Neoclassical Political Economy, the State and Economic Development. *Asian Development Review* 3: 38–58.

Stigler, G. J. 1971. The Theory of Economic Regulation. *Bell Journal of Economics and Management Science* 2: 2–21.

Sutton, J. 1986. Noncooperative Bargaining Theory: An Introduction. *Review of Economic Studies* 53: 709–724.

References

Taylor, F. M. 1929. The Guidance of Production in a Socialist State. *American Economic Review* 19: 1–8. Reprinted in *On the Economic Theory of Socialism*, 1938. New York: McGraw Hill.

Tignor, R. L. 1976. *The Colonial Transformation of Kenya*. Princeton, N.J.: Princeton University Press.

Tirole, J. 1986. Procurement and Renegotiation. *Journal of Political Economy* 94: 235–259.

Toynbee, A. 1936. *A Study of History*, vol. 12. London: Oxford University Press.

Trimberger, E. K. 1972. A Theory of Elite Revolutions. *Studies in Comparative International Development* 7:191–207.

Truman, D. 1951. *The Governmental Process: Political Interests and Public Opinion*. New York: Knopf.

Tullock, G. 1967. The Welfare Costs of Tariffs, Monopolies, and Theft. *Western Economic Journal* 5: 224–232.

——— 1971. Charity of the Uncharitable. *Western Economic Journal* 9: 379–392.

——— 1976. *Toward a Mathematics of Politics*. Ann Arbor: University of Michigan Press.

——— 1980. Efficient Rent-Seeking. In J. Buchanan, R. Tollison, and G. Tullock, eds. *Toward a Theory of the Rent-Seeking Society*. College Station: Texas A&M University Press.

——— 1988. Rents and Rent-Seeking. In C. Rowley, R. Tollison, and G. Tullock, eds. *The Political Economy of Rent-Seeking*. Boston: Kluwer.

von Neumann, J., and O. Morgenstern. 1945. *The Theory of Games and Economic Behavior*. Princeton, N.J.: Princeton University Press.

Wallis, J., and D. C. North. 1986. Measuring the Transaction Sector in the American Economy, 1870–1970. In S. L. Engerman and R. E. Gallman, eds. *Long-Term Factors in American Economic Growth*. Published in the series *Studies in Income and Wealth*, Vol. 51. Chicago: University of Chicago Press.

Warren, B. 1973. Imperialism and Capitalist Industrialization. *New Left Review* 81: 3–44.

Weingast, B. W., and W. Marshall. 1988. The Industrial Organization of Congress; or, Why Legislatures, like Firms, Are Not Organized as Markets. *Journal of Political Economy* 96(11): 132–163.

Wilks, I. 1975. *Asante in the Nineteenth Century: The Structure and Evolution of a Political Order*. Cambridge: Cambridge University Press.

Williamson, O. 1975. *Markets and Hierarchies: Analysis and Antitrust Implications*. New York: Free Press.

——— 1981. The Modern Corporation: Origins, Evolution and Attributes. *Journal of Economic Literature* 19: 1537–1570.

——— 1985. *The Economic Institutions of Capitalism*. New York: Free Press.

World Bank. 1981. *Accelerated Development in Sub-Saharan Africa: An Agenda of Action*. Washington, D.C.: World Bank.

——— 1984. *Toward Sustained Development in Sub-Saharan Africa: A Joint Program of Action*. Washington, D.C.: World Bank.

——— 1987. *World Development Report 1987*. Washington, D.C.: World Bank.

Young, C. 1976. *The Politics of Cultural Pluralism*. Madison: University of Wisconsin Press.

Index

257

Index

Index

Fanon, Frantz, 34
Farquharson, R., 24
Farrell, J., 235
Faulkner, William, 198–199
favoritism, 157
Feddersen, T., 180
federal origins, law of, 171, 175
Federalism (Riker), 171
Ferejohn, J., 179, 180
Fiedler, R., 33
finite state automata, 143
firm, theory of the, 95–98, 99, 108–111
firms
  and acquisitions, 84–85
  amenity potential, 154
  and asset ownership, 70–71, 72
  authority role of, 92–93
  bureacracies in, 228–229
  business strategy of, 90–91
  and capital ownership, 98–99
  and centralized authority, 86
  and collective consumption, 151–153
  and communication, 125–126
  compared to political parties, 4, 147–160
  decision making in, 93–94
  definition of, 94–95
  and employees, 71
  and equilibrium theory, 96–97
  and external constituency, 154
  and influence costs, 80–85, 88–89
  and internal constitutency, 156–159
  mergers of, 64
  nationalized, 228
  and output mix, 152–153
  product mix, 147
  and profit maximization, 148–151
  and reputation, 92–93, 100–111, 142
  and residual rights, 98–100
  and selective intervention, 70, 71, 72
  and transaction-cost theory, 57–65
  and transactions, 108–111
  and trust-honor, 102–105, 106–111, 113
  and unforeseen contingencies, 92–93
  and utility maximization, 148–151
  See also organizations
fiscal illusion, 16
Fischel, D., 241
Fishburn, P., 23, 233
Fisher Body, 63, 68–69
fixed-point theorem, 13
focal points, 73, 129–130, 143
  and equilibrium, 120–123
  in organizations, 93
folk theorem, 102–105
  and reputation, 94, 142–143

Ford, Henry, 157
Ford Motor Co., 159–160
framing, 182
franchising, 97
free markets, 51
free riding, 41–42, 44–45, 53, 191
free trade, 49
Friedman, M., 195, 243
Fudenberg, D., 69, 102, 104, 143, 237

Gallini, N., 235
game theory, 11–12, 91
  and bargaining, 73–74
  cooperative, 27–28, 29
  and corporate culture, 95
  and development studies, 54
  extensive-form, 4
  and focal points, 120–123
  and hierarchical transactions, 111–116
  and interdependent decision making, 26
  noncooperative, 21, 29, 100–111
  and political science, 21–22
  and reputation, 94, 106–108
  subgame perfection, 81
games
  extensive form, 28–29
  market, 27
  nonatomic, 27
  noncooperative, 29, 91, 181
  prisoners' dilemma, 101
  repeated, 94, 100–102
  sequential, 28–29
Geertz, C., 54
General Foods Co., 151, 152
General Mills Co., 151, 152
General Motors Corp., 63, 68–69, 157, 159–160
generalizations and intentions, 174–175
genetics, 30
Ghana, 47, 49
Gibbard, A., 23, 25, 28
Gilligan, T., 179
Glorious Revolution (England), 88
Goffman, I., 54
Goldwater, Barry, 159
goods, *see* private goods; public goods
government
  discretionary authority of, 87–88
  economic analyses of, 195
  and economic growth, 38
  goods and services produced by, 215
  incentives of, 85–86
  influence costs in, 86–89
  information problems of, 226
  intervention of, 52, 85
  price regulation by, 41–42
  public reaction to, 226–227

261

Index

Index

Index

Index

satiation points, 19–20
Satterthwaite, M., 23, 25, 28, 77
Savage, L., 10, 117, 118
scant set, 223–224, 225
Scheinkman, J., 90
Schelling, T., 73, 93, 95, 121, 230
Schleifer, A., 241
Schoumaker, F., 122, 123, 127
Schultz, George, 87
Schultz, T. W., 52
Schwartz, T., 23
Schwodiauer, G., 27
science, 164–166
scientific discourse, 166–170
Scitovsky, T., 233
Scott, J. C., 36–37
Scrinivasan, T. N., 39
Scudder, T., 34
second-sourcing, 235
selective incentives, 43
selective intervention, 70, 71, 72, 79, 81
selling, 239
Selten, R., 104
Sen, Amartya, 23
Senate, U.S., 199–200
Sened, I., 180
sexual harassment, 80
Shepard, A., 235
Shepsle, K. A., 46, 173, 179, 180, 234
Showa Denko, 239
Shultz, George, 240
Simon, H., 95, 99, 114, 182–183, 240
Singapore, 59
single-peakedness, 19–20, 179
situations, 168–169
Skinner, W., 130
Smith, Adam, 49–51, 59, 171, 177, 183, 217, 230
Social Choice and Individual Values (Arrow), 11
social choice theory, 21, 23–24, 28, 215, 230
social decisions, 14–15, 16–17
social democrats, 46
social interactions, 175–177
social science
  classes in, 168–169
  development of, 177–181
  events in, 169–170
  history of, 212
  lack of progress in, 164–166
  and rational choice, 172–177
  unified view of economics and, 213–231
socialist economies, 78
Socialist Party, 145, 150
sociology, 9, 12

South America, 49
South Korea, 59
spatial preference conceptualization, 17–20
special interest groups, 243
  constituencies of, 144–145, 149–151
  and inefficient technology, 208
  see also interest groups
specialization, 183, 186–187
  and attributes, 192
  and contracts, 192
  and economic growth, 217
  enforcement in, 189
  and personalized exchange, 193
Spence, A. M., 90, 241
Spitzer, M. L., 237
Srinivasan, T. N., 234
Stachetti, E., 138, 143
Stalk, G., Jr., 239
state space, 118
Stigler, G. J., 234
strategic manipulability, 25–26
subgame perfect, 81
subjective probabilities, 182
subsidiaries, 83
subsidies, government, 204
substantive rationality, 173–174
substitution, rates of, 218–219
suicide, 214
Sumitomo Chemical, 239
Summers, L. 241
supergame equilibria, 143
supply and demand, 9, 17, 52
surplus, 5; *see also* rent seeking
Sutton, J., 238
symmetry, 121

Taiwan, 59
takeovers, 241
task difficulty, 132–138
Tax Reform Bill, 200, 243
tax revenues, 28, 189–191
Taylor, F. M., 78
technology, inefficient, 201–204, 205–211
Tenneco, 84–85
Texas Railroad Commission, 200–201
Theory and Decision (journal), 23
Theory of Committees and Elections, The, (Black), 11, 24
Theory of Political Coalitions, The, (Riker), 11, 27, 28, 29
Theory of Voting, The, (Farquharson), 24
Third World, 4
Thomas, R., 38, 78
Tignor, R. L., 33
Tirole, J., 142, 236
Tollison, R., 86, 87, 205, 207, 243
tort litigation, 87